BLACK HEROES IN OUR NATION'S HISTORY

Other Books by Phillip T. Drotning

A Guide to Negro History in America
A Job with a Future in the Petroleum Industry

BLACK HEROES IN OUR NATION'S HISTORY

A Tribute to Those Who Helped Shape America

by Phillip T. Drotning

COWLES BOOK COMPANY, INC.
NEW YORK

To the courageous Americans—black
and white—who for two centuries
have fought side by side for freedom

Library of Congress Catalog Number 69-17306
Published simultaneously in the United States and Canada
Printed in the United States of America
First Printing, May 1969
Second Printing, June 1969

FOREWORD

America of the late 1960's is a nation suffering agonies of dissension attributable to a multiplicity of problems. Of these, racial unrest and conflict probably are the most volatile and pressing. Their criticality lies in their genesis—the historic but declining denial of opportunity by white America for black America on the one hand, and the resultant growing frustration and impatience of black America on the other hand.

The obvious solution is to extend full equality of opportunity to all Americans. Unfortunately, many are so blinded by prejudice or self-interest that universal equality remains a distant goal despite the great efforts by concerned leaders of our society. It is this obstructionism that has nurtured a monstrous situation in which the lines of battle are being drawn and in which the voices of moderation are endangered. It is this obstructionism that has blurred the vision and distorted the judgment of otherwise rational men.

The question repeatedly asked is: "What is to be done?" There is no simple solution or answer. There is, however, a simple beginning—a concerted effort, using all available media, to convince all of America that the hour is late, but not too late, to extend the blessing of full opportunity to all.

In this book, the author has contributed significantly to that effort. He has clearly documented the repeated efforts of blacks to sacrifice themselves on the field of America's battles. With equal clarity, he has shown how these efforts first were accepted, then were rejected, and finally, with gradually decreasing reluctance, again were accepted.

Throughout the book a recurring theme persists, a theme of unjust denial of rewards for work well done. It should stimulate in any reader both recognition and resentment for the cruel manner in which white America has refused to grant to black America the full fruits of victory, won with a mixture of black and white blood.

The thoughtful reader will recognize a muted counterpoint, however. This is the increasing willingness to admit the black man to full partnership in efforts to defend the nation, the ever-improving degree to which he has been equipped to contribute as a partner, and the tragically lagging, but nonetheless measurably increasing, tendency toward reward without discrimination for duty under fire.

By combining these two themes, Mr. Drotning has given us a meaningful message while developing an informative chronology of Negro contributions to the national defense since the earliest days of our country. The message is one that cries for acknowledgment by the American people. It reminds white America of the shame of past and present injustices. It tells black America that progress and justice are attainable within the framework of our society. It tells both that the joint efforts of able men of all races can overcome obstacles to national victory.

Although the book primarily addresses black participation in military actions, its thrust is equally applicable to all aspects of American life. That there have been and are gross inequities in opportunities and rewards has finally been recognized by all rational Americans. That substantial improvements have been made also is generally recognized. The crisis of today derives from the rate at which progress is being made. For some white men who are reluctant to change, progress is too rapid; for the frustrated black, progress is all but imperceptible. Until these extreme viewpoints and attitudes approach a reconciliation, the crisis will endure and may even deepen.

Mr. Drotning has made no overt attempt to do other than present a factual picture of the Negro's military contributions and the struggle for equal rights. He has, in fact, done far more. He has founded a clear call for justice—for equality of opportunity and full participation in rewards. Similiarly, he has shown that progress has been made and that greater and more rapid progress can be expected. Perhaps his approach may be the most effective in reaching individuals, of even the most divergent views. If so, his style of presentation could be employed in all media and could be of incalculable value to the nation.

Certainly the reader will be richer because of this book and the knowledge it affords. From such knowledge could come a measure of tolerance and understanding that might help to ease our domestic crisis. Unquestionably it will serve to strengthen our internal bonds.

Frederic E. Davison
Brigadier General, U.S.A.

CONTENTS

	Foreword	v
	Introduction	ix
I.	Bold Adventures in a New World	1
II.	The Struggle for Independence	15
III.	Building a New Nation	34
IV.	Taming the Western Wilderness	52
V.	The War That Saved the Union	73
VI.	Black Soldiers and Red Men	95
VII.	New Look at the Old Cowhand	121
VIII.	Heroes of San Juan Hill	143
IX.	Saving the World for Democracy	162
X.	The Revenge of Pearl Harbor	176
XI.	Fighting for Freedom in Asia	192
XII.	The Long Struggle for Freedom	209
	Bibliography	225
	Index	231

INTRODUCTION

America was born of courage. It owes its discovery to fearless men who sailed uncharted seas, undaunted by terrifying myth and superstition, in search of the unknown. It was inhabited by others who valued ideals and ideas more than physical comfort and personal safety. It gained independence because gallant men dared to place the quest for freedom above life itself, and to challenge a superior foe to win it. It grew and prospered through the courage and zeal of pioneers who risked all the perils of hostile Indians and the relentless environment to establish new lives and to build new hopes in the wilderness. It survives because generation upon generation of Americans has had the tenacity and the valor to resist any challenge—however menacing and merciless—to liberty and justice.

American democracy is unique for the amalgam of human resources that joined in its creation. It was built on the imagination, determination, and courage of men and women of many races and nationalities, encompassing a vast array of religious beliefs and political philosophies. Their bond was a common desire for freedom and the uncommon courage to risk their lives to win it.

Throughout our history, ancient national rivalries have been put aside in this common struggle for freedom. Religious intolerance has vanished in the presence of death and the awareness that each of its victims would, after all, be judged by one God for what he was as a man, not for what his doctrine proclaimed him to be. Courage, not color, has distinguished black men and white men who fought shoulder to shoulder for survival against a common threat from man or nature.

This may be the most precious lesson to be learned from our history: Prejudice, intolerance, and discrimination are vain and hollow luxuries in which none but the ignorant, the idle, and the indolent can indulge. Courage, competence, and comradeship come in many colors, and these characteristics have meaning to men who stand together in the face of adversity.

General William Westmoreland, chairman of the Joint Chiefs of Staff, observed this while commanding the United States forces in Vietnam. "Over here," he said, "we have found out one thing—that cowards and heroes and geniuses and idiots come in all colors. Nobody gets excited and exercised about open occupancy in a foxhole."

Most Americans are aware of the enormous contribution made by black soldiers in Southeast Asia. This is due in part to the fact that it is the first conflict since the American Revolution in which integrated forces have been the rule and not the exception. Unlike the editors and writers who ignored black achievement for most of three hundred years, the television cameraman cannot edit history, for a black man is as obvious when he rescues a white comrade on the battlefield as when, out of frustration and hopelessness, he smashes a store window in Detroit.

This was not the case at other stages in our history. Despite the deep involvement of black men and women in every aspect of our nation's growth and progress, the press, the historians, even the dramatists of stage, screen, and television have rarely accorded them the place they have earned in history. Until recently, even in textbooks provided for schoolchildren, Afro-Americans were seen only as slaves, and all the major participants in the American drama were recorded as white.

The exclusion of black men and women from creditable roles in American history arose, at the outset, from the peculiar needs of a society that tolerated slavery. Unlike the slaveholders of other cultures, those in America could not in good conscience condone the enslavement of other human beings without first persuading themselves that the practice was justified on moral grounds. Thus, the African was viewed as a pagan subspecies whose condition was enhanced by the "largesse" of his master.

There emerged the portrait of the slave as a smiling, loyal, servile idiot whose greatest joy was singing happily as he toiled from dawn to dark in the cotton fields. This image, maintained in fiction and drama for two centuries, was no accident. It was part of a grand design to preserve the myth that black men were indolent, idiotic, incompetent, and childishly fearful, a myth that was essential to the image the conscience of the slaveholder required.

Obviously, the myth and the reality could not coexist. The image of black indolence could scarcely be perpetuated if history was permitted to record the exploits of the black man, York, during the intrepid expedition of Lewis and Clark, or of James Beckwourth and Edward Rose with the fearless mountain men. The image of idiocy could not be generalized to the entire black race if a black man, Benjamin Banneker, was credited with his role in planning the nation's capital, or Lewis Temple with the invention that spawned the Yankee whaling industry.

How could one denigrate an entire race if history recorded the presence of black participants in every major voyage of discovery that reached our shores? How could one stigmatize the black with cowardice if his history books confronted him with the exploits of black Americans such as Crispus Attucks, the first to die in the American Revolution; Prince Whipple, who crossed the Delaware in General Washington's boat; Prince Estabrook, who stood with the patriots at Lexington; or other thousands of black heroes in the Revolution and the War of 1812?

The exclusion of the black man from history, and the conscious efforts to minimize and obscure the achievements of those who broke the chains of slavery, stemmed also from the fear that examples of black success would cause those still enslaved to revolt. The reality of these fears is evident in the hundreds of slave uprisings that did occur. Their consequence, however, was the further denial to black Americans of a valid record of the contributions their race had made to America, a denial that persists to this day.

In recent years, this neglect has aroused concern among contemporary historians, and many scholars have sought to reconstruct the role of black men and women in our history. It is difficult work: Black Americans were so thoroughly excluded from the historical and newspaper accounts of the times that their participation must be ferreted from the official records and original manuscripts that survive. Even the latter are rare: Most blacks were denied by law the education that would have enabled them to record what they did.

The author experienced these handicaps during the research that preceded the writing of his first venture into the field of black history, *A Guide to Negro History in America*, which was published in 1968. It plagued him to an even greater degree in the preparation of this work, and he owes a great debt to a team of patient researchers—John E. Feehery, Richard F. Gavitt, Jim Mayes, and Robert O'Rourke—who uncovered many of the facts included in this book.

During these years of research, it became apparent that the role of the black man in the creation of America was far more extensive than the author had been aware. The first task was to write him back into our history, which inevitably produced a segregated book. Yet there emerged from its pages the clear thread of sacrifice, achievement, and raw courage—involving black and white men together—throughout all the great moments in our history.

This book is an effort to reconstruct the great episodes in American history the way they really happened, reflecting the achievements of black men and white men who *together* made America the great nation it has become. For the most part, its black heroes were ordinary men who responded in extraordinary ways to the challenges of their times. In this respect, they were no different from the white heroes of our history.

The difference is that the stature of the principal white figures in the American drama has grown through the retrospective glorification of their role. There are few black heroes in our history books not because they weren't there but because their story is rarely told, and thus their story has not become legend in the telling.

Phillip T. Drotning
Glenview, Illinois
November 1, 1968

BLACK HEROES IN OUR NATION'S HISTORY

CHAPTER I

BOLD ADVENTURERS IN A NEW WORLD

The young colony at Jamestown, Virginia, in late August of 1619 gave little promise of the bright future that was in store for America. The tiny peninsular settlement on the left bank of the James River was little more than a tenuous foothold for the British in North America, a vagrant speck on the edge of the vast and awesome unknown that lay beyond.

In the dozen years since the first one hundred and five colonists had ventured ashore from three frail craft, the "Susan Constant," the "Godspeed," and the "Discovery," the colony had grown but little. Often, indeed, its survival had been in doubt. Many still recalled the terrible winter of 1609-10, when nine in every ten of the half-frozen settlers had starved to death. Only the timely arrival of spring, and with it a new governor, Lord Delaware, had saved the colony then. With him had come an eager group of immigrants and a shipload of sorely needed supplies.

But now, with the first breezes of fall, the colonists sensed the new feeling of permanence that had begun to permeate the colony. It did not stem from any great physical evidence of growth; fewer than one thousand Europeans had yet reached North America, and there were barely twenty crude houses in the village itself. But there were other signs.

One of these was the convening, in midsummer of 1619, of

the House of Burgesses, the first legislative assembly in America and the forerunner of the representative system that was to build on these shores the greatest democracy in the history of the world. Another was the knowledge that, after years of hardship and privation, more prosperous times were in sight. The colony at last had a stable source of income; the year had seen the shipment of the forty thousandth pound of tobacco since John Rolfe had first cultivated the crop in 1612.

Less obvious in its implications, but equally exciting to those in the isolated and primitive colony on the James, was a third event that would have a profound influence on the colony and the nation it was to spawn. It came with the arrival in August of a sailing ship; not one chartered by the London Company, which had founded the colony, but a Dutch frigate that came out of a storm with a remarkable cargo to trade.

John Rolfe, the English tobacco planter who married the Indian maiden Pocahontas, dutifully recorded the event in his journal. In a single unemotional sentence he described the event that was to scar our national history and undermine the concepts of freedom that were stirring in Jamestown that very year:

"About the last of August came in a Dutch man of warre that sold us twenty Negars."

Historians commonly date the arrival of Africans in America to this event noted by Rolfe in 1619. The surviving records are few, but presumably the Dutch privateer took on provisions in exchange for the twenty black men and women it had on board. The Africans remained in Jamestown, not yet as slaves but as indentured servants in the colonial households. They were required, as were many white immigrants of the time, to give seven years of service in exchange for their passage to America.

Little is known of the fate of these black immigrants. Two of them, Antony and Isabella, married in 1624 and became the parents of the first black child reportedly born in English America. They named him William Tucker, after an English planter in the Jamestown colony.

But, if little is known of the individuals, the arrival of the group was of great significance to the young colony. The labors of those first black immigrants, and of millions who were to follow, helped establish an agricultural empire in the South. It was the prelude to slavery in America, because it was not long until economic pressure caused tradesmen and plantation owners to seek and win legal sanction for the lifetime enslavement of their black servants. Slavery thus became the dominant role of black Americans until the Emancipation Proclamation was issued by President Abraham Lincoln in 1863.

It is in their capacity as slaves that most historians write of the black role in America during the first two and one-half centuries of the nation's history. Perhaps this is not altogether reprehensible, for certainly it was as slaves that the vast majority of blacks left their mark on the country. Yet the emphasis on slavery obscures the far more vigorous scientific, intellectual, and cultural contributions of many black men and women to the growth and development of a great nation.

The practice of indenturing Africans for life became widespread after the 1660's, when Maryland and Virginia enacted a series of statutes legalizing lifetime servitude for black men and women, and other southern states followed suit. As southern agriculture converted to the production of cotton, the demand for slaves increased and slave traders—many of them "respectable" Yankees and some of them black—brought blacks to America in an ever swelling stream.

Wrested from their families and their native lands, the captives endured indescribable hardships in the congested, filthy, disease-ridden holds of the slave ships that sailed between Africa and the Atlantic and Gulf coasts. Those who survived the journey arrived in America in chains to be sold on the auction blocks of Washington, Norfolk, Charleston, New Orleans, and a dozen other cities. They spent their lives working as household servants and artisans, or in the cotton and tobacco fields from dawn to dark, rewarded with a handful of cornmeal and a piece of salt pork if they did their best, or the lash of an overseer if they failed to please him.

The misery of these Africans enriched slave traders, merchants, and planters, in North and South alike. By 1790 there were nearly seven hundred thousand slaves in America and by 1830 more than two million, most of them in the South. In 1860, shortly before the Civil War, the federal census recorded nearly four million black slaves, about half of them toiling in the fields, shops, and gracious plantation mansions of the "cotton kingdom."

The black American, even in slavery, enriched the national economy and the national culture with his courage, endurance, muscle, artistry, and wit. Much of his influence on our heritage persists today.

Most of the cherished antebellum mansions were the product of black slave-artisans. Much of southern industry flourished on the labor of slaves. The idealized image of plantation hospitality —the mint julep syndrome of such films as *Gone with the Wind*—depended on the efforts of talented house slaves who provided courtly service, and often talented and cultured musical entertainment as well.

Rarely portrayed is the South that lived in constant fear because its black slaves, far from happy in arduous and degrading lifetime servitude, frequently displayed their displeasure by burning the house.

At its peak, the cotton-based agriculture that was the foundation of the South's economic progress and growth owed its very existence to the backbreaking labor of almost two million black slaves, male and female, and of every age. Their influence, and that of an equal number of blacks engaged in other pursuits, had a positive impact on the southern culture that can still be heard in the southern "drawl" and southern music, both folk and jazz. It can be seen in the delicate wrought-iron grillwork of a New Orleans balcony and the exquisite carving of an antebellum chair. It can be tasted in the epicurean delicacies of which the South is so justly proud.

Although the economic contribution and cultural impact of the black slaves was enormous, more spectacular contributions were made by blacks who managed to earn their freedom or were manumitted by grateful or conscience-stricken masters. For example, after lifetimes of luxury supported by their slaves, two Virginia statesmen, Thomas Jefferson and John Randolph, willed them freedom when they died.

Free blacks, by 1860, numbered nearly half a million, about

half of them in the South. Many of these black Americans made significant but largely unheralded contributions in science, medicine, business and industry, literature and the arts. Often they owed their freedom and their education to white patrons who themselves risked punishment and even death to act on the conviction that men were born to be free, that all deserved an equal chance.

Although the commonly recorded history of black men and women in America begins with the Jamestown colony, there are many earlier chapters that remain largely untold. Despite the emphasis given them in history, those in the tragic black contingent that was put ashore at Jamestown in 1619 were not the first Africans to touch American shores. They had been preceded by countless others who accompanied British, French, Italian, Spanish, Dutch, and Portuguese adventurers throughout the sixteenth and early seventeenth centuries on daring exploratory voyages to the North and South American continents.

Some historians believe that when Christopher Columbus embarked, in 1492, on his voyage in search of a new route to the riches of the Indies, a black pilot, Pedro Alonso Niño, was a member of his crew. Certainly it was a black cabin boy, Diego el Negro, who sailed with him on his fourth voyage in 1502.

In the years that followed, hardly an expedition put to sea that failed to number one or more black men in its company. Some of them were slaves, others descendants of the slaves who were imported into southern Europe in numbers after 1441, when Portuguese Prince Henry the Navigator sent a caravel to Africa for a cargo of oil, and she returned with a cargo of slaves.

American history faithfully records the establishment of the first permanent white colony in America at St. Augustine, on the Florida peninsula, in September, 1565. Although blacks were with the Spanish founder of the settlement, Don Pedro Menéndez de Avilés, their presence is rarely noted, nor is the fact that St. Augustine was not the first black colony as well.

That honor had already gone to one hundred black slaves who were with Lucas Vásquez de Ayllón nearly forty years earlier, in 1526, when he and five hundred other Spaniards established a settlement near the Pedee River on what is now the

South Carolina coast. Curiously, in an unheeded warning of things to come, the first colonization of America was born out of a slave revolt. Not long after their arrival the black men turned on their Spanish captors and then disappeared into the nearby forests to join the Indians who were already there.

The Spaniards found life in a wilderness infested with hostile Indians more than they could bear, and the burden, no doubt, was not eased by the departure of their slaves. Within a few months only one hundred and fifty of the original five hundred Spaniards survived. Discouraged by the hazards and privation they had experienced in the new land, they returned to Haiti, leaving the blacks behind.

It was thus that black men became the first humans, other than the aborigines, to remain permanently in what is now the United States. They were here well over a quarter century before Menéndez' Spanish and African party built the colony at St. Augustine, almost eighty years before the first permanent English colony was established at Jamestown, and nearly a century before the Pilgrims landed at Plymouth Rock.

The fate of these first black settlers is lost in history. It is possible that none of them survived the rigors of the hostile environment or the reception of their Indian hosts. But it is equally possible that their blood is with us still in the veins of descendants of the Indian tribes they joined. In either event, the black man clearly has an early priority on the right to call himself an American.

Within a few years of the initial voyages to North America of Christopher Columbus, most of the seafaring nations of Europe began dispatching expeditions to find and claim territory in the New World. In each of these, almost without exception, were black men who together with whites braved the tempestuous Atlantic and the hazards of the wilderness to establish colonies and extend Europe's knowledge of the new continent.

Among the early adventurers was Henry Hudson, who in 1609 explored the Hudson River area as an agent of the Dutch East India Company. His discoveries later led the Dutch to outfit a company that would establish their claim to the area by founding a colony.

Eleven blacks were in the party that, after a long and stormy voyage over the Atlantic, established a trading post on Manhattan Island in 1624, which they named New Netherland. In 1626, Minuit, director general of the Dutch settlement, secured Dutch title to the property by purchasing the island from the Indians for goods worth about sixty guilders, then the equivalent of about twenty-four dollars. Eventually, however, the Dutch were forced to cede the territory to the British.

A few years later, not far to the south, Cecilius Calvert, the second Lord Baltimore, sent an expedition across the Atlantic on the "Ark" and the "Dove" to settle lands north of the Potomac. Three blacks, Francisco Peres, Mathias DeSousa, and John Price, were with the party that landed in March, 1634, and thus made a place for themselves in history among the first settlers of what is now the state of Maryland.

DeSousa, in the years that followed, carved out an even larger role. Initially he worked as the indentured servant of two Jesuit priests, paying for his passage, and then he was given fifty acres of land, tools, and three suits of clothes.

The black immigrant soon became an important citizen of Maryland. He was licensed to trade wth the Indians and established a reputation as an unusually competent trader, whose understanding, tact, and common sense gave him an advantage over the Virginia traders in dealing with the Indians. Before long, he became the pilot of a pinnace that traded with the Susquehanna Indians. The respect he established among the other colonists was so firm that he was selected to serve in the General Assembly that met in March, 1641, and joined the most distinguished white citizens of the colony in enacting the laws by which it was governed.

Black men also accompanied the French Jesuit missionary-explorers who ventured into the forests around the western Great Lakes and down the Mississippi River. Among these missionaries was Père Jacques Marquette, who explored the head of Ashland Bay and settled there briefly until driven away by the Indians.

In 1671, Marquette founded the mission of St. Ignatius, at Mackinac, and was working among the Indians there two years later when Louis Joliet arrived with a message from Frontenac, the governor of Canada, urging the priest to guide an expedition to the Mississippi River.

Marquette and Joliet assembled a party of explorers, some French and some African, chosen for their courage and stamina, not their color. Both qualities were needed for the difficult journey that took them to Green Bay, on Lake Michigan's Wisconsin shore, and then up the Fox River to Lake Winnebago. There, after crossing the lake, they lifted their canoes from the water and made the exhausting portage overland to the Wisconsin River, down which they traveled to the Mississippi.

The adventurous Jesuits and their party, living on what little the land had to offer, explored the Mississippi as far south as the mouth of the Arkansas River and then returned to Illinois, where Marquette became a missionary among the Indians. Ultimately the French Jesuit settlement at Kaskaskia, Illinois, included about seventy blacks, some of them farmers and others engaged in a variety of trades.

Typically, only the leaders of the early exploratory expeditions are identified in history, but occasionally an individual member of one of the parties stands out. Such is the case with one of the men who accompanied the French expeditions, a tall, well-proportioned, handsome black who would have been set apart by his features even if they had not been dark.

Jean Baptiste Pointe du Sable came to America after being educated in Paris, arriving in the Midwest with the French explorers in 1765. He found the country to his liking, and, being more an entrepreneur than an adventurer, he established a trading post at the mouth of the Chicago river about 1779.

Du Sable's enterprise prospered, and soon a small community began to develop around it. Today his forty-foot house, bakeshop, and dairy have been supplanted by skyscrapers and luxury apartments—the site that Du Sable had chosen grew to be the city of Chicago, and he is now honored as that city's first settler.

Even in the Pacific Northwest, which was settled much later than the rest of the country, discovery and settlement were the joint effort of black and white men, facing danger together.

A fearless young black was with some of the first explorers

to set foot in the state of Oregon, and the bay in which they landed was named in long-forgotten tribute to the fate that befell him there.

The date was August 16, 1788, and the landing party was sent ashore by Captain Robert Gray, who commanded the sloop "Lady Washington." Among those who entered the dark forests on the shores of Tillamook Bay, seeking to replenish the ship's wood and water supply, was a black crew member named Markus Lopeus.

The sailors had scarcely entered the forest when they were startled by the wild whoops of a party of Indians who leaped from the underbrush to attack them. The seamen resisted vigorously in the hand-to-hand encounter, and in the struggle the young black lost his knife to one of the Indians. Before the Indians were driven off, Lopeus had also lost his life in an effort to recover the weapon.

The death of the young black gave him one niche in history, for Gray named the landing spot Murderer's Harbor because of the sailor's fate, but it denied him another. Gray's sloop was the consort vessel to the ship "Columbia Rediviva," commanded by Captain John Kendrick. Later in the voyage Gray assumed command of the "Columbia" and sailed back to Boston by way of China, carrying the United States flag around the world for the first time.

As exploration of the Northwest continued, black men did not relinquish the role they shared with white adventurers in discovery and settlement. In 1845, the British dispatched two army officers, Henry J. Warre and Mervin Vavasour, to the mouth of the Columbia River to map it and determine whether it was feasible to erect a battery there to hold the river for England.

When they arrived at the mouth of the Columbia, the Englishmen observed a towering promontory, today known as Cape Disappointment, which clearly offered the most favorable site for the battery. To their astonishment, when they explored it they found an American already in possession. He was James D. Saule—also known as De Saule, Saul, or Sanlos—a shipwrecked black sea cook who had been a member of the galley crew of the sloop-of-war "Peacock," of Commander Charles Wilkes' United States Exploring Expedition.

Wherever one turns in the early history of America, black and white men are there, together, sharing the hardships, the danger, the victories, and the disappointments. Nowhere was the impact of the black explorers as great as during the golden age of the Spanish conquistadores in Mexico and the Southwest. Blacks were valued members of virtually all the Spanish expeditions to the New World. Their worth was often noted in the letters of King Ferdinand of Spain, and at one point in the mid-sixteenth century the Spanish governor of Mexico noted that they were "indispensable for the cultivation of the land and the royal revenue."

His observation about the importance of Africans in Mexican agriculture is not surprising, because it was a black member of the expedition of Hernando Cortés who planted and harvested the first wheat crop in America. Cortés, however, was not the first of the Spaniards to rely on both black and white explorers in the conquest of new territory. Another was Balboa, who first visited the north coast of South America in 1501 as a member of a trading expedition. In 1510 he established a settlement at Darién, in what is now Panama, and three years later led a band of explorers that included three blacks overland to the Pacific Ocean. The three helped to build the first ships constructed on the Pacific coast.

Other blacks served with Pizarro in Peru, and in 1532 worked shoulder to shoulder with a white member of Pizarro's expedition, Hernando de Soto, who was later to gain his own place in history for his explorations of much of the southern United States. After assisting in the capture of Cuzco, the Inca capital, in 1533, De Soto returned to Spain a wealthy man. In 1536 he secured permission from King Charles V to finance and organize an expedition to Florida, which had been claimed by Spain but not developed.

De Soto, perhaps recalling his experience with Pizarro, recruited a number of black adventurers to join the thousand-man expedition that landed on Florida's west coast in 1539. For more than three years it ranged through the uncharted territory that now includes North and South Carolina, Alabama, and Mississippi. In 1541 De Soto and his men reached the Mississippi River and crossed into the territory that later became Arkansas, Oklahoma, and North Texas, in a fruitless search for treasure that would equal what he had brought home from Peru.

In 1542, the disappointed Spaniard abandoned his search and led his expedition back to the Mississippi, where he became ill with fever. He soon died, and members of the party buried him in the river, where they hoped his body would escape the attention of marauding Indians.

Many others of De Soto's party died while making their way back to the coast, but not all of them sought to return to Spain. One black man, according to historian W. E. B. Du Bois, remained among the Indians as the first of the tens of thousands of black men who would ultimately make their homes in Alabama.

Perhaps the most ambitious of the Spanish conquistadores was Cortés, whose expeditions pillaged the Aztecs of the treasure that graced their temples and established a permanent Spanish foothold in Mexico. He also appears to have placed the greatest reliance on black explorers. When he first arrived in Mexico from Cuba in March, 1519, he commanded an expedition of nearly six hundred men, seventeen horses, and ten cannon. In the party were three hundred blacks, whose great strength and stamina were employed to drag the heavy Spanish artillery that brought terror to the Aztecs.

In the years that followed, black men accompanied other explorers who ventured northward into the arid deserts above the Rio Grande, where they were plagued by hunger and thirst and besieged by savage Indians. As always with the Spaniards, the motivation was the quest for riches, the pursuit of legends about great treasures of jewels and gold.

In 1539, Francisco Vásquez de Coronado was granted the right to search the American Southwest for the fabled Seven Cities of Cíbola, whose streets were said to be paved with gold. As a result of this expedition, Coronado is generally credited with the discovery, in 1540, of Arizona and New Mexico. In this he gets more than his due, for his enthusiasm for the expedition was actually kindled by a report on the adventures of a black explorer who preceded him. The exploits of that predecessor, a black Moor named Estevanico, or Little Stephen, are rarely recounted, but they remain among the most astonishing in the early history of our nation.

The arrival of Estevanico in America was inconspicuous, considering the stature he was to achieve in the years that followed. He came as the mere servant or slave of Andres Dorantes, who was a member of a Spanish exploratory party headed by Pánfilo de Narváez. The group had left Spain in 1527 on a mission to explore the north coast of the Gulf of Mexico, landing in Florida, probably in Sarasota Bay, in April, 1528.

The explorers, constantly harassed by Indians, fought their way through tangled underbrush and almost impassable swamps, and finally made their way up the coast to a point near the mouth of the St. Marks River. There Estevanico helped his white companions beat swords into tools to build and launch the first ships made in North America. The ships were to be of little value, however, because the explorers were plagued by disease and slaughtered by Indians until all of them, including Narváez, perished. All, that is, but four—Cabeza de Vaca, Castillo, Andres Dorantes, and Estevanico, his slave. They escaped the fate of their companions because they had been captured by Indians—a misfortune that proved to be their salvation.

For six years the three Spaniards and their black companion—all now slaves—remained among the Indians. They gradually won the confidence of their captors, until finally they found an opportunity to escape. For a time they must have wondered whether captivity was not preferable to hunger and privation in a wilderness hundreds of miles from civilization. For two years they wandered, with Estevanico often posing as a medicine man when hostile Indians were encountered. They were but half alive when the black guide finally led them, with some unerring sense of direction that even he could not explain, to the distant Spanish settlements in Mexico.

Dorantes and Castillo, grateful to be alive, lost no time in returning to the comforts of their native Spain, but the adventures of the black Moor had only begun. Antonio de Mendoza, the viceroy of New Spain, learned from his white companions of Estevanico's great courage and remarkable skill and stamina during their eight years in the wilderness. He perceived that the black would be of incalculable value as an explorer and guide, so he purchased him from Dorantes.

Apparently Mendoza was also fascinated by a tale that the wanderers had heard during their long journey, the story of a fabulously rich settlement north of the Rio Grande called the Seven Cities of Cíbola. The viceroy dispatched a Spanish explorer, Fray Marcos de Niza, on an expedition to find the cities and bring back their treasure. Estevanico was chosen as its guide.

An account of the expedition, written by Father de Niza on his return, still survives. He reported that after the expedition had crossed the Rio Grande he sent Estevanico ahead, with a group of Indians, to scout the territory for the rest of the party. The guide, identified by De Niza as "Stephen Dorantez the Negro," adopted the disguise that had served him so well in his earlier wanderings among the Indians. As a symbol of his supernatural status as a medicine man, he carried a gourd trimmed with bells and feathers.

De Niza instructed Estevanico to keep the expedition advised of his progress by sending back wooden crosses whose dimensions would indicate the magnitude of his discoveries.

"I agreed with him," De Niza wrote, "that if hee found any knowledge of any people and riche countrey which were of great importance, that hee should goe no further, but should returne in person, or shoulde sende mee certaine Indians with that token which wee were agreed upon, to wit, that if it were but a meane thing, hee shoulde sende mee a White Crosse of one handfull long; and if it were any great matter, one of two handfulls long; and if it were a Country greater and better than Nueva Espana, hee should send mee a great crosse."

Estevanico set off boldly into the desert, accompanied only by a small band of friendly Indians, while the leader of the expedition waited impatiently in the comfort and security of his camp. Four days after Estevanico's departure a group of breathless Indians arrived at De Niza's camp with "a great Crosse as high as a man." They brought information from the black scout that he had found Indians who informed him that he was thirty days' journey from the Seven Cities, whose stone houses were studded with turquoise.

The vision of fabulous riches spurred De Niza along the route that his black scout had taken, and after several days they were again met by another of his Indian guides. The exhausted and trembling native told them that Estevanico had reached Cíbola, where he had encountered hostile Indians with whom he was negotiating.

De Niza hurried on, but shortly he received the last word of the black adventurer: His incredible luck had run out at last, and he had been murdered by the Indians.

Estevanico had apparently reached the Zuñi pueblo, becoming the first nonaborigine to enter New Mexico, but De Niza did not pursue him to find out. Instead, he rushed back to Mexico with a much embroidered tale of the incredibly wealthy cities that he had never seen.

It was this vision of unimaginable riches that inspired Coronado, in 1540, to lead another expedition northward into Arizona and New Mexico. Less timid than De Niza, he ventured far, but the gold he envisioned was not to be found. When the disgusted conquistador returned to Mexico, he told the viceroy that De Niza had "said the truth in nothing that he reported. . . ." Instead of gold and jewels he had found only "great houses of stone."

Yet in the course of history the new land that Estevanico had discovered proved worthy of the "great Crosse" that he had returned, for surely it was "a country greater and better" than New Spain.

CHAPTER II

THE STRUGGLE FOR INDEPENDENCE

Men who quench their thirst for freedom by risking their lives to win it are inclined to be most discriminating in their selection of comrades-in-arms. Their discrimination, however, is a tribute to their character, not a condemnation of it. It is based on judgment, not prejudice, on reality, not rancor, on courage, not color.

So it was during the long struggle for American independence, as black men and white men fought together for the right to govern themselves. No official edict promulgated by those whose selfish interests led them to attempt the exclusion of Negroes was able to deter black patriots from fighting or white ones from welcoming them into the fray.

Even before the Revolution began, black men joined white Americans as active and outspoken advocates of resistance to British authority. They were among those in Boston, during the decade preceding 1775, who were aroused and incensed by acts of Parliament that they considered oppressive threats to the unusual liberty Colonial America had enjoyed for more than 150 years. Protests against "taxation without representation" became their battle cry, and the British regiments stationed in the colonies to enforce the taxes were the targets of their wrath.

Ultimately, it was a black American who was the first to die in the conflict between colonist and grenadier. He may, indeed, have been the leader of the rebellious patriots who touched off the event that Daniel Webster said launched the American Revolution. Neither he nor his white companions were men who seemed destined for heroic roles in American history. John Adams, the second American president, later said that they were "the most obscure and inconsiderable that could have been found upon the continent." Yet the runaway black slave, Crispus Attucks, and his four white companions who also died are enshrined in the pages of the American pageant.

For nearly two years prior to March, 1770, Boston had been the vortex of the maelstrom of discontent that was sweeping the American colonies. There had been almost incessant friction between Boston's townspeople, who then numbered less than 16,000, about a tenth of them black, and two regiments of British regulars that were quartered in the town to protect the customs officials. Verbal abuse was heaped upon the British soldiers, who were regarded as unnecessary and unwelcome intruders on American soil, present only to enforce His Majesty's harsh and unjust laws. Physical clashes between residents and soldiers were a common occurrence.

The climax came on a crisp, clear Monday evening–March 5, 1770–from a spark that seemed too small to ignite a military and political conflagration that would profoundly alter the history of the world. It came in the person of a small boy who ran through the streets, clutching his bruised head and crying that a British sentry had struck him. The cast of characters he rallied with his cries was not so much a gathering of blue-blooded patriots as of tavern idlers and waterfront bums.

The historic importance of the incident lies less with the provocation and the participants than with the tense atmosphere in which it occurred and the effects it produced. Already inflamed by passionate opposition to British rule, a crowd formed quickly in King Street, threatening and jeering the lone sentry in front of the Town House. The soldier, frightened by the hostile crowd and threatened by volleys of snowballs and bits of ice, loaded his musket and called for help.

When eight men of the British Twenty-ninth Regiment charged out of the barracks and ran to the sentry's aid, someone rang the town fire bell, and the angry crowd grew. It pressed toward Captain Thomas Preston and the semicircle of British soldiers who stood, bayonets fixed, before the Town House. Taunts of "coward" and "bloody-back" were shouted at the soldiers, who nervously stood their ground with bayonets poised against the threatening crowd.

The mob suddenly swelled again, as a group of twenty or thirty men, brandishing clubs and sticks, made its way into King Street. A well-known figure on the Boston docks was trotting in the lead—husky Crispus Attucks, who had been described twenty years earlier by his master as "a mulatto fellow, about 27 years of age, named Crispus, 6 feet 2 inches high, short, curl'd hair, his knees nearer together than common."

What happened is confused in the accounts that were written at the time. Samuel Adams, one of the most outspoken opponents of British rule and the leading colonial propagandist, maintained that the forty-seven-year-old runaway slave from Framingham, Massachusetts, was shot down without provocation.

His cousin, John Adams, who was later to become the second president of the United States, took an opposing position in his defense of the British soldiers at their trial. It was Crispus Attucks, he told the jury, who apparently undertook "to be the hero of the night; and to lead this army with banners, to form them in the first place in Dock square, and march them up to King Street with their clubs." Attucks, according to John Adams, was so ferocious that his "very looks was enough to terrify any person," and it was he who had "hardiness" enough to grab a soldier's bayonet and knock the man down.

This assertion of Attucks' role, which became the most widely accepted version, was based on the testimony of Andrew, the slave of a Boston selectman, who said that Attucks had struck the first blow. According to Andrew, the crowd appeared to be breaking up, on the arrival of British reinforcements, when a group of men came from a nearby corner, "huzzaing and crying, damn them, they dare not fire, we are not afraid of them."

The slave testified that Attucks was armed with "a long cord wood stick" with which he struck at Captain Preston and then at the grenadier, Hugh Montgomery, who stood at his side. Then, Andrew said, Attucks grabbed the grenadier's bayonet with his left hand "and twitched it and cried, kill the dogs, knock them over." The rest of the crowd took up the cry, crowding in on the soldiers, one of whom, in the confusion, apparently thought he heard an order from the officer to fire. He shot off his musket. Crispus Attucks was the first to fall, and before the crowd dispersed eleven Americans had been hit. Five of them–Samuel Gray, Samuel Maverick, James Caldwell, Patrick Carr, and Crispus Attucks–died of their wounds.

The bodies of Crispus Attucks and James Caldwell, neither of them natives of Boston, were carried off to lie in state in Faneuil Hall, the site of Boston town meetings, which John Adams later called "the cradle of liberty." There the runaway slave received the last respects of the leading citizens of Boston.

Three days later, on March 8, the church bells pealed throughout Boston, Charlestown, Roxbury, and all the other nearby towns, shops closed, and the citizens turned out en masse for a funeral procession that was witnessed by more people than any previous event in Colonial history. The hearses moved down King Street, "the theater of the inhuman tragedy," proceeded through Main Street, and finally reached the Granary Burying Ground.

There the five martyrs, one black and four white, were buried together in a common grave. They rest there today, a mute reminder of the improbable event that united America in the struggle for independence.

Colonial propagandists seized on the Boston Massacre as evidence of the intolerable oppression the colonies would face if they remained subservient to British rule. The British had yielded on some of the taxes they levied, but they stubbornly held to the duty on tea until finally, on December 16, 1773, the Bostonians again took the law into their own hands. Masquerading as Indians, a group of them moved silently through the darkness to the British ships docked in the harbor, broke open casks of tea, and emptied them into the sea. The Boston Tea Party became another milestone on the road to revolution.

During the early months of 1774 this new show of resistance

to the British crown brought a series of reprisals against the Massachusetts Colony that became known as the Intolerable Acts. In the first of these acts, Parliament ordered the port of Boston closed until payment was made for the eighteen thousand pounds' worth of tea that had been destroyed. Later acts prohibited public meetings without government sanction, provided that British officials accused of capital offenses would be tried in England rather than Massachusetts, and forced residents of the colony to house and feed British troops.

Tension mounted rapidly in the colonies, and in May Rhode Island issued the first call for an intercolonial congress, an appeal in which New York and Philadelphia quickly joined. On September 5, 1774, the First Continental Congress was convened in Philadelphia, with delegates from all the thirteen colonies but Georgia on hand. In little more than a month it issued the first Declaration of Rights of the colonists, including those of "life, liberty and property."

As the Congress met, local militia in towns throughout Massachusetts were holding crude military drills and storing weapons and powder against the day when it might become necessary to take up arms against the British. Black and white men stood together in the ranks. Patriots throughout the colonies began to speak out openly against the British. Patrick Henry, on March 23, 1775, electrified the colonies with his immortal plea, "Give me liberty or give me death!"

This was the situation in early April of 1775, when patriots in Boston began hearing rumors that the British governor of Massachusetts, General Thomas Gage, was planning an expedition to nearby Concord to seize the arms and ammunition stored there by the colonial minutemen. The minutemen reacted promptly, moving most of their military supplies out of Concord to safer hiding places.

The inept British general, apparently unaware that his intentions were secret only to his own men, proceeded with his plans while the Boston patriots warily scouted every British move. A plan was prepared to warn the countryside the moment the Redcoats began their march. If they moved by land over the Boston Neck, the narrow isthmus that connected Boston to the mainland, the Committee of Safety at Charlestown would be alerted by a single lantern in the belfry of the Old North Church. If they took the shorter route and crossed the Charles River to Cambridge by boat, two lanterns would gleam from the tower of the church.

Early in the morning on "the nineteenth of April in '75," a column of seven hundred of the King's Regulars, with Lieutenant Colonel Francis Smith in command, embarked on the short boat trip across the Charles. Almost before the first Redcoat took his place in a boat two lanterns flashed briefly atop the North Church. Watchful eyes in Charlestown spotted the signal, and a rider was dispatched to Lexington to warn the minutemen there. At almost the same moment William Dawes leaped on his horse and set off for Lexington by the land route while Paul Revere, under the guns of the British navy, made it to Charlestown by sea. There he, too, mounted a fast horse and rode off to arouse the countryside.

The British column, marching through Cambridge and then out the Lexington road, found the mute woods and the darkened colonial houses ominously quiet. In Menotomy, later known as West Cambridge and today as Arlington, a British patrol approached the Newell Tavern but passed on, unaware that three members of the local Committee of Safety, all in their nightshirts, were peering out at them from a window on the second floor.

Not until they passed Menotomy on their way to Lexington did the advance scouts of Smith's brigade encounter signs of activity on the part of the colonists. One by one the redcoats captured three scouts who had been sent out from Lexington to report back on the approach of the British force. In the distant woods they saw armed minutemen hurrying toward Lexington. Putting together the information gleaned from the captured scouts, the British falsely concluded that they would face a thousand minutemen or more when they arrived at the Lexington Common.

Meanwhile, standing before his pitiful band of minutemen stretched out in two thin lines behind the meetinghouse on the green, Captain John Parker fervently wished he had that many men in his command. Instead of a thousand, there were barely seventy half-trained, homespun-clad minutemen to stand up against seven hundred well-trained British troops.

Among those who had answered to the rattle of young William Diamond's drum were men in their dotage and boys in their teens. There were tradesmen, shopkeepers, and farmers, many of them fathers and sons. Among them was Prince Estabrook, a black slave who before the day was out would become one of the forty-nine casualties on the American side.

It was daylight before two hundred men of the British Light Infantry, marching ahead of the main column, approached the Lexington green. The two ragged lines of patriots waited silently as the British approached and formed to face them in crisp, red-coated lines. The commander of the Light Infantry, Major John Pitcairn of the Royal Marines, ordered the patriots to disperse, but the men stood fast.

What happened next will never be resolved. A shot rang out, from whose musket no one knows, and the British soldiers opened fire and charged with their bayonets fixed. Within minutes, eight Americans lay dead and ten had suffered wounds. The Battle of Lexington was over, but the Revolution had begun.

When Smith's main group overtook the forward unit, the British regrouped and continued their march to Concord. Smith, stunned by the resistance that had been encountered, sent an urgent appeal to General Gage in Boston to send more troops. Meanwhile, black and white farmers, tradesmen, and slaves throughout the countryside were putting down their tools, shouldering their muskets, and hurrying toward Concord.

The minutemen came from all the surrounding towns. There was Captain Simon Edgel's company from Framingham, which numbered Peter Salem in its midst. Salem, a slave of the Belknap family, had been given his freedom so he could enlist. From Braintree came Seth Turner's company, which included a black private named Pompey, and from Brookline came Thomas White's company, which included "Joshua Boylston's Prince."

Arriving in Concord, the British soon discovered that most of the arms they sought had been removed. Seven companies proceeded to the North Bridge, and three were left to guard it while the other four went on to search for supplies at the farm of Colonel James Barrett, about a mile beyond.

By this time about four hundred minutemen had gathered on the hills above the bridge, gazing down on the bright red jackets. Soon, seeing smoke rising from the town, they marched toward the bridge, and the British retreated to the other side. Some of them fired, and two Americans fell dead. The minutemen, armed with muskets, fowling pieces, and every other conceivable weapon, returned the fire. They killed three redcoats and wounded nine others, including half of the British officers. The remainder turned and fled.

It was the last action of the day to be fought on British terms. The growing colonial forces, recalling the success of wilderness fighting tactics during the French and Indian Wars, chose to solidify their victory while the British made their long and weary march back to Boston. Taking advantage of the protection afforded by forests and stone fences along the roadside between Concord and Lexington, the minutemen harassed the now outnumbered redcoats. The men fired on the British as the dwindling columns passed, then raced through the woods to new positions farther down the road. There they waited patiently until the frightened and exhausted grenadiers approched, and opened fire again.

Black Americans shared the protection of the trees and stone fences with their white comrades-in-arms as they traded fire with the Redcoats. There were Cuff Whittemore and Cato Wood of Captain Benjamin Locke's Arlington company, and Cato Stedman and Cato Bordman of Cambridge, who served with Captain Samuel Thatcher's company. Pomp Blackman had joined the minutemen by the time the British reached Lincoln. Prince Estabrook, who had returned to the fray with the other surviving members of Captain Parker's Lexington company, was wounded when the last shots were exchanged as the retreating British reached the Boston Neck.

While the weary survivors of Colonel Smith's expedition fought their way back along the narrow, dusty road from Concord, under constant fire by the minutemen along the roadside, a relief expedition commanded by Earl Hugh Percy was making its way slowly out the Lexington road. His First Brigade had suffered numerous delays, one of the most aggravating at the great bridge over the Charles River, where the colonials had removed all the planks and stacked them on the Cambridge side.

Percy sent some of his grenadiers over the stringers of the bridge and they retrieved enough planks to enable the foot soldiers to cross. He then hurried on, leaving a detachment of men to replace the remaining planks so that the supply wagons could follow.

In Menotomy, Percy encountered Lieutenant Edward Gould, of the King's Own Regiment, and Lieutenant Hull. Both had been wounded at the North Bridge in Concord and had left in a carriage ahead of the main British party. Apprised of the desperate situation of Smith's forces, Percy hurried on.

His departure was the signal for one of the most humorously heroic episodes of the day. When Captain Locke's company had departed for Concord, he had left behind in Menotomy, a dozen old men, those whose age or infirmity precluded service in the militia but who were on the "alarm list" to guard the town. No sooner was Percy out of sight than they emerged from places of concealment, captured Lieutenants Gould and Hull, and sent them off to Medford to avoid having them retaken when the British returned.

They had scarcely accomplished this when they received word that the supply wagons left behind by Percy, the bridge having been repaired, were again on their way. The old men—among them Jason and Joe Belknap, James Budge, Israel Mead, Ammi Cutter, and David Lamson—held a hurried strategy session at Cooper's Tavern. They decided to capture the supply train when it reached the town.

Menotomy, in 1775, was not a model of racial tolerance. The town records reveal the construction in that very year, of "new seats over the gallery stairs [of the meetinghouse] made for Negroes to sit in." But on April 19 such mundane matters were forgotten. The old men needed someone to direct their operation, and "they chose for their leader David Lamson, a mulatto, who had served in the [French] war, a man of undoubted bravery and determination."

Lamson situated his army of ancients behind a bank of earth and stones, across the road from the meetinghouse, and the old men waited for the supply train to appear. As the wagons came abreast, he ordered his men to their feet, took aim at the horses, and ordered the grenadiers to surrender.

The well-armed British soldiers, hearing the command from a handful of elderly farmers, refused to take it seriously. The drivers whipped up their horses, and Lamson's men opened fire. Accounts of their marksmanship vary, but they apparently killed two British soldiers, one a lieutenant, and four horses.

The incredulous drivers leaped from the wagons and ran, with their guards, to the shores of nearby Spy Pond. They threw their guns into the water, walked a short distance along the shore of the pond, and surrendered to old Mother Batherick, whom they found there digging dandelions. The old lady returned her prisoners to Lamson's men and gave the colonists a new slogan: "If one old lady can capture six grenadiers how many troops will King George have to send to conquer America?"

As for the black veteran and his elderly army, they had captured the first British troops and the first supplies in the American Revolution!

While Lamson and his men were burying the British horses, after first thriftily removing the horseshoes, Percy was joining forces with Smith at Lexington. The British column now had swelled to eighteen hundred men. Percy was a much more capable leader, and he promptly ordered a series of flanking maneuvers designed to trap the minutemen who were concealed in houses and behind the stone walls along the road. Lieutenant Frederick Mackenzie, of the Royal Welsh Fusiliers, described the action in his diary:

"Before the column had advanced a mile on the road we were fired on from all quarters, but particularly from the houses on the roadside and the adjacent stone walls, and the soldiers were so enraged at suffering from an unseen enemy that they forced open many of the houses from which the fire proceeded and put to death all those found in them."

The most successful of these maneuvers began when the

returning British force reached the flat country around Menotomy. Although the day's engagement is known as the Battle of Lexington and Concord, it was at Menotomy that the colonials sustained more casualties than at any other place. Among the twelve who died was a leading citizen, Jason Russell, two town drunks who lingered over their rum at Cooper's Tavern when the British approached, and the village idiot. In death, they shared the stature of heroes and were buried in a common grave in the town cemetery.

By the time the British were safely back in Boston, the day of fighting had cost them 273 casualties—about 20 percent of their force. Seventy-three grenadiers were dead, 174 wounded, and 26 missing. The colonials had not fared nearly so badly; their total casualties—including many who were not members of the militia—totaled 93, of whom 49 were dead.

The cost to Britain, however, was far greater than the casualties its army sustained. Ultimately, the day's events precipitated the loss of the American colonies, the American dead becoming the second installment on the price of freedom.

Three weeks before the battle at Lexington, Samuel Adams and other colonial leaders had agreed that, if war with the British began, the king's soldiers would attempt to isolate New England from the remaining colonies by marching along Lakes Champlain and George in New York and down the Hudson River to New York City. The colonists had already scouted the British defenses at Fort Ticonderoga, on Lake George, and found them undermanned and in bad repair.

Seizing the opportunity, the Massachusetts Committee of Safety had delegated Benedict Arnold of Connecticut to enlist a force of militia in New England and take Fort Ticonderoga from the British. Meanwhile, others had entrusted the same responsibility to Ethan Allen and his Green Mountain Boys.

Arnold went to Vermont, met with Allen, and, after a dispute over who would command the expedition, the two strong-willed men agreed to share a position at the head of the colonial columns. They arrived in front of Ticonderoga on the night of May 9 and found the entire forty-two-man garrison asleep, except for a lone sentry. The Americans seized the fort without a struggle and hauled its cannon back to Boston, where they were put to good service in driving the British out of that city.

Three blacks participated in this first offensive action by the American forces. Lemuel Haynes, who had served at Lexington and later would become an eloquent black missionary to white Vermont, was with the colonials. So were Epheram Blackman and Primas Black, who served with Allen's Green Mountain Boys.

The Second Continental Congress convened the day Ticonderoga fell, May 10, and two weeks later the British force in Boston was reinforced by troops under the command of Major Generals Howe, Burgoyne, and Clinton. On June 15, George Washington was elected supreme commander of the scattered colonial militia companies, which were brought together into the Continental Army.

Two days later, British and American soldiers met in the Battle of Bunker Hill, a hard-fought contest that actually took place on Breed's Hill, in the heights of Charlestown that overlooked Boston from the north side of the Charles River.

The stage for the Battle of Bunker Hill was set when the colonial leaders learned, on June 16, 1775, of a British plan to occupy Dorchester Heights, on the opposite side of Boston, two days later. As a countermove, they decided to fortify Bunker Hill.

On the night of June 16, responding to the call of General Artemas Ward, the American commander, militia regiments from all the nearby Massachusetts towns began to gather on the Charlestown peninsula. They were a ragged, undisciplined force, but what they lacked in military bearing was compensated for by courage, determination, and zeal.

When darkness fell, more than twelve hundred men had gathered on the peninsula. Shoulder to shoulder, the black and white patriots began the backbreaking task of building a first line of defense on Breed's Hill and a second line on Bunker Hill, which would shelter reinforcements and provide an avenue for retreat if that became necessary. As the night wore on, Colonel William Prescott, who was commanding the operation, frantically urged the men to work faster, least dawn catch them with the fortifications unfinished.

At dawn, Peter Salem, the black minuteman who had fought at Concord, arrived on Breed's Hill with the other soldiers of Colonel John Nixon's Fifth Massachusetts Regiment. They seized tools and began shoveling earth to complete the fortifications as the first shells began raining on their position from the British fleet at anchor in the harbor.

The men worked feverishly throughout the morning while a British force commanded by Sir William Howe waited for the tide so it could cross the Charles River in boats and land on the peninsula. By noon, despite the constant shelling from the British guns, they had finished a central redoubt and a series of breastworks designed to protect its flank. Then, protected from the barrage by their newly built fortifications, Colonel Nixon's regiment and several others rested and waited for the British attack. Behind them, on Bunker Hill, General Israel Putnam waited with reinforcements.

Howe's first attack came in early afternoon. It was a deceptive frontal assault intended to divert attention from the main attack on the American left flank. Because of the breastworks that had been placed there by Colonel Richard Gridley, the Continental Army's first chief engineer, the attack was repulsed.

The British regrouped and tried a frontal assault on the hastily built redoubt, but again they were thrown back by the determined defenders. The Americans had a brief respite while the British prepared for their third attack. The patriots' powder was running low, and Colonel Prescott moved among them, cautioning them not to waste it but to "hold your fire until you see the whites of their eyes." The Americans listened as Barzillai Lew, a thirty-year-old black cooper from Chelmsford, played his fife. Lew, who had fought in the French Wars, could also beat a drum if need be.

Cuff Whittemore, the black veteran of Lexington and Concord, was also among the patriots who awaited the Redcoats' third charge. He took a bullet through his hat. Caesar Brown of Westford was less fortunate. He took one through his chest to become one of the about 440 American casualties of the day, as compared to more than 1,000 for the British. Other black patriots who awaited the final British attack included Cato Tufts, Caesar Dickerson, Sampson Talbot, Grant Cooper, Cuff Hayes, Titus Coburn, Seymour Burr, Prince Hall, who would later found the Negro Masonic Order in America, and Caesar and Pharaoh, who were serving in Colonel James Scamman's York County "Regiment of Foot."

With bayonets fixed, the redcoats poured up the hill. Heeding Prescott's admonition to save their powder, the colonial soldiers held their fire until the forward British ranks mounted the wall. Peter Salem saw his officer, Colonel Nixon, fall. At almost the same moment he noticed, in the front rank that had just leaped to the parapet, the British commander, Major John Pitcairn, the villain of Lexington. Peter took careful aim. He heard Pitcairn shout, "Surrender, you rebels. The day is ours!" The black soldier's musket flashed, and the British officer fell dead.

The name of Peter Salem stands out among all who fought at Bunker Hill. Peter's comrades, impressed with his gallantry, took up a collection that they gave him as a reward, but an even more impressive moment came when he was presented to General Washington, his commander in chief.

Salem remained in the Continental Army through most of the Revolution—at least until 1780, and possibly until 1782. Such long service was rare in a war fought by civilians who often interrupted their service to tend to their business or look after crops. He spent the remainder of his life weaving cane in Leicester and Framingham, where he died in 1816. A memorial to him, erected by the Sons of the American Revolution, stands there today.

Another hero at Bunker Hill was Salem Poor, an ex-slave who had also been in action at Lexington and Concord two months before. There are no specific accounts of his service with Colonel Frye's regiment on that day, but it must have been extraordinary, because Colonel Prescott and thirteen of his officers petitioned the Continental Congress in his behalf.

"To set forth the particulars of his conduct would be tedious," the officers wrote, but "in justice to the Caracter of so Brave a Man . . . We declare that a Negro Man called Salem . . .

behaved like an Experienced officer, as well as an Excellent Soldier. . . ." The officers left to Congress the decision as to what reward was due "so great and Distinguished a Caracter" as this "Brave and gallant Soldier."

During the months that followed the Battle of Bunker Hill, the newly formed Continental Army began a policy of exclusion as far as black enlistments were concerned. Blacks who had already served in local militia companies were permitted to continue in service, but the recruiting of additional black soldiers was prohibited. In practice, the policy was not honored by many of the colonies, and as the war wore on it was abandoned because of the need for first-class soldiers, which blacks had already proved themselves to be.

One of the most persuasive arguments in behalf of the enlistment of black soldiers, which is also a social commentary still worth reading, was made by Alexander Hamilton. Writing to the president of the Continental Congress in March, 1779, he said:

"I foresee that this project will have to combat much opposition from prejudice and self-interest. The contempt we have been taught to entertain for the blacks, makes us fancy many things that are founded neither in reason nor experience; and an unwillingness to part with property of so valuable a kind will furnish a thousand arguments to show the impracticability or pernicious tendency of a scheme which requires such a sacrifice. But it should be considered, that if we do not make use of them in this way, the enemy probably will; and that the best way to counteract the temptations they will hold out will be to offer them ourselves. An essential part of the plan is to give them their freedom with their muskets. This will secure their fidelity, animate their courage, and I believe will have a good influence on those who remain, by opening a door to their emancipation. This circumstance, I confess, has no small weight in inducing me to wish the success of the project; for the dictates of humanity and true policy equally interest me in favour of this unfortunate class of men. . . ."

When the draft began, many black slaves were sent to serve in their masters' places, often gaining freedom as a reward. As the war shifted to the south, even states such as Virginia and Maryland began enlisting blacks. One black family in Virginia had nine men under arms.

Before the war ended with the surrender of Cornwallis at Yorktown, about five thousand blacks had served in the Continental army, and two thousand more with the American naval forces. For the most part, black soldiers served in integrated units, facing the enemy with white patriots at their side.

There were, however, occasional all-black regiments that, without exception, distinguished themselves. One of these served in the attempted siege of the British garrison at Newport, an American defeat that was, in fact, a successful withdrawal made necessary when a supporting French force was delayed by a hurricane at sea.

The colonial forces, pinned on an island without naval aid, included six brigades under General John Sullivan. Among them when the British counterattack came on August 29, 1778, was Colonel Christopher Green's First Regiment, a newly enlisted unit made up of 125 blacks. The assault was made by Hessian mercenaries, who directed it towards the all-black regiment, which, they believed, would offer the softest spot in the American line because of its inexperience. Instead, they encountered stubborn and unrelenting opposition from the black soldiers, who withstood three charges without giving ground.

Although the British force eventually drove the Americans across the Sakonnet River, it was an orderly withdrawal in which the king's troops sustained nearly five times as many casualties as the colonial brigades. The black soldiers' performance and courage won high praise from the white defenders of other sections of the line and from colonial military authorities.

William Eustis, an army surgeon who later became governor of Massachusetts, described the service of the black Rhode Island regiment the preceding fall in the defense of Red Bank:

"Among the traits which distinguished this regiment was their devotion to the officers [white]: When their brave Col. Greene was afterwards cut down and mortally wounded, the sabres of the enemy reached his body only through the limbs of his faithful guard of blacks, who hovered over him and protected him, every one of whom was killed. . . ."

Eustis, noting the paradox that in the Revolution, as in every war since, black soldiers had fought for freedom that they have never fully won, added the comment:

"The war over, and peace restored, these men returned to their respective states; and who could have said to them, on their return to civil life, after having shed their blood in common with whites in the defense of the liberties of the country: 'You are not to participate in the rights secured by the struggle, or in the liberty for which you have been fighting.' "

Throughout the remaining years of the struggle to win independence for America, black patriots participated in every major encounter with the British. Salem Poor, continuing to display the courage for which he had been cited at Bunker Hill, remained in George Washington's command to endure the bitter winter at Valley Forge, shoeless and half-starved, and then to fight at White Plains.

David Lamson, the black man who had led the old men of the town in the capture of the first British soldiers at Menotomy, tramped off at Washington's call for four days of service to help drive the British from Boston with the capture of Dorchester Heights in March of 1776. His name turns up again in the town records five years later, when he was taxed twenty shillings and sixpence to supply Washington's army with beef.

In December, 1775, at the Battle of Great Bridge, which took place on the Elizabeth River about twelve miles below Norfolk, Virginia, a band of colonial troops faced a superior British force under Lord Dunmore. When the Americans were finally forced to withdraw, the last to leave was a free black named William Flora, who got off eight last shots at the advancing redcoats before he followed his retreating comrades "amidst a shower of musket balls."

Black soldiers were with General Washington when he crossed the Delaware; one, Prince Whipple, was in the general's own boat. A black soldier in Captain Pelton's company of the Second New York Regiment, Phillip Field of Dutchess County,

New York, died at Valley Forge during the bitter winter of 1778.

In July, 1777, in one of the most daring and audacious exploits of the Revolution, a party of colonial soldiers raided the British headquarters at Newport, Rhode Island, and captured General Richard Prescott, who was in his nightshirt, asleep. It was a black soldier named Jack Sisson who arrived first at the general's bedroom and broke down the door.

Many black soldiers served as spies for the American forces. One of them, Pompey, obtained the British password and helped overpower a picket when General "Mad Anthony" Wayne attacked Stony Point, New York, in July, 1779. The Americans won a British fort, more than five hundred prisoners, and some badly needed supplies. Pompey, a slave, was a double victor. He was given his freedom. Another who won his freedom for espionage was James, the slave of Virginia planter William Armistead. Before the Battle of Yorktown, he served as a spy for French General Lafayette, bringing valuable information from the British camp.

After the British surrender, Cornwallis was startled to see James in Lafayette's quarters: while the black slave had been spying for Lafayette, the British had thought he was spying for them. James was emancipated and awarded a pension by the Virginia legislature. In later years, when the French general visited Richmond, he was reunited with his spy and found that he had taken the name James Lafayette.

The mixed crews on the colonial naval vessels contained many blacks, some of whom served as pilots because of their intimate knowledge of the coastal waters. They were with John Paul Jones, David Porter, and James Barry. One of them, James Forten, was only fourteen when he served as a powder boy with Stephen Decatur on the "Royal Louis." Captured by the British and offered freedom in England, he declined. "I am here a prisoner for the liberties of my country," Forten said. "I never, never, shall prove a traitor to her interests." Forten later became a wealthy sailmaker in Philadelphia.

Virginia, which floated the largest of the state navies during the Revolution, used many black pilots, among them Caesar, who was the slave of Carter Tarrant of Hampton. The Virginia legislature purchased Caesar's freedom after the schooner "Patriot" captured the British brig "Fanny" while the black sailor was at the wheel.

Examples of courage during the Revolution were not confined to men. Molly Pitcher, for one, has been idealized in American history because of her fearless response during the Battle of Monmouth, when she carried water to the American soldiers and then seized a gun herself when her husband fell.

Unsung, but even more gallant, were the actions of a black woman, Deborah Gannett. She enlisted on May 20, 1782, as a regular soldier in the Fourth Massachusetts Regiment under the name of Robert Shurtliff and served for nearly a year and a half before her masquerade was detected. Nearly ten years later, the Massachusetts legislature gave her an award of thirty-four pounds for her "extraordinary instance of female heroism."

Male and female, the patriots who won America's freedom truly wrote a story of courage in black and white.

CHAPTER III

BUILDING A NEW NATION

The early years of the nineteenth century found a young America struggling to consolidate its victory over the British and establish itself as a nation of power and influence on the world scene. Meanwhile, many of the blacks who had won their freedom through valorous service in the War for Independence were joined by white abolitionists in the fight to win freedom for all black people in America. The inconsistency of denying freedom to a race that had fought and died to win it for the nation was a powerful argument for the gradual abolition of slavery in the states north of the Mason-Dixon Line.

The nation's hopes for greatness were emphasized when President Washington engaged Pierre L'Enfant, a French engineer and architect who had served as an officer in the Revolutionary Army, to lay out a grand design for the new capital at Washington, D. C. Secretary of State Thomas Jefferson provided L'Enfant with maps of the great cities of Europe, and the Frenchman set out to design a plan "drawn on such a scale as to leave room for that aggrandisement and embellishment which the increase of the wealth of the nation will permit it to pursue at any period however remote."

At Jefferson's suggestion, L'Enfant enlisted to assist him a black surveyor, Benjamin Banneker, a free Marylander of great brilliance, dignity, and charm. Although self-taught, Banneker published an almanac that so impressed Jefferson that he sent a copy to the head of the French Academy of Science as evidence that "the want of talents" ascribed to blacks "is merely the effect of their degraded condition."

Banneker and George Ellicott, a Quaker friend, selected the sites for the Capitol, the White House, and other major government buildings. The black surveyor also helped L'Enfant lay out the ingenious arrangement of broad avenues, mall, circles, and parks that make Washington such an attractive city even today. When a dispute arose between L'Enfant and George Washington in 1792, resulting in the French architect's dismissal, the plans disappeared. The design might have been lost had not Banneker and Ellicott been able to reconstruct it from memory.

At the time of the black surveyor's death in 1806, Thomas Jefferson was occupying the White House, built on the site that his black friend had selected. Jefferson, no mean architect himself, found time to design the east and west terraces and one-story offices that were attached to the original structure, but he was mainly preoccupied with the new nation's effort to develop its resources and build a stake in international trade. This, in a nation greatly dependent on imports from abroad, meant the building of an effective merchant fleet.

Many blacks served aboard the vessels that sought to establish American eminence at sea. Three of them were participants in an episode that ultimately led to the second war with England in less than three decades.

Harassment of American shipping by the British navy was growing steadily as England, warring with Napoleon on the European continent, resorted to increasingly harsh measures to halt the flow of contraband goods to France. American ships were often fired upon, boarded, and searched by British seamen.

American resentment reached its peak in June, 1807, when the "Chesapeake," a United States naval vessel, was fired upon by the royal man-of-war "Leopard" almost within the harbor at Norfolk, Virginia. Three American sailors were killed, eighteen wounded, and four seized and held on charges of desertion from the British navy. One of the four prisoners did prove to be a deserter and was executed. The other three—all black sailors—were able to prove that they were Americans and were finally released.

Bitterness over the incident was inflamed by a British practice that was even more unpalatable to freedom-conscious Americans, that of impressing American seamen into service with the Royal Navy. Although John Strachan, Daniel Martin, and William Ware, the three black sailors taken from the "Chesapeake," were released, many others were not so fortunate. British officers, searching American vessels for deserters, had few scruples about forcing able-bodied men—deserters or not—to serve under the British flag. From 1809 onward, the total of impressed American seaman ranged from 750 to 1,000 a year.

Meanwhile, the purchase of the Louisiana Territory from France in 1803 seemed to spur, in the new nation, the conviction that America's destiny lay in the expansion of its borders. With the desire to explore and settle the great expanse to the west came the ambition on the part of many Americans to include Canada within the nation's borders. American eagerness to expand northward and control the rich fur trade, along with anger at the British for their support of Indian raids on the western and northwestern settlements, helped quite as much as the maritime grievances to set the stage for President Madison's formal declaration of war on England on June 19, 1812.

War, when it came, found the nation with few resources other than courage and determination. It was weak in ships and the materials of war, and weaker than need be in fighting men because of laws that prohibited the enlistment of blacks in the military services. Despite the valor of black patriots in the recent struggle for independence, Congress in 1792 had limited enrollment in the militia to white citizens. A policy directive in 1798 forbade the use of blacks in the army, navy, or marines.

The directive was widely ignored, particularly by ship captains who knew the value of the blacks in their crews. Yet, even for the "free men of color"—blacks who had escaped from slavery or managed to buy their freedom—there was little opportunity to prove again their courage or their loyalty to the country they regarded as their own. It was not until 1803 that

Congress so much as resolved to "enquire into the expediency" of granting black sailors the same protection that was afforded white seamen.

Underneath the overt actions that limited the black man's hope of full participation in citizenship, in war and in peace, were sentiments directly opposed to those expressed by Jefferson and other thoughtful men of the time. A southern writer, Rev. Dr. Joseph Ingraham, put into words the self-delusion, unsupported by science or history, that the black was "wholly destitute of courage. . . . Cowardice is a principal of his soul, as instinctive as courage is in the white man." How black men were forced to disprove that belief, time and again through all the major episodes of American history—and that they remained willing to do so—is one of the most inspiring facets of human achievement in America.

The United States, at the outbreak of war in 1812, had a fleet woefully small in numbers. In the face of a much larger British fleet that had clamped an effective blockade on all the major American ports, there was no possibility of a concerted effort to slug it out, fleet to fleet or even squadron to squadron.

The nation's naval leaders were compelled to adopt tactics not unlike those of the minutemen during the British retreat from Concord more than forty years before. Given great freedom to act independently, the fleet struck where and when it could, evading a watchful enemy if his force was too great but battling fiercely, ship to ship, when a vulnerable target presented itself.

Thus, America's earliest victories in the war at sea were battles between single vessels: "Constitution" versus "Guerrière" in August, 1812; Decatur's "United States" versus "Macedonian" in October; David Porter's amazingly successful raids against British shipping in both the Atlantic and the South Pacific in 1813.

Equally telling were the blows struck by American privateers. Their crews, out for booty as much as for glory, included more black seamen than the naval vessels in the early stages of the war because they were not subject to the same restrictions against the use of blacks. Prowling the Atlantic with speed and daring, they harassed British merchant shipping, occasionally engaged an enemy warship, and at one point captured and held an Irish island and a town on the Scottish coast.

It was on one such privateer, the "Gov. Tompkins," that two black sailors—John Johnson and John Davis—displayed the kind of courage that has won respect and admiration for black fighting men in each of our nation's wars. In a letter written on January 1, 1813, the ship's commander, Nathaniel Shaler, described how at sunrise his privateer had come upon three British ships, the largest of which appeared to be a large transport:

"Before I could get our light sails in, and almost before I could turn around, I was under the guns, (not of a transport) but of a large *frigate!*—and not more than a quarter of a mile from her. I immediately . . . commenced a brisk fire from our little battery; but this was returned with woeful interest.

"Her first broadside killed two men and wounded six others. . . . The name of one of my poor fellows who was killed ought to be registered in the book of fame, and remembered with reverence as long as bravery is considered a virtue; he was a black man by the name of John Johnson; a 24 lb. shot struck him in the hip and took away all the lower part of his body; in this state the poor brave fellow lay on the deck, and several times exclaimed to his shipmates, 'Fire away my boys, no haul a color down.'

"The other was also a black man, by the name of John Davis, and was struck in much the same way: he fell near me, and several times requested to be thrown overboard, saying, he was only in the way of others. While America has such tars, she has little to fear from the tyrants of the ocean."

However brave their black and white crews, the combined forces of raiding privateers and American naval vessels were never enough to break the power of the Royal Navy's blockade of the coast. And in the west, during the first months of the war, American efforts on land were even more frustrating.

The first was an abortive attempt by troops under General William Hull to invade Canada. Hull's weeks of weary marching and building trails across western Ohio—after more weeks of indecisive probing and failure to mount an offensive—gave

British Major General Isaac Brock time to organize a stout defense that brought Hull's expedition to an inglorious end with his surrender at Detroit on August 16, 1812.

Near Niagara, a second drive to penetrate the British colony two months later was driven back by a superior and better disciplined force at Queenston Heights. Coupled with the loss of Fort Dearborn and the massacre of the American garrison by Potawatomi Indians, these early defeats left the northwestern territory of the Americans with little or no defense against a possible British invasion.

What soon became apparent to the Americans—aside from the revelation that some of their generals were less than competent—was that the strategic key to victory in the Northwest was not to be found on land at all, but in the control of the Great Lakes. There is reason to believe that the British, lulled by the relative ease with which they had disposed of the first American attacks, overlooked the possibility of an American offensive in these inland waters until it was too late.

In 1813, the Americans set to work building a fleet of fighting ships to operate on the Great Lakes. Four ships were built at Presque Isle (near the present site of Erie, Pennsylvania), five others at Black Rock, on Lake Ontario. The latter, in order to reach Lake Erie, where a British fleet of six vessels was being assembled, had to be warped up the Niagara River.

As the American ships left the ways, completed on crash schedules by teams of black and white artisans, the American fleet commander, Oliver H. Perry, had other problems. Chief among them was his difficulty in mustering crews for all of the vessels. Captain Perry complained to Commodore Isaac Chauncey of the Navy Department that he was being sent nothing but "blacks, soldiers, and boys."

Chauncey replied that Captain Perry should be happy with the blacks he was getting because "they are not surpassed by any seamen we have in the fleet and I have yet to learn that the color of a man's skin or the cut and trimming of the coat can affect a man's qualifications or usefulness. I have nearly fifty blacks on board of this ship, and many of them are among my best men."

By late August, Perry had four hundred men and, despite his reservations, more than one hundred of them were black. In early September, his ships gunned, manned, and provisioned, Perry set out westward on Lake Erie to engage the British.

He found the enemy on September 10 at Put-in-Bay, near the western tip of the lake. The British, with superior long-range guns, blasted Perry's leading ships with heavy fire. The Americans, with no alternative, continued to close in as the hail of enemy shot poured among the crewmen.

Perry's flagship, the "Lawrence," was put out of action; he escaped, took command of the "Niagara," and returned to battle. As the battered American vessels moved within close range of the outnumbered British, they poured the full power of their broadsides into the enemy vessels. One by one, the British ships were sunk or captured. When the battle was over, the British fleet had disappeared as an effective force in the Great Lakes, and control of the water remained in American hands.

A single phrase of Perry's report on the Battle of Lake Erie is recalled in every textbook of American history: "We have met the enemy and they are ours." Rarely mentioned is the praise he lavished on the black members of his crew, the men of whom he had complained a few months earlier. These sailors, the captain said, "seemed absolutely insensible to danger."

Control of the lakes, gained by Perry's men at Put-in-Bay, enabled the Americans to transport soldiers by water in one last attempt to invade Canada and wrest control of the territory from England. While never successful in reaching their objective, Montreal, the American troops were able to recoup their earlier losses in the west by recapturing Detroit and pursuing the British northward to defeat at the Battle of the Thames on October 5, 1813. It was in this battle that the Shawnee Indian leader, Tecumseh, was killed.

Although the Americans did not win new territory in Canada, the black soldiers who fought with the American forces found new hope for freedom there. Their reports of the potential of the country north of the border as a haven for fugitive slaves were in large measure responsible for the development of the

Underground Railroad that carried runaway slaves to Canada in the years after the War of 1812.

The final defeat of Napoleon ended England's need to commit troops to battle on the European continent and enabled the British to bring additional pressures to bear in the defense of Canada and, offensively, against the United States.

With the Americans in firm control of the west, that theater never again became the scene of major military action. There was no further significant activity west of Niagara and a siege of Fort Erie in 1814 was beaten off. Lake Erie remained under United States control, although the British navy, commanded by Sir James Yeo, dominated Lake Ontario.

The black and white sailors of the American navy had another opportunity to display their valor in September, 1814, when a British force of eleven thousand men crossed the border near Lake Champlain and began a drive down the western side of the lake. The assault was intended to be a combined land and water operation, with ground troops attacking the fortified American base at Plattsburgh while British ships engaged the American fleet on Lake Champlain. The effort failed, again because of a naval battle, when the American vessels met and destroyed the British fleet in Plattsburgh Bay. Without the support of naval guns, the British land forces were decisively beaten at Plattsburgh and retreated to the north.

The most successful British venture, particularly because of its effect on American morale, was the attack on the nation's capital in the summer of 1814. A large force of British troops, under Major General Robert Ross, moved up Chesapeake Bay under the protection of the Royal Navy and landed near Washington in late August of that year.

In the capital, feverish preparations were made both for the defense of the city and for evacuation of the government to a place of safety. President and Mrs. Madison abandoned the White House–Dolley Madison, at the last moment, taking with her a portrait of George Washington–as the enemy force approached the town of Bladensburg, where a defense of the capital was to be made.

The mayor of Washington, James Blake, issued an order that all able-bodied citizens—including "all free men of color"—were to report for duty to help build redoubts for the American troops who would meet the British at Bladensburg. The order went out on August 21, and the following day an issue of *The National Intelligencer* reported:

"An immense crowd of every description of persons attended to offer their services. . . . It is with much pleasure also we state that on this occasion the free people of color in this city acted as became patriots . . . conducting themselves with the utmost order and propriety."

Considering that the newspaper conspicuously ignored black Americans on most other occasions, and in the same edition offered them for sale in the slave markets of Washington, this was high praise indeed. Blacks again had showed their determination to act, side by side with white Americans, in the defense of their country.

The combined efforts of both races, in this instance, were not enough. The British pushed through to occupy Washington on the twenty-fourth of August, burning the Capitol and other government buildings, including the White House. They were not able to hold the city, however, and abandoned it to reembark on their transports in less than a week.

As 1814 drew to a close, the battle that young America had been fighting for nearly three years against her former rulers was virtually a stalemate. In the Northwest, the confederation of Indian tribes that had supported the British in assaults on American forces in Canada had been broken up. The victory of Perry's fleet on Lake Erie and the defeat of the English on land and water at Plattsburgh had effectively put an end to any serious threat of invasion from the north. The national capital, although raided and held for a few days by the enemy, was again safely in American hands.

Only in the South did it appear that the British might yet be able to mount a successful offensive. Even as the British were attacking Washington, there were strong indications that this was, in fact, the British plan.

In August of 1814, British troops landed in West Florida and took Pensacola. General Andrew Jackson, in command of the Seventh Military District, led his forces in the recapture of the city, an action that was only a prelude to a much more decisive and memorable encounter that was to come a few months later and a few hundred miles to the west.

Jackson was convinced that the British would make their major assault in the South on Mobile. Even later, when it became apparent that New Orleans—with its sea trade and its strategic control of the most important inland water route, the Mississippi—was the eventual goal of the enemy, he continued to believe that the attack would come overland from Mobile. When he was called upon to organize the defenses of New Orleans, that conviction continued to influence his actions—and very nearly led to one of the great blunders of American military history.

Wherever the attack might come from, there was no doubt in the fall of 1814 that New Orleans was such an inviting prize that the British would seize the first opportunity to take it. Jackson moved from Mobile to take personal charge of organizing the defenses, and from the outset it was clear that the black population of the charming old French and Spanish city would have a significant role in his plans.

That Jackson should consider the use of black troops indispensable to his defense of New Orleans is not surprising. He had been given ample opportunity to observe the performance of black soldiers elsewhere. Moreover, after 1809 "free men of color" had become as numerous in New Orleans, or very nearly so, as white men. An 1805 census counted about 3,500 white residents and nearly 1,600 free blacks, and to the latter had been added, in 1809, nearly 2,000 free blacks who had arrived by way of Cuba from the revolution in Santo Domingo.

Jackson was also encouraged by the fact that many of the free Louisiana blacks had already received extensive military training. Under Spanish rule, two large companies of black militia had been organized and entrusted with maintaining law and order in the streets of the often brawling seaport.

Even before he arrived in New Orleans, Jackson had been confronted with the question of whether the former black militiamen should be called into service and rearmed. White sentiment was generally against it; the threat of slave rebellions had engendered terror over the suggestion that black people be given weapons.

This fear was not totally unreasoned, because there were many examples of rebellion or attempts by slaves to rebel. Many recalled the abortive rebellion organized by Gabriel Prosser, a slave, in Henrico County, Virginia, in 1800. Some had estimated that as many as fifty thousand slaves would have been involved in the revolt if the plot had not been found out in advance. The numbers were frightening, but even more unnerving was the calm, cold courage with which thirty-five of the plotters who were executed had met their fate. One, asked whether he had anything to say at his trial, had replied:

"I have nothing more to offer than what General Washington would have had to offer, had he been taken by the British officers and put to trial by them. I have ventured my life in endeavouring to obtain the liberty of my countrymen, and am a willing sacrifice to their cause; and I beg, as a favour, that I may be immediately led to my execution. I know that you have predetermined to shed my blood, why then all this mockery of a trial?"

In his decision to rearm the black militiamen, Jackson also had to contend with a feeling that, having served under Spanish rule, they might be less than dedicated to the United States.

No supporter of the "free men of color" was more determined or influential than the governor of the Louisiana Territory, William C. Claiborne. Within a week after the transfer of the territory to the United States in 1803, he had written to Secretary of State James Madison that the black militia were "esteemed a very serviceable corps" and that "not to recommission them would disgust them, and might be productive of future mischief." The territorial House of Representatives in 1807 advised Governor Claiborne to "give to the Battalion of free men of Color the activity which their zeal sollicits." They were used on several occasions after that, including one, in 1811, requiring them to put down a serious slave rebellion in the Parish of St. John the Baptist.

So it was that Governor Claiborne, at the time of the British capture of Pensacola, was able to report, in a letter to General Jackson about the future defense of New Orleans, that there were units of free blacks ready to assist. He pointed out to Jackson that these men, under the Spanish, "were always relied on in time of difficulties, and on several occasions evinced in the field the greatest firmness and courage." Claiborne added that he had interviewed officers of the companies, themselves black, and that "they expressed their devotion to their country and their readiness to defend it."

There apparently was never any serious question in Jackson's mind about the desirability of joining black and white forces in the defense of New Orleans. Some insight into his feelings about black soldiers can be gleaned from a stern note he wrote to an assistant paymaster of the Seventh Military District when the man objected to paying black troops in cash:

"Be pleased to keep to yourself your opinions upon the policy of making payments to particular Corps. It is enough for you to receive my order for the payment of troops with the necessary muster rolls, without enquiring whether the troops are white, Black, or Tea."

Even if Jackson had misgivings that he never revealed, they were set to rest by his first review of the militia after his arrival in New Orleans. Fewer than six hundred volunteers appeared for the first parade, but more than a third of them were "free men of color" from the Santo Domingo battalion.

In the end, it proved to be Jackson—even more than Claiborne—who upheld the right of the black man to defend his country on equal footing with the white soldier. His "Proclamation to the free colored inhabitants of Louisiana," dated September 21, 1814, was held up for more than a month before Governor Claiborne mustered the courage to release it. The proclamation told the blacks, in part:

"Through a mistaken policy you have heretofore been deprived of a participation in the glorious struggle for national rights in which our country is engaged. This no longer shall exist.

"As sons of freedom, you are now called upon to defend our most inestimable blessing. . . . Your country, although calling for your exertions, does not wish you to engage in her cause, without amply remunerating you for the services rendered. . . . To every noble-hearted, generous, freeman of color, volunteering to serve during the present contest with Great Britain, and no longer, there will be paid the same bounty in money and lands, now received by the white soldiers of the U. States. . . . On enrolling yourselves in companies, the major-general commanding will select officers for your government, from your white fellow citizens. Your non-commissioned officers will be appointed from among yourselves."

The proclamation, in an apparent effort to justify the segregated character of the units, assured New Orleans blacks that they would not be "exposed to improper comparisons or unjust sarcasm" but would, as an independent battalion or regiment, "receive the applause and gratitude of your countrymen."

The two groups of black militia were under the general supervision of a wealthy white merchant, Colonel Michel Fortier, Sr., who provided them with much of the war material—arms, ammunition, and supplies—they needed. In actual command of the first battalion was a white planter, Major Pierre LaCoste.

Although formation of the second battalion is also credited to Fortier, it appears that Joseph Savary, referred to as "a mulatto from Santo Domingo" and at various times as a captain, major, and colonel, had much to do with organizing it into an effective fighting force. Actual command of the second battalion was held by Major Louis Daquin, or D'Aquin—a white man from Santo Domingo. It is believed that the black troops themselves selected him as their leader.

Nearly five hundred free blacks who had enlisted in the two battalions were among the six thousand soldiers who stood at attention before General Jackson in his final review before the British attacked the city. The general singled them out for special praise when, after the review, one of his aides read an address to them:

"Soldiers—. . . . you surpass my hopes. I have found in you, united to those qualities, that noble enthusiasm which impels great deeds.

"Soldiers—the President of the United States shall be informed of your conduct on the present occasion, and the voice of the representatives of the American nation shall applaud your valor, as your general now praises your ardor. The enemy is near; his 'sails cover the lakes;' but the brave are united; and if he finds us contending among ourselves, it will be for the prize of valor and fame its noblest reward."

In preparing his defenses, Jackson attempted to cover all the likely approaches to the city, including the multitude of swampy bayous and long fingers of shallow water that lead from the Gulf of Mexico through and around the Mississippi Delta. Despite these precautions, however, Jackson held to his conviction that a British trek overland from Mobile was the most logical approach. If such an attack were to come, the probable route would lie across the Plain of Gentilly, north and east of the city. The main artery of transport across the plain was the Chef Menteur Road, which Jackson ordered guarded by several batteries.

It is significant that the troops the general chose to guard the spot he considered most vulnerable included the battalion of blacks under Major LaCoste. The battalion commanded by Daquin was kept in New Orleans, on the alert to be moved to help repel an attack that might come from another direction.

When the attack finally came, neither Jackson's intuition nor his supplementary precautions proved to be of value. The British chose a route of attack that very nearly succeeded in taking Jackson completely by surprise. At no other time in the War of 1812 had the enemy been able to approach so close to an American general's headquarters without warning.

The British, under Major General Sir Edward Pakenham, chose to move by water, seeking out a route that wound its way through the bayous east and south of New Orleans toward the city itself. Whether through chance or superior knowledge of the general's preparations, the route they chose was one that Jackson had left unguarded. The King's soldiers had moved inland to the Villeré plantation only nine miles east of the city, disembarked, and set up camp before word reached Jackson on December 23 that the enemy was on his doorstep.

If it is true that Jackson's oversight almost brought disaster to the Americans, it is also true that his reaction was swift and sure, and that the choice he made was perhaps the only one that could have saved his position. The general decided to attack immediately, before the British had time to organize the march that would surely result in the capture of New Orleans. Seeking to disorganize the British, thus giving the city time to prepare new defenses, Jackson ordered a night assault on the British camp.

Taking about fifteen hundred of his men into action under the cover of darkness and a heavy, swirling fog, Jackson pounced on the British camp. His force was a motley one that included, in addition to Savary's two hundred well-disciplined "free men of color" under Daquin's command, an assortment of Creoles, farmers, Choctaw Indians, and even the Barataria pirates of Jean Laffite. Supporting the attack was the American gunboat "Carolina," moored in the Mississippi and firing into the British lines.

The now legendary hero of the engagement was a black soldier who served with neither of the black battalions, but with the United States Seventh Regiment, which moved early into the fray. Forty years later, as a bearded veteran of two wars, he would march at the head of New Orleans' patriotic parades, but on this occasion he was a small, fearless, fourteen-year-old drummer boy.

In the fog, darkness, clamor, and confusion that followed the American attack, the role of this youngster was crucial to the American victory. It was Jordan B. Noble's drum, rattling incessantly in the center of the battle—"in the hottest hell of fire" —that held Jackson's troops together. Marcus Christian, in a monograph written for the 150th anniversary of the battle, described the course it took:

"As the men swarmed into action on the cold, foggy night of December 23, it was 'give and take' on both sides, whereupon the British, finding that there was not enough 'give' in the American lines, attempted to force the left flank. Meeting this threat, the Forty-Fourth began to oblique. Then, Major Plauche's highly vaunted Creoles, in company with Savary's colored troops under Daquin's command, and Jegeat's Choctaws, all advanced to meet the flanking movement of the oncoming British. The British, intent upon outflanking the 44th regiment, stumbled within pistol shot of the colored battalion.

"It was then, according to Gayarré, that 'instantly a well-sustained fire began and was warmly kept up on both sides.' It was probably at this point that Savary's cry, 'March on! March on, my friends, march on against the enemies of the country!' was first raised in his Santo Domingo French. . . .

"The December night was very cold. After a half-hour of fighting, the heavy fog dropped lower, mixing with the smoke of battle. There was, at times, considerable confusion among troops on both sides. When the fight came close, it often developed into a series of duels between regiments, battalions, companies, squads, and even individuals. Under such circumstances, the Negro troops fared well, although some of the guns which Colonel Fortier had repaired for the free men of color failed at the crucial moment, and in the hand-to-hand fighting they were used as clubs. Of the valor of the men from Santo Domingo, Jackson said in his report: 'Savary's volunteers manifested great bravery.' "

The outcome of the battle itself was indeterminate—a victory for neither side. But it was the prelude to victory for the Americans and to a shattering defeat for the other side. The British were thrown off balance by the suddenness and savagery of Jackson's night attack, and morning found them in no condition to press on toward New Orleans.

Jackson and his improbable collection of heroes, with a daring stroke, had bought the time they needed. The general used it to draw his troops closer to the city and to build a defensive line along the Rodriguez Canal. It extended along the north bank of the canal—the bank nearest the city—from the Mississippi on the west to a nearly impenetrable swamp on the east.

His call went out to the men of New Orleans—black and white, slave and free—to assist in building the wall of mud, logs, and cotton bales behind which his troops would shelter while turning their fire into the advancing British. Nearly two thousand blacks were among those who labored on the building of the redoubts. Some were "free men of color" not fit for service with the militia, but one historian reports that they "might as well have been slaves," considering the backbreaking work required of them.

An artillery duel on New Year's Day, 1815, foreshadowed the main engagement, which came exactly one week later. A small force of British was sent up the west bank of the Mississippi in an attempt to turn the American flank, but the main body of British troops made its assault on January 8, 1815, against the strongly fortified line that Jackson had built on the opposite bank of the canal.

Behind the stout fortifications—at the very center of the line—was the largest assembly of black troops ever gathered on American soil. Both the LaCoste and Daquin-Savary battalions were there, side by side, in the line held elsewhere by Generals Carroll, Coffee, and Adair. Black companies were scattered throughout the regiments that held other sections of the line.

Pakenham sent the bulk of his British troops against the largely white regiments, apparently believing that they were untrained militiamen who would quickly give way. He was wrong, and the unerring fire of the Tennessee and Kentucky riflemen mowed down column after column of the advancing British.

The eager black militiamen of LaCoste and Daquin chafed at the inactivity before their position at the center of the line. Finally, their impatience became so great that their officers could no longer restrain them, and black soldiers began leaving the ranks to make unauthorized sorties against the British, who otherwise were too far away.

A man of Plauche's battalion, Vincent Nolte, wrote in a letter to *The Niles Register* that Daquin's battalion was next to his and that the "New Orleans colored regiment were so anxious for glory that they could not be prevented from advancing from over our breastworks and exposing themselves."

One of the thirteen Americans killed in the battle was black, and about one-third of the wounded were from the black battalions. The British lost more than two thousand men, including General Pakenham. In the confusion of the battle it was impossible to be certain who had fired the shot that brought Pakenham down. Jackson himself thought the credit should go to one of his black soldiers. In a letter written some time later to President Monroe, Jackson commented:

"I heard a single rifle shot from a group of country carts we had been using, and a moment thereafter I saw Pakenham reel and pitch out of his saddle. I have always believed he fell from the bullet of a free man of color, who was a famous rifle shot and came from the Attakaps region of Louisiana."

The withering American fire held the British so far from the American lines that they never reached a position from which to storm the redoubts. With their general dead, the survivors finally withdrew. The audacity of Jackson, and the mutual courage of his black and white troops, had won the day.

Ironically, had it been a century later the battle would never have been fought. It occurred two weeks after the hostilities between the two nations had been halted with the signing, in Europe, of the Treaty of Ghent. Because of the primitive communications of the day, the news had not yet reached either Jackson or Pakenham in New Orleans.

Jackson's victory, nevertheless, served a purpose that might not have been quickly accomplished in any other way. The decisive American defeat of Pakenham's army settled forever the fate of the Louisiana Territory. The western lands were, from then on, unquestioned American territory—open to American explorers and traders—settled by American farmers and cattlemen and miners.

The War of 1812, born out of America's desire to develop its commerce on land and on sea, had accomplished its purpose. Commerce was to be free, and the West was open to hardy men—black and white—who would blaze its trails and lead its settlers to new homes on the new frontiers.

CHAPTER IV

TAMING THE WESTERN WILDERNESS

Western America was a vast and unexplored wilderness on the January day in 1815 when Jackson's motley army defeated Pakenham at New Orleans, sealing the nation's authority to explore without British interference the territory that lay beyond the Mississippi.

Only along the Rio Grande and on the Pacific coast south of San Francisco Bay were there the embryonic signs of civilization. The adventures of Estevanico and Coronado, although they had yielded no gold, had captured the imagination of other explorers and settlers—many of them black—and led to continuing Spanish efforts to settle the territory that is now Texas, Arizona, and New Mexico. The Spanish had also pushed into California by both land and sea.

The initial permanent colonies on the west coast were established by Captain Gaspar de Portolá, the Spanish governor of Baja California, whose land and sea expedition led to the settlement of San Diego in 1769. The party then ventured northward to Monterey and San Francisco Bay, the explorers eating their pack animals along the way. In the half century that followed, a chain of missions was established along *el camino real* ("the king's highway"), with Africans as well as Spaniards residing in most of them.

The presidio of San Francisco was established in 1776, while the American colonies were engaged in their struggle for freedom. A Spaniard, Don Juan Bautista de Anza, had marched overland with a thirty-man army and two hundred colonists, to establish the colony on the shores of San Francisco Bay. Los Angeles had its inconspicuous beginnings only five years later, in September, 1781, when a party of eleven families, recruited in Mexico by Fernando de Rivera y Moncada, ended its weary trek and began building a crude village from bricks made of clay. Of the forty-six settlers, more than half—twenty-eight—were black. Governor Felipe de Neve, perhaps envisioning a day when the tiny cluster of adobe huts would become a great city, romantically named the unimpressive colony *El Pueblo de Nuestra Señora la Reina de Los Ángeles de Porciuncula* ("The Town of Our Lady the Queen of the Angels of Porciuncula").

Between California and the sparse settlements at St. Louis and St. Charles along the Mississippi and the lower Missouri was a region of mountain, plain, and forest, inhabited by buffalo, grizzly bear, and Indian, into which no American, white or black, had ever ventured. Although explored by only a few, and only on its fringes, the territory was desired by many.

The French explorer La Salle had established France's claim to the Louisiana Territory in 1682, when he descended the Mississippi and declared the entire drainage basin of that great river to be French. The Spanish held similar claims by virtue of their explorations from the south. Britain, which held Canada to the north, still coveted the rich furs that were believed to exist in the unexplored territory. None of these nations, however, was in a position to exploit its claims.

The legal status of Louisiana Territory, so far as European interests were concerned, was resolved by military might in Europe in 1800, when Napoleon forced Spain to return the territory to France. Thus, when Thomas Jefferson became president of the United States in 1801, France was holding a huge territory on America's western borders. In the interests of security as well as expansion, Jefferson wanted these lands for America.

Knowing that France had been weakened by Napoleon's military ventures, Jefferson instructed the American minister to France, Robert R. Livingston, to make overtures for the purchase of a portion of the Louisiana Territory. Later, he dispatched his friend James Monroe to Paris as a special envoy to press for the purchase. Monroe, on his arrival, was delighted to discover that the French foreign minister, Talleyrand, had already asked Livingston what America would pay—not for part of the Louisiana Territory, but for all of it. Although they lacked the authority, the two Americans agreed to purchase Louisiana for fifteen million dollars.

With the reluctant approval of Congress a few months later, America had a legal claim to much of what is now the western United States. All that remained was to discover what America had bought and to enforce its right to hold it.

Jefferson for some time had been considering an expedition that would explore the upper reaches of the Missouri River and continue on to the Pacific Northwest, which had already been visited by American naval parties. He now resolved to launch such an expedition. Politically, his problem was a delicate one, because each person whose approval he required would need to be given a different reason for the expedition, and none of the reasons the real one.

Jefferson's basic intention was to establish, through exploration, American claims to the territory that extended all the way to the Pacific coast. This, obviously, he could not reveal to the Spanish, with whom he was trying to maintain friendly relations. To overcome their objections, it was necessary for the President to maintain that the expedition would be a mere "literary pursuit," intended to broaden knowledge of flora, fauna, and geography.

With Congress, his problem was even more difficult. Many of its members, along with many in the nation, already considered Louisiana a foolish purchase. To appease a cost-conscious Congress, already skeptical of the value of the lands to the west and without Jefferson's vision of the nation's future expansion in that direction, the President portrayed the mission as an effort to prevent the potentially rich Indian fur trade from being seized by the British.

The Spanish accepted Jefferson's explanations, and his overtures to Congress were sufficiently convincing to yield an appropriation of $2,500 with which to launch the Lewis and Clark Expedition of 1804–1806. It was not the only or the last great exploration of the continent, but as a display of courage and determination it has few rivals.

Meriwether Lewis, the man chosen by Jefferson to organize and lead the expedition, was twenty-nine years old and an infantry captain who had served for a time as private secretary to Jefferson. Lewis himself selected as his co-commander thirty-three-year-old Captain William Clark, who had once commanded a rifle company in which Lewis served. Together, the men assembled an exploratory party, organized along military lines, that included four sergeants, twenty-two privates, an interpreter, and a black man who was referred to throughout Clark's journals as "my servant" but who was, in fact, Clark's slave. Ultimately included were another interpreter and his Indian wife. Throughout the long and arduous expedition, the Indian woman, Sacajawea, and the black slave, York, performed roles that far exceeded their formal status.

It is difficult, in a push-button world whose geography is largely known, to appreciate the supreme test of courage involved in the exploration of territory into which man has never ventured before. By today's standards, Lewis and Clark's journey is a comfortable four-hour jet airplane trip from St. Louis to Portland, Oregon, and back. The explorers who started off on the same trip in 1804 knew nothing of luxury. They carried their own food—fourteen barrels of "parchmeal," twenty barrels of flour, seven barrels of salt (which did not even last through the outward leg of their journey), fifty kegs of pork, and fifty bushels of meal. Worried about hostile Indians, the travelers also took with them "eighteen tomahawks, fifteen scalping knives, fifteen dozen pewter looking glasses, three pounds of beads, six papers of small bells, three dozen tinsel bands, two dozen earrings, five hundred brooches, seventy-two rings, three gross of curtain rings to adorn copper-colored fingers or ears." The trip, by boat, foot, and horseback, took two years four months, and nine days.

Seven soldiers and ten rivermen were also attached to the

expedition when it began the long voyage up the Missouri, departing from Rivière du Bois, on the Illinois bank of the Mississippi above St. Louis. In its early days of travel the party established the pattern that would be continued as it moved up the lower reaches of the river: Clark, the more experienced riverman, spent most of his time in one of the three boats, the largest of which had a fifty-five-foot keel; Lewis was most often on shore, directing the men who towed the boats and the hunters who supplied the expedition with game, and making notes on the topography and wildlife of the region.

York, the lone black member of the expedition, appears often in Clark's journals, the first note coming on June 5, when the party passed the Osage River. ". . . here my Servent York Swam to the Sand bar to geather Greens for our Dinner, and returned with a Sufficient quantity wild Creases or Tung grass."

The party was not long in encountering Indians, and in July held a peaceful meeting with Ottawas on the Nebraska shore above the present site of Council Bluffs, a name given the steep cliffs by Lewis and Clark in honor of this initial powwow.

The ability of both Lewis and Clark to deal fairly with the Indians and to gain their confidence was to be revealed time and again during the next two years, and rarely was the party seriously threatened by the tribes with which it talked and bartered. Often it was York who helped engage the interest and friendliness of the Indians as they assembled in council with the expedition's leaders.

In October, as the party neared the Mandan villages, Clark described a meeting with the chiefs of the Arikaras: ". . . the three great Chiefs and many others Came to see us to day, . . . much astonished at my black Servent, who did not lose the opportunity of [displaying] his powers Strength &c. &c. . . ."

York, whose sense of humor was apparently as huge as his frame, soon got into the spirit of the occasion and enjoyed it immensely. Clark's entry of the following day reports: "Those Indians were much astonished at my Servent, they never Saw a black man before, all flocked around him & examined him from top to toe, he Carried on the joke and made himself more turribal than we wished him to doe." A week later, Clark noted that another band of Arikaras "are much pleased with my black Servent."

Reaching the Dakotas in late October, the expedition prepared to spend the winter in the Mandan Indian villages, about 1,600 miles from the start of their journey. They built cabins of cottonwood logs and for five months endured the bitter cold, short rations, and raging blizzards of the northern plains. Clark reported that at times the "Murckery . . . stood at 40° below 0 . . .", and he frequently recorded the return to camp of men, including York, with frostbitten feet and hands.

Even so, despite cold, inactivity, and hunger, there were moments of gaiety. On Christmas Day ". . . we fired the Swivels at day break . . . & continued firing dancing and frolicking dureing the whole day." Prominent in such festivities throughout the journey was the fiddle of the Frenchman, Cruzat, and the dancing of the black man, York. On New Year's Day, Lewis and Clark decided to share their gaiety with the Indians and sent Cruzat, York, and fourteen others to the nearest of the Mandan villages.

"I found them much pleased at the Dancing of our men, I ordered my black Servent to Dance which amused the Crowd verry much, and Somewhat astonished them, that So large a man should be active. . . ."

With the arrival of milder weather in March, York and the others began making cottonwood dugouts to be used in ascending the shallower reaches of the Missouri that lay ahead. The big keelboat returned to St. Louis with the first report from the expedition, and the remainder of the party, now numbering thirty-three (plus an infant born during the winter to Sacajawea), set out up the Missouri. After two near disasters caused by the treacherous currents, during which the Indian woman rescued many valuable articles that washed overboard, the party reached the mouth of the Yellowstone River on April 25. It was still so cold that the "water friezed on the oars."

Here the party had the first of many encounters with grizzly bears. Lewis killed a three-hundred-pounder with a single shot and concluded that "in the hands of a skillful rifleman they are by no means as formidable or dangerous as they have been represented." Within two weeks, experiences with other grizzlies caused him to change his mind. A particularly vivid description is that of the attempts of six hunters to kill one unusually ferocious bear. Shot six times, the beast rushed at them, a broken shoulder only slowing it for a moment. Two of the men took refuge in the river; the others hid on the bank, reloaded, and fired several additional shots. The enraged grizzly then attacked two of the men on the bank, forcing them to throw aside their guns and leap into the water. The bear followed, but a shot fired by one of the men still on shore went through its head and finally killed it. When the men skinned the animal, they found that eight balls had passed through its body.

A few days after the adventure with the grizzly, a huge bull buffalo swam the river during the night and stampeded through the camp. Only the barking of Lewis' dog diverted the buffalo from running down the commander in his tent. No one was hurt, but when the animal finally fled the camp, York discovered that it had stepped on his rifle and left it "much bent." The black man was fortunate that the huge beast's hooves had so narrowly missed trampling on him.

In June the party passed Great Falls, after an exhausting portage of more than eighteen miles, for which it had built carts to haul the heavy dugouts and all the expedition's heavy equipment. It was during this portage that Clark nearly lost his life.

Clark, York, Sacajawea and her child, her husband Charbonneau, and one other member of the party had gone to view the falls. When a violent thunderstorm arose, Clark led Sacajawea and her baby into a ravine in an effort to find shelter for themselves and their guns and equipment. Within moments they were trapped by a torrent of water.

York, who had ventured away from the others in search of game, returned to find Charbonneau in a panic and the others struggling to scramble out of the flood. The black man quickly calmed Charbonneau and, with his help, dragged Clark, Sacajawea, and the baby from the swirling water. York, Clark recalled, was "greatly agitated for our wellfar."

As the expedition neared the headwaters of the Missouri, its leaders became eager to make contact with the Shoshone Indians, knowing from Sacajawea, whose father was a Shoshone chief, that they would be able to obtain horses with which to continue their journey. On July 18, 1805, Clark, with York and one other man, set off in advance of the main party in an effort to find the Indians. The mission was unsuccessful, and it was not until August 13 that they finally encountered the first group of sixty Shoshones. Among them was Chief Cameahwait, Sacajawea's brother, who was, she discovered, the only surviving member of her family. With the Indian woman's help, Lewis and Clark were able to barter for horses and also to gather information on the route they would take to the Pacific Northwest.

The trail over the Bitter Root Range was rough and precipitous (". . . over Rocky hill Sides where our horses were in [per] petual danger of Slipping to their certain destruction. . . . Several horses fell . . ."), and the game on which the expedition had fed previously was nowhere to be seen. The entire party subsisted mainly on berries, and hunger became a constant companion.

The explorers were in the high mountains for all the first half of September, and even then had many miles of difficult country left to traverse. They could still find no game, although they shot some grouse and one stray horse. On September 20, on the western slopes of the range, they encountered the first of the Nez Percé Indians and got their initial taste of dried salmon and camass root, staples of the Nez Percé diet. Neither was much to their liking, but these readily available foods became their diet for the remainder of the westward journey.

On September 26, the expedition reached the Canoe Camp Site, in what is now the huge Nez Percé National Historical Park. There they camped for twelve days while York and the others built the canoes that would enable them to return to water travel.

Among the Nez Percé, as among the previous tribes that had been encountered, the black explorer was again the center of attention. The Indians called him "Tse-mook-tse-mook to-to-kean," Nez Percé for "black white man." By now, York was apparently tiring of his role as the expedition's principal curiosity. He joined the others in dancing for the Indians as usual, but, when one of the natives moistened his finger to see if the black would rub off, York pulled his knife and glared at him. The gesture and the expression needed no interpreter, and the legend of the event persists among the Nez Percé, who recall that the black man "make big eyes much white in eyes and look fierce at Chief."

As soon as the canoes were completed, the party embarked on a route that took it west, through the perilous rapids of the Snake River. The Indians were astonished at the courage of the explorers when, to avoid long and troublesome portages, they shot the most hazardous rapids in their canoes. Finally, on November 8, the explorers made their first camp within hearing of the ocean surf, and on the fifteenth made camp at the mouth of the Columbia.

The purpose of the expedition had in essence been fulfilled, inasmuch as Jefferson had authorized the commanders, if the return journey across the continent seemed too great an ordeal, to "return by sea, as you should be able." No ship was available, however, and the expedition prepared to winter in Oregon, until it could begin the eastward ascent of the Columbia in the spring. When there was disagreement over the location of the winter campsite, the commanders, long since humbled by the adversity they had shared with the others in the party, abandoned military tradition and took a vote to decide where to build the camp, which they called Fort Clatsop. The Indian woman, Sacajawea, and the black slave, York, were permitted to vote along with the rest.

On March 23, 1806, grateful for the end of the cold, wet winter at the river's mouth, the expedition reembarked for the return journey up the Columbia. On July 3, at a spot on the Bitter Root River that they named Traveler's Rest, the partners in discovery put together a plan they had conceived during the long months at Fort Clatsop. The expedition split into two units, Lewis taking one toward the northwest to explore a short-cut route across the Continental Divide—a route they were convinced existed, although they had not been able to locate it on their westward journey—while Clark headed back along the route the expedition had previously covered, with the intention of branching off later to explore the Yellowstone.

Both enterprises were successful. The pass that Lewis found and used on the return trip was named Lewis and Clark Pass, and it did lead to the upper waters of the Missouri. Lewis was able, in the course of his exploration, to cover a considerable portion of the Marias River as well, mapping some territory to the north that might prove useful in establishing a water route for the northern fur trade.

Lewis had one bitter experience en route to his reunion with Clark. He and the French fiddler, Cruzat, went into the woods in search of game, and soon had killed one elk and wounded another. The two men took off on separate trails in search of the wounded animal, with Lewis apparently unconcerned over the fact that Cruzat was blind in one eye and nearsighted in the other. Suddenly a shot rang out and the leather-clad Lewis felt a bullet pass through his buttocks; the half-blind Cruzat, mistaking him for the elk, had shot him.

Clark, for his part, had a relatively easy time in carrying out his assignment. Arriving at Three Forks, he sent a part of his group down the Missouri by canoe to join forces with Lewis at the mouth of the Marias River. Clark and the others headed east to the Yellowstone. They rode horses for a portion of the trip, until bands of Crow Indians stole them, and then transferred to dugout canoes for the rest of the journey.

Meanwhile, Lewis' wound had worsened, and he was unable to stand or sit by the time the two elements of the expedition met at the mouth of the Yellowstone for the return to the Mandan villages. Lewis lay stretched out in a boat for several days, but the party finally reached the Mandans, with whom Charbonneau, Sacajawea, and the baby remained. After an uneventful journey, the explorers arrived in St. Louis on September 23, astonishing many who had seen them off more than two years before and given them up for dead. Clark recorded joyfully, "we were met by all the village and received a harty welcom from it's inhabitants &c. . . ."

Early in 1807, Captain Meriwether Lewis was appointed by

President Jefferson as governor of the Louisiana Territory, but two years later he was mysteriously murdered in a tavern along Tennessee's notorious Natchez Trace. His old partner, Captain Clark, assumed the same post in 1813, after a major portion of the Louisiana Purchase had become the Missouri Territory.

As to the fate of York, history is clouded with doubt. On the return of the expedition to "civilization," the black man, who for more than two years had faced the perils of the wilderness with Clark, saving his life, nursing his wounds, guiding the expedition and hunting its food, once again became his master's slave. He returned with Clark to Louisville, where he was hired out to a local family so that he could be near his wife. Ultimately, however, Clark's conscience must have got the better of him, for he freed York and bought him a wagon and six horses, with which the Negro established a freight line between Richmond and Nashville.

Clark's account of subsequent events, as related to Washington Irving, portrayed York as an inept businessman, which he may well have been. Allegedly, two of the horses died and the others were sold in a worthless bargain. Clark reported that York then became a free servant, but was so ill-treated that he longed for his former master, tried to rejoin him in St. Louis, and died of cholera along the way.

This version of York's fate was probably soul-satisfying from Clark's point of view. He even quoted the ex-slave as saying, "Damn this freedom. I have never had a happy day since I got it." However, Clark's account is very much in doubt.

A trapper named Zenas Leonard, trading among the Crow Indians in 1832, met a black chief who was an exceptional warrior and had a fluent command of the Crow tongue, which he exercised volubly on his four wives. The chief told Leonard that he had accompanied Lewis and Clark on their expedition, had gone home with Clark, and later had returned to the West with a Missouri River trader named MacKinney. If his story was the truth, the black chief could only have been York.

With the successful completion of the Lewis and Clark expedition, the way to the West was open, and the exploration and settlement of all the territory beyond the Mississippi began.

To the pioneers it seemed a forbidding and almost endless domain, and the initial penetrations of the new territory were largely made by hardy, venturesome, devil-may-care traders and trappers who went among the Indians in search of the rich furs that the mountain rivers produced. Among these adventurers were the mountain men—now legendary figures such as Jim Bridger, Kit Carson, Jim Beckwourth, and Edward Rose—who sallied into the wilderness alone, or as guides for trapping and trading expeditions.

Bridger, Beckwourth, and Rose all served as guides for William H. Ashley, a general of the War of 1812 who established the Rocky Mountain Fur Company trading post at the mouth of the Yellowstone River in 1822. Two of these mountain men—Beckwourth (also spelled "Beckwith") and Rose—were black.

Rose, recalled in history as "morose and sullen," had lived among the Crow Indians for a time, knew their language, and was wise in the lore of the West. On one occasion, the refusal of Ashley to take his advice on the best route to follow forced that explorer to abandon an expedition and return to St. Louis.

Beckwourth was Rose's opposite in personality, a garrulous and friendly black who trapped and explored alone in the West in the early years of the nineteenth century and later became a guide for fur traders, trappers, and wagon trains.

Rose finally said farewell to civilization and returned to the Crows for good. Not so Beckwourth. Born in Charlottesville, Virginia, in 1789, of a slave mother and a Revolutionary War officer, he became a primary figure in western exploration—in legend as well as fact. Beckwourth made countless claims about his own exploits, enough of which were true that it is difficult to separate fiction from fact. Among those that appear to be supported by history is his assertion that he established one of the most renowned meeting places of the pioneer traders and mountain men—the Gantt-Blackwell Fort, at Pueblo, Colorado.

There is no doubt that Beckwourth discovered the lowest pass through the Sierra Nevada mountains; it still bears his name. The intrepid mountain man laid out the trail through this pass that was to carry an endless stream of wagons from Reno to the California border. The black trailblazer, in fact, could claim credit for putting Reno on the map. In 1868, his trail was followed by the first railroad built through the territory, and the site that became Reno was picked for development by the railroad company, which was amply rewarded when hundreds of eager speculators gobbled up the lots.

Beckwourth described his adventures in a highly romanticized autobiography that yielded many legends about his exploits. Most sensational of all, however, was a legend that he did not create, because at the time it became current he was no longer alive to tell the story.

When the black adventurer was in his sixties, he got into a dispute in Denver that didn't end until the other man lay dead at Beckwourth's feet, the victim of an ailment laconically referred to in that boisterous frontier town as "lead poisoning." Beckwourth was held in jail for a time, but was finally acquitted on a plea of self-defense. The result was virtually a foregone conclusion in the pioneer West, where a man was rarely found guilty of murder except when his adversary was unarmed or had been shot in the back.

After his acquittal, according to the legend, Beckwourth went to live among the Crow Indians, a tribe in which he had long claimed to be a chief. He carried a medicine bag containing a hollow bullet and two oblong beads that made him welcome among the Crows. They believed that the black man's medicine brought them luck.

Beckwourth tired of life among the Crows and announced one day that he planned to depart, a decision that the Indians received with moody silence. If Beckwourth left, they reasoned, he would take their good luck with him. So, on the pretense of bidding him an appropriate farewell, they staged an elaborate feast in his honor. The Indians poisoned his stew so that death would keep his good luck with them forever.

The persistence of this legend is not surprising, but the facts seem to be far less romantic. After leaving Denver, Beckwourth, apparently died on the trail two days before he reached the Crows. Either way, though, it was an appropriately active end for the black mountain man who carved such an important niche in the history of the West.

Another major stage in the development of the West, and particularly of California, centered around the four expeditions of John C. Frémont, a soldier, explorer, mapmaker, writer, and politician who through intrigue and action helped bring the Golden State into the Union.

Frémont, a U. S. topographical engineer, led a government scientific expedition west as far as South Pass, in Wyoming, in 1842. He mapped details of value to those who moved west along the Oregon Trail, and he climbed to the summit of the second highest point in the Wind River Mountains, now known as Frémont's Peak.

Kit Carson was Frémont's guide on this first expedition, but on the second Frémont expedition, a year later, Carson was accompanied by another guide–Jacob Dodson, who was a free black employed by Frémont's father-in-law, Senator Thomas Hart Benton of Missouri.

This time the party traveled down the Snake River to Fort Boise, on to The Dalles, and then down the Columbia River to Fort Vancouver. After exploring the region around Klamath Lake, Frémont, Dodson, and the others went south to the Truckee and Carson rivers in northwestern Nevada and, on a spur-of-the-moment decision by Frémont, made an incredibly difficult midwinter crossing of the Sierra Nevada mountains near Lake Tahoe, arriving in March at Sutter's Fort on the Sacramento River. They returned east via Tehachapi Pass, near the south end of the Sierra Nevada and Great Salt Lake.

The facts about Frémont's third expedition are somewhat confused because he apparently acted in part under secret orders that were never revealed. Traveling again to California, he supported a minor revolt against Spanish control and fortified a small hill on which he and a handful of soldiers raised the American flag. The gesture was the first in a series of events that led to the annexation of California. Frémont, however, made some rash moves that led to his court-martial and eventual resignation from the army. The incident tarnished the luster of the reputation that had developed from the reports on the highly successful second expedition in which Jacob Dodson had participated.

In 1848, Frémont decided to return to California and make his home on a forty-thousand-acre property near Mariposa that he had purchased on an earlier expedition. He financed this journey with the aid of Senator Benton, intending, additionally, to map a route for a railroad through the mountain passes.

Frémont was again accompanied by a black employee of Senator Benton, Saunders Jackson, who volunteered because he wanted to earn $1,700 to purchase his family out of slavery. After a series of unexplained blunders, magnified by bad weather and deep snows during the mid-winter mountain crossing, the expedition lost its way in the Sierra Nevada. Eleven men died before the party found its way out of the mountains in 1849 and reached California by a southern route.

A great controversy developed over the results of the disastrous expedition, and for a time it appeared certain that the explorer's career would end in disgrace. Frémont's luck was not all bad, however. Gold had been discovered on some land that he had purchased on one of his earlier expeditions.

If Frémont's capacity as an explorer was not vindicated by the success of his first three expeditions, judgment of his leadership may have been tempered by the fact that he was now a millionaire. In any event, when the first California legislature met in December of 1849, Frémont was elected as one of the state's first United States senators. He was not reelected, however, because of his antislavery views.

Saunders Jackson, meanwhile, was granted permission to mine a section of Frémont's land and within a few days had accumulated his $1,700. He returned to Missouri, redeemed his family from slavery, and disappeared from history.

Westward migrations along the Santa Fe and Oregon trails had already been well under way when Frémont made his last expedition. Many of the wagon trains assembled at Independence, Missouri, where a Negro blacksmith named Hiram Young was on hand to help shoe the horses. Young prospered as the number of emigrants increased, finally building an enterprise that included a wagon factory with fifty men at its twenty-five forges. Young and his men built many of the ox-drawn wagons that lumbered west over the trails.

Many black pioneers were among those who risked the hazards of the elements, wild beasts, and Indians to seek new homes on the fertile western plains. When the first party of Mormon pioneers arrived in the valley of the Great Salt Lake in 1847, three blacks were among those who had gone on ahead to establish homes and plant the crops that would get the main body of settlers through their first season. The names of these men—Oscar Crosby, Green Flake, and Hark Lay—are inscribed along with those of Brigham Young and their other white companions on the monument that stands in Salt Lake City at the mouth of Emigration Canyon.

At least two black men had died of "winter fever" along the trail that the first Mormon party blazed. The main parties that followed a year later also included many black individuals and families; the Mississippi company, for example, was made up of fifty-seven white persons and thirty-five blacks.

One of the most incredible stories of personal courage in the long saga of western settlement originated in the family of James Madison Flake, from North Carolina. Flake, a white man, joined the Church of Jesus Christ of Latter-day Saints in 1844 and went to Nauvoo, Illinois, to accompany Prophet Joseph Smith on his journey to the Promised Land.

With the Flake family, as they shivered in a Nauvoo dugout during the winter of 1846–1847, was a little black child, not yet in her teens, known only as "Liz." The slave child had been a wedding gift from Mrs. Flake's father.

When spring arrived, Liz and the three small Flake children started off with the family across the plains, herding loose cattle before them during the long months on the hot, dusty trail. Their hazardous journey ended in the Salt Lake valley in October, 1848.

Two years later, with the family barely established in Utah, James Flake died and his widow decided to take her family west to California. They joined a company that was destined for the San Bernardino Valley and again set out over rugged mountain trails and fiery desert sands. When they arrived in California in 1851, the black child helped to make the bricks for the first home built by Mormons in the lush San Bernardino Valley.

Liz was now entering her teens, but her trials were not over. Soon after the family's arrival in California, Mrs. Flake became ill and died. Liz was left alone with the three Flake children and cared for them for three years, until they went to live with another family. Ultimately, Liz married a free black named Charles H. Rowan, who became a prosperous San Bernardino businessman. When one of Liz's former charges married, he and his bride received—and the family still treasures—a fine set of silver that arrived as a wedding gift from his mother's former slave.

At about the time that Liz Flake arrived in California, other Americans were rushing to the riverbeds of its mountain foothills, lured by the cry of "gold." Many blacks joined these pioneer prospectors, some of them slaves who hoped to buy freedom with the treasure they found. Most came overland, some by sea. The first black "around the horn" was Waller Jackson, who came from Boston to mine at Downieville in 1849.

By 1850, the census recorded nearly one thousand blacks in the state, and there were undoubtedly many more. They were mining at Placerville, Grass Valley, Negro Bar, Mormon Hill, Murphy's Diggings, Diamond, and Mud Springs. At Mokelumne Hill, a group of white miners tried to play a joke on a black man who asked them where to dig. They pointed to the most unpromising location in sight, and cursed themselves a day or two later when the black returned to thank them carrying a sackful of gold.

A black named Dick, mining near Tuttletown in Tuolumne County, staked a claim so rich that it soon yielded one hundred thousand dollars in gold. Like most miners—black and white—Dick couldn't resist the temptation to begin enjoying his new-found riches. He repaired to the gaming tables of Sacramento and killed himself in remorse a few days later when he found that he was broke.

More fortunate were the blacks who came to mine but found ways to acquire a more reliable income serving the needs of others. One such man was Robert Anthony, who owned what may have been the first quartz mill in California, established in Yuba County on the banks of Horn Cut Creek. Another,

Moses Rodgers, lived in Hornitos Camp and owned a group of mines near Quartzburg. He became one of the most renowned mining engineers and metallurgists on the Pacific coast, a remarkable accomplishment for a man who had bought his freedom after coming to California a slave.

Other venturesome black Americans found employment driving freight wagons and even carrying mail for the Pony Express. George Monroe, a black stagecoach driver who was to take former President Ulysses S. Grant into the Yosemite Valley in 1879, became renowned as "the third best stagecoach driver in the West." The names of the two men who surpassed him aren't recorded, but the black driver's name lives on in perpetuity, because Monroe Meadows, in the beautiful Yosemite Valley, is named for him.

Other black slaves were less fortunate, because nineteenth century masters were not above agreeing to allow their slaves to earn their freedom and then appropriating the money without keeping their part of the bargain. This was the experience of Alvin Aaron Coffey, who came to California a slave and labored from dawn to dark working his master's claims. The owner told Coffey that he could buy his freedom for one thousand dollars, so the black man, after a grueling day with pick and shovel, began working nights as a cobbler, repairing the boots of other miners. When he had accumulated five hundred dollars of the agreed one thousand, his master took it from him.

Coffey's master later became discouraged with California and returned to Missouri, taking his slave with him. On their arrival, Coffey was promptly sold to another owner, fortunately a more compassionate one. His new master agreed to allow him to return to California so he could earn enough money to buy freedom for himself and his wife and children.

Once again, Coffey set off on the arduous trip across the plains and mountains and, on arrival in California, labored for three years in the mines at Shasta. Finally he accumulated the seven thousand dollars he needed to set his entire family free. In later years Coffey became a respected farmer at Red Bluff, and the first black member of the Society of California Pioneers.

Even before the Mormons ventured into Utah and the gold

miners to California, another black American was approaching the Pacific Northwest along the route laid out by Lewis and Clark, leading a wagon train over the Oregon Trail. He and his family, along with several white ones, sought to establish new homes in the fertile valleys along the Columbia River.

This adventurous pilgrim, George William Bush, was a free black born in Pennsylvania who later braved the western wilderness with the French trader Robideau. It is believed that Bush actually reached the Pacific coast on one of his expeditions before returning east to work for the Hudson's Bay Company.

Eventually, Bush migrated to Tennessee and Illinois, where he raised cattle, and then moved on to Missouri, where he became prosperous as a cattle trader. His days of adventure were far behind him in 1844, he thought, and he considered himself a permanent resident of Missouri, when the territory enacted a law that banned free blacks from the state. Bush was forced to sacrifice his holdings and move on, renewing his search for freedom in the new territory to the west. He teamed up with a white friend, George Simmons, and other white families in a wagon train that set off through the perilous hazards of the Oregon Trail.

The other members of the party considered themselves fortunate to have so stalwart and experienced a guide as George Bush, and his knowledge and judgment were of constant value as the lumbering oxen of the wagon train plodded westward, through the Pawnee country along the Platte and then over four hundred miles of monotonous plains to Fort Laramie.

The miles disappeared slowly behind the weary party during months of burning heat, choking dust, and broken wagon wheels, but finally it had endured the torturous trail through the Rocky Mountains and emerged into the green and fertile valley of the Columbia River, which lay beyond. For George Bush, what should have been a day of rejoicing proved to be no more than another in a lifelong chain of disappointments. Oregon, too, had recently banned free blacks from the territory.

The black pioneer and his family had but two choices: to turn back, which was unthinkable, or to go north into territory then considered British, which most Americans avoided.

Bush decided to head north, come what may. And then came the discovery that restored his faith in his fellowmen. The remainder of the Simmons party, learning of his decision, quietly concluded that if Oregon would not have the black guide and friend who had brought them safely through their journey, they wanted no part of Oregon. They would go north, too.

The wagon train wintered along the Columbia while Simmons and others scouted the territory as far north as Whidby Island, in Puget Sound. When spring came they again hitched up their oxen and the entire party crossed the Columbia and pushed on north to a promising prairie that Simmons had discovered near the present city of Tumwater, Washington.

There Bush staked a land claim and soon established himself as a prosperous farmer and a valued citizen. His reputation as a provident and generous man grew as he befriended countless white immigrants who arrived on Bush Prairie, ignorant of the territory and often without tools or supplies. During a near famine in the winter of 1852, Bush was the only man on Puget Sound with a surplus of wheat. Although he was offered a fortune for it by Seattle speculators, the black farmer was unwilling to profit from the misfortunes of others. He kept his wheat and distributed it among the hungry on the basis of need.

George Bush and his son, William Owen Bush, became highly proficient in the cultivation of the fertile Tumwater soil. By 1854, they had developed one of the most valuable farms in the territory, but again their world seemed about to crash at their feet. Their claim to the property was held invalid because George Bush was black.

The countryside around the Bush homestead was literally populated with white farmers whom Bush had befriended in their time of need, and now they stood by him in his. At their urging, the first territorial legislature adopted a memorial to Congress in 1854, successfully urging that Bush's land claim be confirmed despite his color.

In the years that followed, William Owen Bush won national attention for the territory and brought many settlers to Washington with the prizewinning crops he exhibited throughout the country. He brought the first reaper and binder to Washington, and is still considered one of the state's most distinguished pioneers.

The most curious quirk of fate, however, was the great benefit to America that came from the inadvertent presence of the Simmons-Bush party in the territory north of the Columbia—born though it was out of indefensible discrimination against a black American. When the Canadian boundary dispute was finally resolved, the fact that American settlers were already well established in the territory was a powerful argument against the British.

And so it was throughout the West during much of the nineteenth century. Jean Bonga, a black man, settled at Michilimackinac in 1782. His grandson, George Bonga, was born in 1802 near the present site of Duluth and lived to become "a thorough gentleman in both feeling and deportment . . . a man of wealth and consequence" who served as interpreter for Governor Lewis Cass of the Michigan Territory and at the signing of the Chippewa Treaty at Fort Snelling in 1837.

In Montana, it was Mary Fields, a black woman who worked as a nurse for the Ursuline nuns at St. Peter's Mission, but left that sheltered environment to run a restaurant in Cascade, haul freight, drive a stagecoach, and finally, in her later years, operate the village laundry. Mary was the kind of rugged pioneer woman who was unabashed when lost in a blizzard, or when a pack of wolves frightened her horses so badly that they overturned the wagon. She was past seventy when she felt the need to prove her womanhood by knocking a man down in Cascade's streets because he had failed to pay his laundry bill.

Her counterpart in South Dakota was "Aunt Sally" Campbell, who arrived in the Black Hills with General Custer's expedition and remained in South Dakota to become the first female resident—black or white—of the territory. Her grave can still be seen in the dying mining town of Galena, carefully tended by a white man whose father knew "Aunt Sally."

CHAPTER V

THE WAR THAT SAVED THE UNION

The sad-eyed young black sat on a hard bench in the tiny, drafty cell in Charlestown, Virginia, looking out at the gallows that stood in Samuel Street. He recalled his horror, a few days before, when he had watched as a troop of twenty-one Virginia Military Institute cadets took his friend and leader to the platform and the hangman sprang the trap.

There had been an air of finality about the event, John Brown hanging there, legs twitching, in the spine-chilling December air. But John A. Copeland, Jr., knew it was not final at all. As John Brown had told a *New York Herald* reporter just before his death:

"This question is still to be settled—the Negro question—the end of that is not yet."

But the end had come for John Brown, and Copeland pondered the events that had preceded it as he sat there awaiting his own. Only a few months before, he had been contentedly pursuing his studies at Oberlin College, in Ohio, enjoying a privilege that, in the mid-nineteenth century, was rare even for free blacks like himself. Then into his life had come Brown, a gaunt and bearded white man whose eyes blazed with a strange fire. The impassioned voice of the stranger, crying out against slavery, had shattered Copeland's complacency.

Copeland had left the security of the Oberlin campus and

the friendship of the nonviolent abolitionists who surrounded him there to join the revolutionary John Brown in Maryland, at the Kennedy farm. There, across the bridge from Harpers Ferry, Virginia, he had found four other blacks and sixteen white followers of the determined and possibly mad abolitionist who believed that only violent action, not crusading speeches, could set the slaves free.

Throughout the summer of 1859 the tiny band had drilled and trained for the mission they hoped would realize John Brown's dream of establishing a stronghold to shelter escaping slaves. It was an ambitious plan for so small a group, but the fanatical Brown was convinced that, once the attack was launched, it would attract the support of the countryside.

Copeland shuddered as he recalled the disaster that had followed when he and his friends descended on the federal arsenal at Harpers Ferry on the night of October 16, 1859. The town, instead of supporting them, had resisted the attack. In a tragic irony, the baggagemaster at the local depot, Heywood Brown, was struck by a stray bullet and was the first to die. How cruel that the first victim of an effort to free the slaves should be a free black.

Copeland recalled the horrible, frightening day and night that had followed, before a company of marines under Colonel Robert E. Lee arrived to put an end to the revolt. Bullets had poured through the tiny arsenal and the floor became slippery with blood as ten of his comrades, including two of Brown's sons, fell dead at his feet.

When Brown had finally been forced to surrender, on the morning of the second day, two of Copeland's black friends, Lewis Leary and Dangerfield Newby, were dead. Osborn Perry Anderson and four others had escaped. Copeland, along with a slave named Shields Green, John Brown, and three other white men, had been captured by the marines.

Copeland recalled the trial, with Brown's defenders tediously reciting the history of mental aberrations among Brown's ancestors while the abolitionist angrily refused to plead that he was insane. And finally, the sentence: death for the six men found guilty of slave insurrection, treason, and the murder of the five Virginians they had killed.

Copeland picked up a pen and began a letter to a friend:

"I am not terrified by the gallows, which I see staring me in the face, and upon which I am soon to stand and suffer death for doing what George Washington was made a hero for doing. . . . Washington entered the field for the freedom of the American people—not for the white man alone, but for both black and white."

A few days later the black student's short life also ended when the trap was sprung.

John Brown's adventure was quixotic and perhaps even insane, but, although it failed to achieve its immediate purpose, the impact of the event electrified North and South alike. Militia commanders immediately began to drill troops as far south as Georgia. Thousands of northerners who had been indifferent to the abolitionist cause were now persuaded that slavery should be eradicated, and many reflected this conviction when they voted for Lincoln and the Republican ticket in 1860.

The southern states, when it became clear that Lincoln would run on an antislavery platform and that he would win, began threatening secession. By the end of 1860, the unsettled, boiling issue of slavery—as John Brown had prophesied—had brought the nation to the most critical domestic impasse in its history. It was clear that the states committed to slavery sheltered an increasingly unpopular policy, an institution that shackled man's freedom in an otherwise free nation, and it was clear that the belatedly conscience-stricken North was no longer willing to tolerate it.

No president-elect has ever confronted so agonizing a dilemma as that which faced Lincoln when he arrived in Washington in late February of 1861. The nation he was expected to administer was tearing apart at the seams. Seven states in the lower South had already seceded from the Union, and it appeared that the other eight slave states might soon follow suit.

Despite his own convictions about the slavery issue, the new President's inaugural address was a moderate political statement aimed at winning friends in the wavering border states in an effort to hold the Union together. This caution was also influenced by Lincoln's knowledge that the North would not support a war in which the cause was abolition.

All this changed on April 12, when South Carolina troops opened fire on Fort Sumter in Charleston Harbor and the Civil War began. Lincoln's only recourse, defense of the fort, cost the North three more slave states and most of a fourth. Although Virginia seceded, forty of its western counties—including the one in which John Brown had staged his famous raid—voted to remain with the Union; two years later, as West Virginia, they achieved statehood on their own.

Faced with the problem of retaining the loyalty of these counties, and of Delaware, Maryland, Kentucky, and Missouri, Lincoln made it clear that his primary goal was preservation of the Union. Hoping that the secessionists might also have second thoughts, he reassured both North and South that he would not tamper with slavery.

Three days after the bombardment of Fort Sumter, President Lincoln issued a call to arms for seventy-five thousand men to quell the uprising. A wave of patriotic fervor swept the North. Eager recruits, old men as well as barefaced boys, queued up at recruiting centers, often chanting what was to become the most inspiring song of the Civil War, the one in which John Brown's soul marched on.

But for more than four million black citizens, regardless of the enthusiasm with which they besieged the recruiting officers, the right to march in the spring of 1861 bore the familiar label: "White Men Only."

Despite the magnitude of the national crisis and the issue in which it had its roots, blacks were not welcome in the Union ranks. The National Militia Act of 1792, precluding blacks from military service, was still in effect. In addition, there existed the innate fears and prejudices of a white majority that, even in the North, believed that freed slaves lacked the qualities required of fighting men, that to arm them would be an admission that the white man was not up to the task of winning his own war, and that putting a gun in the black man's hand might prompt him, in revenge for his years of oppression, to be less than discriminating in selecting the whites on which it was used.

The black Americans did not take their exclusion passively. They knew what the war was all about and they desperately wanted a piece of the action. In city after city, black men continued to offer their time, their money, and themselves.

On the day after Lincoln's call, a group of Boston blacks, meeting in the Twelfth Baptist Church, pledged their lives and their fortunes to the Union cause. In Providence, a black company offered to march with the First Rhode Island Regiment as it prepared to leave for the front. New York's governor was offered the services of three regiments of black soldiers whose arms, equipment, and pay would be furnished by blacks throughout the state.

In Philadelphia, two black regiments were quickly formed and began drilling in Masonic Hall. In Pittsburgh, the army was offered the services of the black Hannibal Guards. Black citizens of Cleveland gathered in National Hall, declared their allegiance to Lincoln's policy, and pledged money, prayers, and men. In Detroit, Captain O. C. Wood and the thirty-five members of his Detroit Military Guard asked for a war assignment.

On April 23, Simon Cameron, the secretary of war, received a letter that should have made him question a policy that regarded black soldiers as unfit:

"I desire to inform you that I know of some three hundred of reliable colored free citizens of this City [Washington] who desire to enter the service for the defence of the City. I have been three times across the Rocky Mountains in the service of the Country with Fremont and others. I can be found about the Senate Chambers, as I have been employed about the premises for some years."

The letter, signed "Jacob Dodson (Coloured)," was from the black frontier scout who had pioneered western exploration with Frémont and had often faced hostile Indians with Kit Carson at his side. Despite the courage he had already demonstrated in behalf of his country, the offer was refused.

The federal policy against black enlistments was maintained for well over a year, but events finally conspired to force a change in Lincoln's policy. One was the climactic turn of events in the war itself. Early setbacks of the Union Army, such as the defeat in the First Battle of Bull Run, made it clear that the North could use all the help it could muster against the stubborn forces of the Confederacy.

Equally influential was the persistent private and public pressure applied by black and white leaders to induce the government to utilize all the human resources of the North in the struggle. Humanitarian reformers hungering for slave freedom joined with pragmatic soldiers and politicians who wanted victory on the battlefield, and wanted it soon. Sensing the growing force of this common goal, Lincoln began to see, as the conflict wore on, that a social war with emancipation as its objective might revitalize the fight to reconstitute the Union.

Ultimately, a series of events and the conduct of his own officers were to force Lincoln's hand. The first of these events was an encounter at Fortress Monroe, Virginia, between Union General Benjamin F. Butler and a Confederate officer. The officer came to Butler to retrieve three fugitive slaves who had taken refuge in the fort. Butler refused to release them, asserting to the enemy officer that "you say you have seceded, so you cannot consistently claim them. I shall hold these Negroes as contraband of war, since they are engaged in the construction of your battery and are claimed as your property. The question is simply whether they shall be used for or against the government of the United States. . . ."

Butler's interpretation that slaves could be considered "contraband" made history, because it triggered a massive exodus of fugitive slaves to Union camps. Many of the Union forts were overrun with blacks, all eager to fight or to serve in any way, but kept from the field of battle by federal restrictions that many officers regarded as ridiculous and perverse.

Although there was no immediate change in federal policy, a number of Union officers elected to jeopardize their military careers and arm the newly freed slaves. Acting on an order of the secretary of war that authorized him to "employ fugitive slaves in such services as they may be fitted for . . . however, not being a general arming of them for military service," Major

General David Hunter, in May, 1862, sent out a call for black fugitives to join the army.

Hunter ignored the second phrase of the War Department order and began forming the blacks into a regiment, an act that might have been overlooked had not his abolitionist convictions led him to take other liberties with his authority. The most grievous of these, from Lincoln's point of view, was an order he issued the day after his recruiting drive began. It declared, "The persons in these three states, Georgia, Florida, and South Carolina, heretofore held as slaves are therefore declared forever free."

Lincoln, still trying to keep the border states from joining the revolt, was horrified. One of his generals, without authority, had done what the President had assiduously avoided doing, had emancipated the slaves in three southern states. Lincoln penned a biting disclaimer, saying that "neither General Hunter nor any other commander or person has been authorized . . . to make proclamation declaring the slaves of any state free."

Hunter's intemperate action cost him his beloved regiment, the First South Carolina Volunteers. It was disbanded within four months without ever having been officially mustered, or even paid. One company, however, was kept intact and turned over to Captain John Trowbridge, the officer who had recruited its members. They formed the nucleus of the first all-black regiment officially mustered into the army, in November, 1862.

Thomas Wentworth Higginson, the white commander of this unit, subsequently wrote a warmly perceptive account of the courageous and devoted blacks of the regiment. One story involved the surviving company of Hunter's regiment, which was ordered to garrison St. Simon Island, off the coast of Georgia. With Acting Captain Trowbridge in command, the black troops arrived on St. Simon to learn that a band of Confederate guerrillas was on the island, which was inhabited by five hundred blacks. Before the company disembarked, twenty-five armed islanders—some of whom later became First South Carolina recruits—had already set off after the guerrillas.

"The rebel party retreated before these men," Higginson wrote, "and drew them into a swamp. There was but one path, and the negroes entered in single file. The rebels lay behind a great log, and fired upon them. John Brown, the leader, fell dead within six feet of the log,—probably the first black man who fell under arms in the war. . ."

Higginson, something of a romanticist as well as an effective and understanding officer, also wrote a touching account of the first parade of his black volunteers through the streets of Beaufort, South Carolina, "the first appearance of such a novelty on any stage."

The men had been drilling for weeks, but they knew that now they were "marching through throngs of officers and soldiers who had drilled as many months as we had drilled weeks, and whose eyes would readily spy out every defect.

"I confess it. To look back on twenty broad double-ranks of men (for they marched by platoons),—every polished musket having a black face beside it, and every face set steadily to the front,—a regiment of freed slaves marching on into the future,—it was something to remember; and when they returned through the same streets, marching by the flank, with guns at a 'support,' and each man covering his file-leader handsomely, the effect on the eyes was almost as fine.

"The band of the Eighth Maine joined us at the entrance of the town, and escorted us in. Sergeant Rivers said ecstatically afterwards, in describing the affair, 'And when dat band wheel in before us, and march on,—my God! I quit dis world altogeder.' I wonder if he pictured to himself the many dusky regiments, now unformed, which I seemed to see marching up behind us, gathering shape out of the dim air."

Many were indeed being formed. Pressures to bring about emancipation mounted as Lincoln's experiments with compensated emancipation and with the relocation of freed slaves to colonies in Haiti and Liberia failed. As the administration counted its losses at Second Bull Run, Antietam, and Fredericksburg in 1862, it became painfully obvious that more manpower was needed to stifle the enemy.

In the fall of 1862, Lincoln permitted the enlistment of some black soldiers in selected locations of the war arena. But, like Hunter, some officers had not awaited his authority. In August, before the President's approval, Kansas Senator James H. Lane had recruited the First Kansas Volunteers, and by October they had already met the enemy at Island Mounds, Missouri, in the first official engagement of black troops in the war. General Butler mustered an entire regiment of freed blacks in Louisiana. General Augustus Chetlain took control of nonwhite volunteers in Tennessee. Before New Year's Day of 1863, black regiments had clashed with their former masters in Louisiana and South Carolina.

After a costly but impressive Union victory in Antietam, Maryland, on September 17, 1862, the time seemed ripe to give northerners an even bigger boost in morale. Lincoln accomplished this five days later by issuing a preliminary emancipation proclamation. In it he declared that on January 1, 1863, all slaves would be free in those states still in rebellion.

When the new year came, the President signed the final Emancipation Proclamation, freeing all persons held as slaves. Lincoln, as he described it himself, issued the historic order "upon military necessity," but to the white and black citizens attending watch meetings on New Year's Eve it symbolized much more. Those gathered in Tremont Temple in Boston—Frederick Douglass, William Wells Brown, William Lloyd Garrison, Harriet Beecher Stowe, Charles B. Ray, and other black and white Americans who had given much of their lives to the abolitionist cause—interpreted the document as one of the great humanitarian statements of all history.

The proclamation dealt a serious blow to the "stomach of the Confederacy," the plantation slaves who tended crops and the artisans who forged the guns and built the ships that were enabling the South to put up such a stubborn fight against superior forces. The document struck a second blow to the South's ambitions by officially authorizing, throughout the North and the occupied South, the enrollment of freed slaves in the Union Army.

With the Union Army ranks open to all citizens without regard to color, the recruiters' drums began to beat a cadence for the benefit of black Americans. On March 2, 1863, Frederick Douglass wrote in his newspaper an impassioned editorial entitled, "Men of Color, To Arms!" The brilliant black abolitionist—an ex-slave who bore whip scars on his back—sensed an opportunity for his race to gain more than freedom; it could also achieve the respect of white comrades-in-arms:

"I urge you to fly to arms and smite with death the power that would bury the government and your liberty in the same hopeless grave."

As the war had dragged on and casualty lists from combat and disease had lengthened, many northern whites had grown apathetic toward military service. The eager black volunteers were welcome replacements in the battle lines, and by the end of the war more than 186,000 had enrolled in the Union Army. One of every four northern sailors—29,511 out of 118,044—was black. In the Union Navy blacks held all ranks in the enlisted grades, and one black sailor, Robert Smalls of South Carolina, held the unofficial rank of captain. In addition, a quarter of a million black men and women labored for the army and navy as teamsters, cooks, nurses, pilots, construction workers, and guards.

The majority of the soldiers fought in one of the 166 all-black units that served the Union. The United States Colored Troops included 145 regiments of infantry, 7 cavalry regiments, 12 regiments of heavy artillery, 1 regiment of light artillery, and 1 of engineers.

For the most part, black soldiers fought with white officers leading them. Only seventy-five or eighty of the seven thousand officers assigned to the USCT were black, and eight of them were surgeons. Those with the highest ranks were Lieutenant Colonel A. T. Augustana, a surgeon; Lieutenant Colonel Reed of the First North Carolina Regiment; and Major Martin Delaney.

In the early stages of black service in the Union Army, even with the abolitionists, the War Department, and the administration supporting the new enlistment policy, many politicians, professonal soldiers, and private citizens doubted that the black man would contribute significantly to the war effort. For more than two centuries, in order to justify a policy of black enslavement, white Americans had been telling themselves that the black was inferior, childlike, shiftless, and unreliable, a second-class human who profited from his relationship with his slave master.

Many blacks, having the lash as their alternative, had acted out this role until the image they presented began to support the canards that were leveled against them. Thus, even many of those who knew that there was no biological merit in the white denigration of the black slave wondered whether he could respond to the challenge of the battlefield after generations of abject subservience. These doubts required that the black man do what no white man was ever asked to do—prove the fitness of his race as well as his courage as a man.

Initially, it was difficult to find white officers willing to assume black commands. Many regular army veterans, particularly the West Pointers, envisioned shattered military careers if they were compelled to rely on incompetent blacks. However, the officers who assumed such commands did so with enthusiasm, and before many months had passed, with the help of their courageous black soldiers, they had won such reputations for themselves and their outfits that white officers were vying with each other for black commands.

Even before emancipation and the wholesale enlistment of black soldiers, Colonel Higginson and his superior, Brigadier General Rufus Saxton of the Army of the South, had proof that black troops could not only shoulder muskets but could use them as well. Cameron's successor as secretary of war, Edwin M. Stanton, had wired Saxton the orders that General Hunter had longed for, "to arm, uniform, equip and receive into the service of the United States such number of volunteers of African descent as you may deem expedient, not exceeding 5,000." Not long afterward, Colonel Higginson began leading his eager black troops on sallies up the rivers that fed into the marshy coast lying between the important port cities of Charleston, South Carolina, and Savannah, Georgia.

In one of their first encounters with the enemy, a detachment of Higginson's men found themselves surrounded by Confederate cavalry during a night march near Township, Florida. The raw recruits might have panicked, but instead they fought ferociously, beating off the attackers and leaving twelve of them dead.

After the skirmish, Higginson recorded in his diary that "the key to successful prosecution of this war lies in the unlimited employment of black troops. Their superiority lies simply in the fact that they know the country, while white troops do not, and moreover, that they have peculiarities of temperament, position, and motive which belongs to them alone.

"Instead of leaving their homes and families to fight, they are fighting for their homes and families, and they show the resolution and sagacity which a personal purpose gives."

The black soldiers, ultimately, won the right to fight on the merits of their own performance in battle. Although they would prove their courage in 449 separate engagements with the rebels before the war was over, only three major engagements in 1863 were needed to settle forever the question of whether blacks could and would fight. They were singled out by Secretary of War Stanton in December, 1863, when he remarked that "the slave has proved his manhood, and his capacity as an infantry soldier at Milliken's Bend, at the assault upon Port Hudson, and at the storming of Fort Wagner." The incredible heroism of the black soldiers who fought in those engagements made it clear that Stanton was right.

Port Hudson, in early 1863, was the last remaining Confederate fort on the lower Mississippi. Because its siege guns and field artillery threatened Union warships, it was a critical obstacle to General Ulysses S. Grant's plans, and he ordered it taken to ease his army's approach to Vicksburg.

The effort to breach the strongly fortified and heavily garrisoned fortress was almost suicidal, yet it was entrusted to five black regiments, one of them barely three months old and none of them experienced in mortal combat. The task given to the Louisiana black regiments–the First and Third Regiments of the Corps d'Afrique, Butler's First and Third Louisiana Native Guards, and Banks's First Engineers–required that they advance over a long stretch of broken terrain, through a tangle of fallen trees, under the very muzzles of the Confederate guns.

The black infantrymen, some of whom had been in uniform for less than two months, charged toward the enemy breastworks and ran head on into a hail of rebel fire. Many fell, and the remainder backed off, regrouped, and charged again. More men fell as they were driven back a second time. Undaunted, they reformed their lines and charged again, and then again, and yet again, but the entrenched enemy could not be dislodged.

General Ullman, one of the regimental commanders, witnessed the action:

"The troops made six or seven charges over this ground against the enemy's works. They were exposed to a terrible fire and were dreadfully slaughtered. . . . all who witnessed these charges agree that their conduct was such as would do honor to any soldier."

As a military maneuver, the charges on Port Hudson were a failure, but they weakened the fort for its eventual capture. As one engineer officer reported at the end of the day, "Port Hudson is doomed. It would make a good iron mine now." Aside from the military significance of the black behavior at Port Hudson, its impact on the nation was profound.

The New York Times, which had been reluctant to commit itself to support the use of black troops, was won over by the incredibly valorous performance at Port Hudson. It belatedly agreed that Banks's report on the engagement "settles the question that the negro race can fight with great prowess."

"These black soldiers," the *Times* reported, "had never before been in any severe engagement. They were comparatively raw troops, and were yet subjected to the most awful ordeal that even veterans ever have to experience—the charging upon fortifications through the crash of belching batteries. The men, white or black, who will not flinch from that, will flinch from nothing. It is no longer possible to doubt the bravery and steadiness of the colored race, when rightly led."

The newspaper obviously was not yet ready to give the black man all he deserved. The qualification, "when rightly led," agreed with a widely held view that black soldiers could triumph only under the leadership of white officers. The *Times* apparently was unaware that two out of every three officers in the Corps d'Afrique were black.

Included among these thirty-eight black officers was Captain André Cailloux, who commanded Company E of the First Infantry. When Cailloux died he was so close to the earthworks of Port Hudson that, despite several attempts, his men were not able to retrieve his body. It was not recovered until after the fort had surrendered.

Cailloux was given a state funeral in New Orleans, and all the city turned out. The great funeral procession wound through the narrow, crowded streets of the Vieux Carré led by the band of the all-white Forty-second Massachusetts Regiment. In the words of one witness, it was "the funeral of the dead hero, the like of which was never before seen in that, nor, perhaps, in any other American city, in honor of a dead Negro."

At Milliken's Bend, the second of the three engagements applauded by Stanton, the position of the two armies was reversed. There it was the gray-clad Confederate troops who decided to eliminate a Union-held camp. In June of 1863, a garrison of 1,400 men in blue—only 160 of them white—was manning the outpost of Milliken's Bend, Louisiana, a tiny town only twenty miles from Vicksburg, Mississippi. The attacking rebels, estimated to be 3,000 strong, stormed the encampment of the Ninth and Eleventh Regiments of the Louisiana Volunteers of African Descent, who were outnumbered two to one.

The Confederates soon swarmed over the camp's fortifications, and with bayonets and clubbed rifles the black soldiers engaged them hand to hand. The longest sustained hand-to-hand, bayonet-to-bayonet engagement of the Civil War ensued. It ended only with the appearance of the Union warship "Choctaw," which caused the Confederates to flee.

The southerners left behind them 130 dead whom they could not carry away. Casualties among the heavily outnumbered Union troops were understandably heavy—652 Union soldiers, most of them black, were dead, wounded, or missing.

"It is impossible for men to show greater gallantry than the Negro troops in this fight," remarked General Elias S. Dennis, commander of the Military District of Northeastern Louisiana. Charles Dana, assistant secretary of war, commented that "the bravery of the blacks in the battle of Milliken's Bend completely revolutionized the sentiment of the Army with regard to the employment of Negro troops." And General Grant, in his memoirs, recalled that the fight was the "first important engagement of the war in which colored troops were under fire. These men were raw," he said, "having been enlisted since the beginning of the siege [of Port Hudson], but they behaved well."

Perhaps the most gallant display of courage was that of the Massachusetts Fifty-fourth Infantry, the first black regiment to be recruited in the North. Commanded by a blue-blooded Boston abolitionist, assembled in the streets where Crispus Attucks had died, and built on the initial enlistments of Charles and Lewis Douglass, sons of the fiery black abolitionist, the regiment seemed fated from the onset to earn a glorious place in history.

"I know not, Mr. Commander, where in all human history, to any given thousand men in arms there has been committed a work at once so proud, so precious, so full of hope and glory as the work committed to you." Those were the glowing words of Governor John A. Andrew to Colonel Robert Gould Shaw on May 18, 1863.

Dignitaries and friends of the men in the Fifty-fourth gathered around the ranks of black soldiers in their Readville training camp that day. The governor presented four silken flags to the colonel as more than a thousand spectators, black and white, stood together on the parade ground. Among them, proud and jubilant, were Frederick Douglass, Wendell Phillips, Samuel May, Professor Louis Agassiz, and William Lloyd Garrison. All of them were witnessing a dream come true.

The send-off in Boston when Shaw and his black troops embarked for the South was even more spectacular. A colorful parade was scheduled, and the cream of Massachusetts society turned out to wish good fortune to the troops. Abolitionist spokesmen led the cheers, with Garrison waving from a balcony, "his hand resting on a bust of John Brown. No regiment on its departure has collected so many thousands as the 54th," reported the *Boston Evening Journal.*

By July, the Massachusetts infantrymen were grouping with other regiments on Union-held islands near the key Confederate city of Charleston, South Carolina. This force faced a formidable challenge in nearby Fort Wagner, a massive fortress on Morris Island that controlled every sea approach to the city.

Charleston's commander, General P. G. T. Beauregard, sensing that the federal troops were massing for an offensive, ordered his outstanding companies to man Fort Wagner's guns. On July 11, these troopers successfully repulsed the first Union attack. On the sixteenth, the Fifty-fourth Massachusetts had its first taste of battle on nearby James Island. In this brief skirmish Shaw's black soldiers acquitted themselves well in a losing cause, saving the Tenth Connecticut, an all-white regiment, from being cut to pieces.

Ever since their impressive farewell ceremony in Boston, Shaw had feared that his men would not be given an opportunity to do what was expected of them. Several weeks earlier he had written to General George Crockett Strong requesting that the Fifty-fourth be sent to a combat area where it could become involved in an important action.

On the eighteenth, after his men had gone two nights without rest and two days without rations, Shaw reported to General Strong for orders. Battle lines were already forming when the general asked: Will the Fifty-fourth lead the next assault on Fort Wagner?

Shaw had his wish, and, as the columns formed in the ocean twilight, Strong and Shaw spoke words of encouragement to the black men of the Fifty-fourth.

"Move in quick time until within a hundred yards of the fort," Shaw shouted. "Then, double-quick and charge!"

Fort Wagner had been the target of artillery shells all day long, but as the Union foot soldiers charged toward the breastworks it became apparent that the bombardment had done little to soften the defenses. Gunners at Wagner opened up, and cross fire from fortresses at Cummings Point, Gregg, and Sumter, as well as from James and Sullivan's Islands, bracketed the exposed Fifty-fourth.

The black soldiers, with Colonel Shaw in the lead, struggled forward, some of them knee-deep in seawater. They double-timed through a hail of bullets, slowed briefly in the deep ditch before Wagner's parapets, and then stormed the walls. Shaw's men, many of them wounded, scrambled up and planted the state and national flags on the parapet. White soldiers from New York and Connecticut rushed up to help, and for three hours the Union soldiers fought with bayonets and clubbed rifles against artillery, rifle fire, and grenades. But they could not hold out against such odds.

Sergeant William H. Carney of Company C was running beside Sergeant John Wall when a shell knocked Wall, the regimental color-bearer, off his feet. Carney realized that it was a mortal wound, so he grabbed the flag and ran to the head of his column. In less than twenty minutes, Carney found himself alone at the fort's entrance. Around him lay the dead and the wounded as they had fallen, stacked up one on top of the other.

Carney dared not enter the fortress alone, so he clung to its sandy outer slope. Half an hour passed, and the Union forces renewed their assault. The sergeant saw through the smoke what he thought was a company of the Fifty-fourth advancing toward him. He raised the flag and started in its direction, but as he got closer he realized that the uniforms were gray. Carney wheeled around, still clutching his flag, and was shot twice as he stumbled into a water-filled ditch. With the help of a trooper from the One-hundredth New York Regiment, the sergeant made his way through the fire to his own company, meanwhile sustaining a third wound, this one in the head.

The flag had never left Carney's hands throughout his long and painful ordeal. When he saw his comrades from Company C, he passed it to one of them and fell to his knees, asserting proudly, "Boys, it never touched the ground."

For his bravery, Carney was awarded the Medal of Honor, the first of twenty won by black soldiers during the Civil War.

Of the 650 black troops engaged that day at Fort Wagner, 272 lost their lives.

When Lewis Douglass returned to Morris Island, South Carolina, he described the battle in a letter to his fiancée:

"DeForest of your city is wounded, George Washington is missing, Jacob Carter is missing, Charles Reason wounded, Charles Whiting, Charles Creamer all wounded. . . . The regiment has established its reputation as a fighting regiment, not a man flinched, though it was a trying time. Men fell all around me. A shell would explode and clear a space of twenty feet. Our men would close up again, but it was no use, we had to retreat, which was a very hazardous undertaking. . . . Remember if I die I die in a good cause. I wish we had a hundred thousand colored troops we would put an end to this war."

The rebel forces at Fort Wagner contemptuously reported that they had buried Shaw in a trench "with his niggers." They considered it a final insult to a man they hated for leading black troops, but Shaw's father saw it otherwise. When plans were made to exhume the bodies of Shaw and his men for reburial in the North, Francis Shaw protested to General Gillmore, writing, "We hold that a soldier's most appropriate burial place is on the field where he has fallen."

The mingled ashes of Shaw and his men still rest there, no longer black and white but, like all soldiers in battle together, a mutual shade of gray.

Shaw and his men are immortalized in a statue by St. Gaudens that stands in Boston Common, directly across the street from the Massachusetts State Capitol. Part of Boston's "Freedom Trail," it is visited each year by tens of thousands who read on it the words of James Russell Lowell:

Right in the van on the red rampart's slippery swell
With heart that beat a charge he fell
                    Foeward as fits a man.
But the high soul burns on to light men's feet
Where death for noble ends makes dying sweet.

July of 1863 proved to be the turning point in the war for

Union forces. With emancipation the declared national policy and blacks welcome in the ranks of the men in blue, there were many new soldiers with the most personal cause–their own freedom–to fight for. After impressive victories at Gettysburg, in Virginia, and at Vicksburg, Mississippi, still fought largely by white soldiers on both sides, the North began to apply relentless pressure on the Confederacy.

Not all the black men who fought donned army uniforms or served in segregated units. Matching the black man's service with the land forces was his contribution to the war effort as a member of the Union Navy. Throughout its history, the navy had never barred free blacks from enlisting. In September, 1861, it adopted the policy of recruiting former slaves to bolster its force. Ex-slaves and freedmen responded with the same enthusiasm as they who had shown to fight on land.

One of the navy's recruits was particularly welcome. He brought his own ship! This daring black was Robert Smalls, pilot of the Confederate gunboat "Planter," which was assigned as a special dispatch boat to the Confederate port commander at Charleston, South Carolina.

On the night of May 13, 1862, the ship was moored in Charleston Harbor and, although the boat was loaded with a cargo of guns and ammunition intended for Fort Ripley, all of its white officers were ashore. Smalls, who had been awaiting such an opportunity, gathered his crew and confided his plan to commandeer the vessel and deliver it to the Union Navy. Some of the men were skeptical, understandably so because the route out of the harbor lay under the guns of half a dozen Confederate installations. But Smalls convinced them, and the men slipped off into the night to gather their meager possessions and their families.

At midnight, Smalls donned the coat and uniform hat of the officer normally in command, took the wheel, and steamed toward the entrance of the harbor. As he passed under the batteries of Forts Sumter and Johnson, he gave the gunners there his captain's customary salute, and they let the "Planter" pass without suspecting that the black man was in command.

"I thought the 'Planter' might be of some use to Uncle Abe,"

Smalls said as he turned the ship over to an astonished officer of the Union fleet. And so it was, for the "Planter" was later used to carry the black men of Higginson's First South Carolina Volunteers on their raids up the rivers of the South Carolina and Georgia coasts. Smalls and his crew enlisted in the Union Navy, were rewarded by Congress for their bravery, and Smalls himself was invited to Washington to meet the President.

The black pilot made many trips to Washington in later years, for he became a national hero, was elected to Congress, and served five terms as a representative from South Carolina. Smalls was idolized by his constituents, although occasionally some of them thought he was being glorified beyond his due. On one such occasion, legend has it, someone claimed that Smalls was a political genius, and a friend protested that he didn't think the congressman was quite that good.

"He isn't God," the man said.

"Yes, that's true," replied Smalls's advocate, "but give him time. He's a young man yet."

Smalls served throughout the war as a pilot for the Union Navy, and when the flag of the United States was again raised over Fort Sumter in April, 1865, it was the "Planter"—with Smalls at the helm—that brought two thousand black Americans to the ceremony. This time there was no fear of bombardment from Sumter's batteries.

By the time hostilities ended, black sailors made up one-quarter of the Union crews. More than 29,000 of them had seen service, facing the prospect of death, injury, or capture aboard at least 49 different vessels. Black casualties in the Union Navy numbered about 800, also about a quarter of the navy's total of 3,200 victims. Another 2,000 black seamen died of disease, which killed more men, on land and sea, than every kind of weapon.

Four black Union sailors won the Medal of Honor during the war. One of these was Joachim Pease, who was cited for "marked coolness, good conduct, and qualities even higher than courage and fortitude."

Behind the stilted language of the official citation lay one of the most dramatic naval battles of the Civil War, an encounter between two ships that were the pride of their respective fleets.

Pease, a native of Long Island who had never experienced slavery, was a navy veteran whose service had already won him promotion. On June 18, 1864, he was serving as a gun loader aboard the U. S. S. "Kearsarge" as she lay off Cherbourg, France, when the Confederate warship "Alabama" hove into view.

The men of the "Kearsarge" had reason for alarm. In her career, the "Alabama" had sunk, burned, or captured sixty-nine vessels, and her confident crew now prepared confidently to add a seventieth victim, the "Kearsarge," to the list.

The duel lasted about ninety minutes, the two ships standing broadside and pouring hot iron into each other. One shell from the rebel ship landed a few yards from Pease, knocking three sailors to the deck. Spurred to action by the sight of their bloodied comrades, Pease and James H. Lee, a sponger, worked like madmen to maintain a constant stream of fire on the "Alabama." Lee fed the powder and Pease loaded the cannon, sending deadly shells at the enemy every four or five minutes. Both men were showered with shrapnel when the Confederate ship pinpointed the gun that was giving her the greatest amount of trouble.

Finally a white flag replaced the Confederate colors on the mast of the rebel gunboat. One of Pease's shells had delivered the mortal blow, and the Confederate ship's bow rose high out of the water. She stood straight up on end for a second or two and then slipped slowly into the sea.

From the day that black men first saw action against their former masters, scarcely a battle was fought in which freed slaves did not engage the enemy.

When Richmond fell, black units were the first to enter the city. They fought in Florida at Olustee, at Vicksburg in Mississippi, and at Savannah during the siege of that vital port city. Blacks fought in major battles in Arkansas, Kentucky, Tennessee, and North Carolina. They had a vital role in the reduction of Petersburg as a Confederate stronghold, and in the Battle of the Wilderness they fought in the leading assaults.

In the final drive of the war, as Grant pursued Lee down the road to surrender at Appomattox, the former slaveholders of the South had an entire black corps—General Godfrey Weitzel's Twenty-fifth—breathing down their necks.

More than 20 percent of the North's 180,000 black soldiers—nearly 40,000 of them—were dead. But the black slave had proved himself a man.

CHAPTER VI

BLACK SOLDIERS AND RED MEN

Officially they were the Ninth and Tenth Cavalry Regiments, but to those who knew them best—the Apache, Comanche, Kiowa, and Sioux—they were known, with fear and respect, as the "buffalo soldiers." Expert horsemen, rugged individuals, implacable adversaries, they are characters in a story that spans more than three tempestuous decades of America's settlement of the West. Billy the Kid and Geronimo knew them well, yet their service on the western frontier, against outlaw and Indian alike, is scarcely remembered today.

They came into being in 1866, little more than a year after the Army of the Republic had staged its last great spectacle, passing in review for two days before the Capitol of the nation it had preserved. As always, in the aftermath of war the millions who had worn the Union blue were reduced to a handful of regular army officers and troops. Yet even as the soldiers exchanged their uniforms for civilian garb savage tides were brewing in the Southwest—in Texas, New Mexico, Arizona, and the territory known today as Oklahoma.

Indian hordes, virtually unchecked during the trying years of war, were reacting with savage hostility to the encroachment on their tribal lands of sometimes rapacious and always unwelcome whites. Footloose veterans, seeking fortune and lusting for adventure that would compare with what they had experienced in war, pursued those aims lawlessly all along the frontier. Meanwhile, conditions approaching anarchy reigned along the Rio Grande.

Among the thousands set adrift by peace were many blacks, onetime slaves who, after serving valiantly in the army that set them free, had no place to which they could return. Congress found a solution to this problem, and to its own, by sending many of the black veterans off to guard the western frontier. The creation of four black regiments—two of cavalry and two of infantry—was authorized on July 28, 1866.

Within days, General of the Army Ulysses S. Grant dispatched telegrams to two of his old comrades-in-arms. He asked General Philip Sheridan, commanding the Division of the Gulf, to organize one of the Negro cavalry regiments, and General William T. Sherman, commanding the Division of the Missouri, the other. The new regiments were designated the Ninth and Tenth U. S. Cavalry, and to command them Grant picked Colonel Edward Hatch of Iowa for the Ninth, and Colonel Benjamin H. Grierson of Illinois for the Tenth.

Hatch and Grierson, both of whom had brilliant Civil War records, moved swiftly to organize the regiments and set up their headquarters. Hatch established headquarters for the Ninth at Greenville, Louisiana, and Grierson took the Tenth to Fort Leavenworth, Kansas. And then their troubles began.

Congress, regarding the peacetime use of black troops as an experiment, had specified that all the officers be white. In addition, it had imposed the more onerous restriction, from the standpoint of potential officer candidates, that each of them appear before a special examining board appointed by the secretary of war.

This restriction, coupled with doubts on the part of many officers regarding the potential of blacks as cavalrymen, made it almost impossible for Hatch and Grierson to find officers who would serve. Months later, as recruits were pouring into Greenville, Hatch complained to the adjutant general that he had several hundred soldiers on hand, was receiving arms and horses, but still was without a single officer present for duty.

Grierson was having the same problem, not only with officers but also with men. The latter problem was of his own making, because his standards were impossibly high. His instructions to Captain L. H. Carpenter, who was on recruiting service in Philadelphia, were typical:

"Recruit men sufficiently educated to fill the positions of non-commissioned officers, clerks, and mechanics in the regiment. You will use the greatest care in your selection. . . . enlist all the superior men you can who will be a credit to the regiment."

So difficult were these standards to meet that by the end of September, 1866, only one man, Private William Beauman, had arrived at Leavenworth, and he had malaria. Eventually, however, the recruiting tempo picked up for both officers and men, and soon both Hatch and Grierson had their manpower situation well in hand.

In the spring of 1867, Grierson found himself plagued with other woes. General William Hoffman, of the Third Infantry, was openly contemptuous of the black troops and of the officers who served with them. The Tenth found itself quartered on low, swampy ground, segregated from white troops even on the parade ground, and discriminated against in scores of petty ways. Grierson, genuinely fond of his black troops, complained bitterly to division headquarters, but got few satisfactory answers to his problems.

Another difficulty arose at Leavenworth that was to plague the buffalo soldiers as long as they remained on the frontier: their horses were very poor. In April, 1867, Grierson went to St. Louis to inspect mounts for his troops. He found not a single one that was suitable for service; many were wind-broken cripples of the war, others were too old. Equipment, too, was often worn and shoddy, much of it the castoffs of more fortunate regiments.

The difficulties that Grierson could not surmount he got around. As a result, eight companies of the Tenth were in the field by midsummer, and soon thereafter Grierson received orders to transfer his headquarters to Fort Riley, Kansas. Three companies were assigned to Indian Territory, while the other five were billeted at temporary posts along the Kansas Pacific Railroad, then under construction across Kansas. At Fort Riley,

Grierson fleshed out his regiment to its full complement of twelve companies, and he and his untried buffalo soldiers moved unflinchingly into a full-scale Indian war.

The initial skirmishes between troopers of the Tenth and their Indian foes were of a minor nature. The regiment suffered its first combat death in August, 1867, when F Company, under the command of Captain George Armes, fought a six-hour battle under a blazing Kansas sun with a heavily armed war party of Cheyenne. Seven Indian braves lost their lives in the encounter that also claimed Sergeant William Christy, a small, tough, wiry farmer from the rolling hills of Pennsylvania.

In July of 1867, Congress created the Indian Peace Commission, which met on Medicine Lodge Creek in Kansas in a week-long powwow with the chiefs of the major tribes. The Comanches, Kiowas, and Kiowa-Apaches signed treaties agreeing to move their lodges to a reservation of about three million acres lying between the Washita and Red rivers in Indian Territory (now Oklahoma). The Cheyennes and Arapahoes received a tract of about four million acres immediately to the north.

On paper it looked good, and for a time it appeared that the black cavalrymen might have respite from their frequent but inconclusive encounters with Indian war parties. The federal government agreed to provide the Indians with ample food, clothing, and other supplies, and the Indians reserved the right to hunt buffalo anywhere south of the Arkansas River. Resident agents would help the tribes to adjust to reservation life and see that their wants were met. In return, the Indians were to keep the peace, refrain from molesting settlers, and stay clear of the railroads.

Although the Medicine Lodge treaties brought a temporary halt to warfare on the central plains, they failed to solve other pressing problems. Numerous influential chiefs had refused to attend the powwow, and, to the south, bands of Kiowas and Comanches continued to make life precarious for settlers and ranchers along the Texas frontier. As a crowning blow, Congress fell to haggling over details of the treaties, and ratification was long delayed.

Colonel Grierson found conditions settled enough during the

winter of 1867–68 to billet most of his troops in the relative comfort of Fort Riley, though Troops D, E, and L remained in Indian Territory, and Troop M was moved to Fort Gibson, southeast of the present city of Tulsa. In the thousands of square miles of Indian Territory and frontier country, there was little that four troops of cavalry and a handful of infantry could do to keep the peace. Kiowa and Comanche raiders made periodic forays on herds of the Civilized Tribes, and whiskey peddlers plied their dangerous and destructive trade with impunity. White captives, brought from Texas into the Territory, usually were recovered only after ransoms had been paid.

Congress continued to dally. As winter and spring became summer, large numbers of Plains Indians gathered at Fort Larned, Kansas, to receive their promised annuities. Indian Agent E. W. Wynkoop had little to offer them, but the ever present bootleggers did. Idle and hungry, disgruntled and often drunk, the Indians were looking for trouble and usually found it. Raids were made on Forts Zarah and Wallace in early May, and later in the same month a large war party of Cheyenne attacked and burned a Kaw village at Council Grove. Sporadic raids were made throughout the summer—on Twin Butte Creek, on Pond Creek near Fort Wallace, near Fort Dodge, at Cimarron Crossing, and yet another near Cheyenne Wells. Colorado's Governor Hall reported that two hundred warriors were devastating the southern section of his state.

General Sherman was determined to punish the offending tribes and, after consultations between the Departments of War and Interior, received presidential approval to do so. However, with only two regiments of cavalry at his command, the Seventh and the Tenth, Sherman found the task virtually impossible. In one month alone, the saddle-sore troopers of the Tenth scouted more than a thousand miles in search of their elusive foe without a single interception. Then, in mid-September, the tide of events changed.

Captain G. W. Graham, with thirty-six troopers of I Company, struck a trail along the Denver road and followed it until he reached the Big Sandy. There, along the banks of that shallow creek, the company found a hundred or more Cheyenne braves waiting for them. For the black troopers of Company I, it was their first encounter with their red adversaries, and one they would not soon forget.

The troopers, fighting back to back, soon found themselves in hand-to-hand combat. Although outnumbered and inexperienced in the ways of Indian warfare, they proved to be more than a match for their enemies. When the Indians withdrew at nightfall, as was their custom, eleven of their braves lay dead and fourteen wounded. Captain Graham counted his losses at only one man wounded and eighteen horses dead or missing.

About a week later, Captain Louis Carpenter and H Troop left Fort Wallace, with the troopers vowing to "finish what I Troop started." About noon on September 22, two troopers were sent from Wallace with dispatches for Carpenter, who had marched to Sandy Creek, about forty-five miles west, made camp, and sent out scouts in search of Indian signs.

The dispatch riders were nearing Carpenter's camp when they were hailed by two bedraggled white troopers who proved to be scouts from Major George Forsyth's Frontier Scout Command, then attached to the Third Infantry. They reported that five days earlier hundreds of Cheyennes had attacked Forsyth's outfit, surrounding it and cutting the men off from escape. The two scouts had managed to slip away in the night to go for help.

While the Forsyth scouts continued on to Fort Wallace to rouse the garrison there, the two H Company riders spurred on to Sandy Creek to advise Carpenter of Forsyth's plight. H Company mounted up almost immediately, and by dark on September 23 had covered about thirty-five miles. The troopers were in their saddles again at dawn, and after covering thirty more miles came upon an Indian burial ground. Inspection of the raised burial scaffolds revealed that most of the Indians had died recently of gunshot wounds.

The men of H Company again made camp, to rest themselves and their horses, and the following day were overtaken by another of Forsyth's scouts, who had made his way back to Fort Wallace but found most of the garrison already out searching for Forsyth. With the scout as a guide, Carpenter took thirty of his men who were riding the strongest mounts and moved out at a gallop. The rest of the troop was told to follow as rapidly as possible.

Carpenter and his black troopers drove their horses to the point of collapse over the eighteen miles of rough country that lay between their camp and the banks of the Arikaree River. Approaching it, they saw movement in the valley, but when they reached it not a Cheyenne remained in sight. Forsyth's camp was a slaughterhouse. Six men of his command lay dead. Fifteen were wounded, including the major, who had been shot through both legs. The stench from the dead men and animals was so overpowering that Carpenter's first move was to transfer the wounded to a position some distance away. The next day, joined by other units that included the Tenth's I Company, the united command took the wounded on the sad and painful trek back to Fort Wallace.

If the buffalo soldiers still doubted the savagery of their opponents, these illusions were now dispelled. Driven by a desire to avenge the deaths of their fallen white comrades, the black cavalrymen turned with renewed vigor to the hazardous task of clearing the western plains of hostiles. Riding hard and fighting fiercely throughout the remaining months of 1867 and most of 1868, sharing a decisive victory with Custer's ill-fated Seventh Cavalry on the Washita River, the relentless buffalo soldiers all but rid Kansas of the bloodthirsty Cheyenne.

Early in 1869, Sheridan assigned a new role to Grierson and the men of the Tenth. Regimental headquarters was moved from Fort Gibson to Camp Wichita, and the regiment was assigned to serve as an "army of occupation" for the Plains tribes as they settled into the "routine" of reservation life. In March, six companies were situated at Wichita and an equal number assigned to Camp Supply (later Fort Supply) in what is now northwestern Oklahoma.

The black troopers at Wichita immediately began to prepare the fort for the vital role it was to serve in the stabilization of the West. Troopers not on scouting duty traded their guns for axes to cut logs in the Wichita Mountains. Others quarried stone, and construction began on quarters, stables, and storehouses. In August, the name of the post was changed to Fort

Sill, and, though it has undergone many changes of command and purpose in the century that has passed, many of the orginal buildings still stand as monuments to the skill and ingenuity of the buffalo soldiers who helped build them.

Grierson's Indian charges found their warlike habits hard to break. With the coming of spring, they began to leave the reservation in small raiding parties, in much the same fashion as they had followed for centuries. Satanta, a totally unreconstructed and unrepentant war chieftain of the Kiowas, was a constant source of trouble in that year and for many years to come.

Late in May, a war party of about thirty-five Arapahoes struck the mail station on Bear Creek, killed two privates of the Third Infantry, and seriously wounded a sergeant. Major Kidd, commanding the Tenth's A and K Companies, drove the Indians off and brought the dead and wounded into Fort Dodge. In June, a government train from Dodge, escorted by Lieutenant J. A. Bodamer and twenty-five troopers of F Company, was attacked by about a hundred well-mounted Kiowas. The buffalo soldiers fought off the attackers and killed three of them. Corporal Freeman and Private Winchester suffered slight wounds.

Three days later a large party of Comanches decided to test the mettle of the troopers at Camp Supply. After an unsuccessful attempt to run off the cavalry horses, they skirmished for an hour or more with the five companies then at the post. Six of their braves were dead and ten wounded before the Comanches had learned more than they wanted to know about buffalo soldiers. They wheeled their horses and disappeared.

Meanwhile, the Kiowas and Comanches were exercising all their ingenuity to make life miserable for the hated "Tejans" along the North Texas frontier. During May and June of 1870, they killed fifteen settlers in Jack County alone. The Kiowa chieftain White Horse made a sweeping raid across the Red River, killed a settler, and took his wife and six children captive. With every settler fearing for his scalp, the Texas newspapers began abusing Indian Agent Lawrie Tatum and Grierson of the Tenth for failing to keep the Indians under control.

The criticism of Grierson was unjustified; his cavalrymen

were allowed to interfere with reservation Indians only when authorized to do so by the Indian agent. Despite this general order, a showdown between the more militant of the reservation Indians and the army was inevitable.

Bombarded with letters and telegrams from Texans, Sherman, now commander in chief of the United States Army, made an on-the-scene investigation of the Texas frontier in early May. He was accompanied by the inspector general and a carefully selected detachment of the Tenth, which served as escort. Sherman made an arduous circuit of the West Texas posts garrisoned by the buffalo soldiers of the Ninth and other regiments, finally arriving at Fort Richardson on May 18, 1871.

The camp was barely astir the next morning when a blood-stained teamster named Thomas Brazeale staggered into the fort to report that a war party of more than one hundred Indians had attacked a ten-wagon train about ten miles west of Jacksboro. Sherman immediately ordered Colonel Ranald S. Mackenzie, the Fourth Cavalry commanding officer, to take every available man and run down the raiders.

Almost bursting with fury, Sherman himself set out for Fort Sill, where he wasted little time in calling the Indian agent, Tatum, on the carpet. Who, he asked Tatum, were these Indians who, with seeming impunity, raided the Texas frontier from the sanctuary of their reservation? Tatum, awed by the outraged general and aghast at the news of the wagon train massacre, replied that the Indians would be in for their rations in a few days and that Sherman could question them then.

On May 27 the Kiowas came to the agency, and Tatum called the chiefs into his office to question them about the raid. Satanta, belligerent and boastful as always, rose immediately to harangue Tatum about his problems—real and fancied—and bragged that he had led Chiefs Satank, Eagle Heart, Big Tree, and Big Bow in the raid. Tatum hurriedly penned a note to Grierson and then went to report in person to both Sherman and Grierson. The three men decided to call a council of the Indian chiefs at Grierson's home on the post, at which time the guilty parties would be placed under arrest. Orders were given to the buffalo soldiers to saddle their mounts and, on a given signal, to seal off all possible avenues of escape. As an added precaution, a dozen troopers with carbines were posted inside Grierson's house.

The self-confident Satanta was the first to arrive; he had heard of Sherman's arrival at the post and was anxious to size up the famous white warrior from Washington. Under questioning, he readily admitted his part in the raid, but then, observing that Sherman's temper was rising, he changed his story and started for his horse. Grierson's alert orderly forced the Indian chieftain to resume his seat. When twenty more Kiowas, Satank among them, arrived for the council, Sherman informed them that the guilty chiefs were to be arrested and taken to Texas for trial. Satanta flew into a rage and clutched at the revolver under his blanket, but Sherman gave a signal and the shutters flew open to reveal the grim-faced black troopers with their carbines at the ready. Satanta regained his composure.

Responding to a signal from Grierson, the mounted troopers trotted into their prearranged positions to bar escape. At about the same time another chief, Lone Wolf, rode up from the trader's store carrying two Spencer rifles and a bow and arrows. Dismounting, he threw one of the Spencers to a brave, the bow and arrows to another, and leveled the remaining carbine at Sherman. Without hesitation, Grierson leaped at Lone Wolf and wrested the carbine from him. He then ordered Satanta and Satank, acknowledged participants in the wagon train massacre, taken to the guardhouse.

A summons was sent for Big Tree and Eagle Heart, the only participants who still remained at the trading post. When they failed to appear, a detail of buffalo soldiers was sent to bring them in. Big Tree, behind the counter helping himself to the trade goods, saw the troopers coming and plunged through the rear window. The cavalrymen galloped in pursuit, surrounded him, and forced his surrender.

Eagle Heart, on his way to answer the summons, witnessed Big Tree's capture and managed to escape. Meanwhile, other Indians who had been standing by began to edge away. Called upon to halt, they opened fire on the mounted troopers, wounding one of them. One Indian was killed when the buffalo soldiers returned the fire, but the others escaped in a mad dash into the Wichitas to the north and west.

The council on Grierson's porch ended with Sherman telling the remaining Indians that Satanta, Satank, and Big Tree would be held for trial and that the forty-one mules taken in the raid on the wagon train must be returned. Within a day the three Indian chiefs had been placed in a wagon for transport to Fort Richardson, but they were still far from subdued. Along the way, Satank was killed after stabbing one of the corporals assigned to guard him. The surviving chiefs—Satanta and Big Tree—were sentenced to hang. They never did. Governor Edmund J. Davis commuted their sentences to life imprisonment, and a few years later they were returned to their people.

For the men of the Tenth, the resolution of the wagon train massacre was a proud feather in their caps. They had remained calm under very trying circumstances, had impressed Sherman with their poise and skill, and had brought three criminals to justice. In a memorandum to General Pope, Sherman said their conduct ranked with the most exemplary he had ever seen.

With the incarceration of two of their most militant chiefs and the death of another, the Kiowas and Comanches became much less aggressive. Brief, sporadic raids along the Texas frontier continued, but even these tapered off with the coming of winter. The troopers settled into the monotony and boredom of winter camp life, relieved only by the occasional nursing of frostbitten feet after a routine patrol.

With the arrival of spring, Grierson was ordered to temporary duty in St. Louis as superintendent of the Mounted Recruiting Service, the only time in more than twenty years with the Tenth that he was separated from his beloved troops. Grierson was replaced as commander by Lieutenant Colonel John W. Davidson, a spit-and-polish soldier whose autocratic and disciplinarian rule quickly alienated officers and men alike. One of his rules—that no man should walk on the parade ground grass—came to a sudden and ignoble end when the first culprit to be arrested was Davidson's own son.

In 1873, seven companies of the Tenth Regiment were ordered to Texas, where for the first time they became closely linked with the army's other black regiment, the Ninth, and together the troops pursued their course of taming the wild frontier. Three companies of the Tenth were garrisoned at Fort Richardson and two each at Forts Griffin and Concho. During the long, cold winter of 1873–1874, events were shaping up that would radically alter the diminished role of the Tenth as an "army of occupation." In December, a detachment of men from the Fourth Cavalry, commanded by Lieutenant C.L. Hudson, intercepted a war party along Texas' Nueces River, and in the ensuing fight nine young braves were killed. Among them were Tau-ankia, the son of Lone Wolf, and Gui-tain, the son of Red Otter, who was Lone Wolf's brother and himself a minor chief.

When the news of these deaths reached the reservation, the entire tribe went into deep mourning. Lone Wolf burned most of his belongings, killed many of his horses, and slashed himself time and again across the chest and arms. At about the same time a disastrous blow was struck against the Comanche tribe. Winter raids had grown so extensive that Davidson had stationed his black troops in stockaded camps on a line from Fort Sill to Fort Griffin. In this way, he could move rapidly to intercept raiding parties, or relay information to Lieutenant Colonel George Buell at Fort Griffin regarding the probable routes and destinations of war parties leaving the reservation. In late January, 1874, dispatch riders carried word to Buell that a party of Comanches had stolen some horses and was heading toward the Double Mountains, about one hundred miles west of Fort Griffin (near the present city of Belton, Texas). On February 5, Buell found his quarry, and in a running fight the buffalo soldiers killed eleven warriors and recovered sixty-five animals.

The blows struck by Hudson and Buell did nothing to allay the warlike mood of the Kiowas and Comanches. Instead, they kindled in the Indian warriors a burning desire for revenge. Thus it was that the spring of 1874 found the Texas frontier a powder keg, with all the explosive elements that foretold major warfare between the black buffalo soldiers and their Indian foes.

The troopers of the Ninth Cavalry, whom the Tenth now had

joined, had also experienced a rugged time during their early years in the West. When Colonel Edward Hatch and his men of the Ninth marched west out of San Antonio to garrison Forts Stockton and Davis—forlorn specks on the West Texas prairie—the task they faced was more than should be asked of any man. The territory was incredibly difficult to patrol. It contained thousands upon thousands of acres of nearly impenetrable brush along the Rio Grande, hundreds of square miles of plains and desert where the lack of water made survival difficult, and some of the most rugged mountain country on the North American continent. It was a land over which savage Indian tribes—the Mescalero Apache, the Lipan, and the Kickapoo—had held sway for hundreds of years, and where Kiowa and Comanche Indians often sought and found refuge when driven by cavalry units and Texas Rangers from the territory farther north and east.

To the south lay Mexico, torn for half a century by almost uninterrupted revolution and counterrevolution, where desperado and government official often were distinguishable from each other only by the uniforms they wore—and even those changed hands frequently. Border bandits, both white and Mexican, based their operations on the side of the Rio Grande that seemed most opportune at the moment, and raided those on the other side.

Lurking always in the background was the shadowy Comanchero with the whiskey, guns, and ammunition that he was eager to trade with anyone who could bring him stolen horses or cattle. The vast area and its multitude of problems were enough to occupy the attention and challenge the courage of several regiments, but for the most part the buffalo soldiers were expected to handle it alone.

When Hatch and the Ninth arrived at Stockton and Davis in July and August of 1867, they found the forts in ruins. Unoccupied during the Civil War years, both forts had been systematically destroyed by Confederate troops. The black cavalrymen lost little time in cutting logs, making bricks, and reconstructing quarters for both enlisted men and officers.

Although rebuilding the forts was the first priority, patrols began within days after the arrival of the still untried troopers. Unfamiliar with the country, they had no success in ferreting out their elusive foe, and the Indians, for their part, seemed to be sizing up their black opponents before engaging them in battle. Not until late in October did a band of savage Kickapoos —feared and distrusted even by other Indians—draw first blood from the Ninth. They did it the easy way, ambushing and killing two mail escorts, Corporal Emanuel Writhe and Private E. T. Jones of D Company. A month later, again making sure that the odds were in their favor, more than one hundred Apaches attacked the eastbound stage from El Paso and killed Private Nathan Johnson, a member of the escort squad.

It was Christmastime before the buffalo soldiers were given an opportunity to test their skill and courage with a unit of company strength. Captain William Frohock and the troopers of K Company were bivouacked at old Fort Lancaster, about eighty-five miles east of Fort Stockton, when a midafternoon attack by a force of nine hundred Mexicans, Lipans, Kickapoos, and renegade whites took them by surprise. K Company, at full strength, had only seventy-five men, but three hours later the black troopers still held the field, and twenty of their attackers would never fight again. Three buffalo soldiers—Andrew Trimble, William Sharpe, and Eli Boyer—were presumed dead after being caught by surprise, roped, and dragged away.

In its first test of fire, the Ninth had proved its ability to meet and defeat the enemy—a tribute to Hatch's training and the innate skill and courage of the men. There was no doubt that the Negro cavalryman was the equal of his white counterpart when the chips were down.

In anticipation of an aggressive spring campaign, Hatch pulled his troops into a tighter circle. Companies L and M moved upriver from Brownsville to Forts Duncan and Clark, while Fort Quitman, on the river southeast of El Paso, was reactivated and garrisoned by a detachment under Major Albert P. Morrow. Before Hatch could put his plans into action, however, he was placed in charge of the Freedmen's Bureau for Louisiana and transferred to New Orleans. His second in command, Lieutenant Colonel Wesley Merritt, replaced him as commander and was eager to carry out his plans. Savage raids across the Rio Grande by small bands of vicious Kickapoos kept the troops so busy "putting out brush fires" that the major offensive never got under way.

One of the Ninth's more impressive victories during 1868 came in September, when nearly two hundred Apaches raided a wagon train near Fort Stockton, ran off all the stock, and, as always, headed for sanctuary across the Rio Grande. Determined to make the Indians pay a bitter price for their dead, Lieutenant Patrick Cusack and sixty-one men of A Company immediately took up their trail. It was not hard to follow, and the Indians were unable to move rapidly because they were driving several hundred head of stock. Cusack and his men overtook them in the rugged Santiago Mountains, just short of the border, and attacked at once. In a running fight to the river, the buffalo soldiers soundly whipped the Apaches, killing twenty-five braves, wounding many more, and recovering two hundred animals and two captive Mexican children. Only two of the troopers were wounded.

The year 1869 was a particularly bloody one on the South Texas frontier, and a most frustrating one for the Ninth Cavalry. Raids began early in the year and continued without letup. Between January and April, hit-and-run raids by the Kickapoos in Bexar, Frio, Uvalde, Zavala, Medina, and Atascosa counties cost the lives of sixteen ranchers and settlers, the loss of hundreds of animals, and thousands of dollars in property damage. With the first warm winds of spring, Kiowa and Comanche raiders resumed their old habit of racing down from their territorial reservations to strike at homesteaders in Central Texas. Burnet, Comanche, Johnson, Parker, and Tarrant counties were particularly hard-hit.

The saddle-sore and bone-weary troopers of the Ninth were in their saddles almost constantly, often sleeping in them, as they pursued but seldom found their will-o'-the-wisp enemy. By September the discouraged and exhausted troopers were in low spirits. It was almost a year since their last major victory, and it had begun to seem that the next opportunity would never come.

Then, near Fort McKavett on the San Saba River, the buffalo soldiers picked up the trail of a strong war party. Their exhaustion forgotten, the black troopers followed the trail for 250 miles until they finally came upon a camp of Comanches and Kiowas near the headwaters of the Salt Fork of the Brazos River.

To the blare of bugles and the drum of horses' hooves, the troopers charged the unwary Indians. The shouting and exultant buffalo soldiers chased the fleeing Indians for nearly a dozen miles, abandoning the pursuit only when their horses became exhausted. Between twenty and thirty Indians were killed or wounded, and their entire camp and all their equipment destroyed or captured.

Hatch, meanwhile, had returned from his temporary assignment in Louisiana determined to reinstate the plans he had been forced to abandon a year before. In his effort to clear the Apaches, Comanches, and Kiowas from the area under his guardianship, he concentrated a detachment of nearly 150 soldiers at Fort Concho under Captain John Bacon. On October 10, Bacon and his buffalo soldiers marched to old Fort Phantom Hill, near the site of present-day Abilene. There he was joined by a small detachment from the Fourth Cavalry and a score of Tonkawa scouts.

Bacon planned to send scouting parties out to find the hostiles he sought, but the Indians made this unnecessary. At sunrise, as the black and white troopers and their red scouts were awakening, about five hundred Kiowas and Comanches pounced on the camp from every side. Although outnumbered more than two to one, the troopers proved, for the second time in a year, that they were more than a match for attacking redskins. After a bitter, hand-to-hand ordeal, the Indians were forced to flee. The buffalo soldiers, in hot pursuit, discovered and destroyed their camp and captured seven squaws and a number of horses. The final tally was forty Indians killed against seven troopers wounded, none fatally.

Although many bitter conflicts lay ahead, the campaigns of late 1869 and 1870 marked a turning point of sorts in the eight-year war between the Ninth Cavalry and the Indians of the southern plains. The Ninth, unable during its first two years on the frontier to find, much less defeat, its foe, had now gained the knowledge of the country and the experience on the trail it needed to meet the Indians on their own terms. By January, 1870, Hatch had sufficiently cowed the hordes of Comanches and Kiowas to turn his attention to the Mescalero Apaches who struck from the mountain strongholds in the almost inaccessible Guadalupes. The first expedition into the Guadalupes led to the discovery of an Apache encampment in the fastness of the mountains, but, more important, it allowed the troopers to map areas never before explored by "white" men and set the stage for successful campaigns of the future. Another major event occurred in 1870: Sergeant Emanuel Stance of F Troop became the first buffalo soldier to earn the Medal of Honor. Twelve other troopers of the Ninth and Tenth were to follow in his footsteps in the years that lay just ahead.

On May 20, 1870, F Troop's commander, Captain Henry Carroll, ordered Sergeant Stance to lead a detachment of nine troopers out of Fort McKavett on a routine patrol along an old Indian trail known locally as the Kickapoo Road. The detachment was about eighteen miles north of the fort when it spied a small band of Indians driving a herd of horses across a nearby hill. Spurring their own horses to the attack, the troopers engaged the Indians in a running skirmish until the foe escaped into heavy hillside thickets of oak and other shinnery.

With darkness coming on, Sergeant Stance ordered an overnight camp near Kickapoo Springs, and at six the next morning the troopers broke camp and cut their own trail back to Fort McKavett. About six miles from the fort, they spotted a band of twenty or thirty Kickapoos pursuing a herd of government horses. The herd guards, outnumbered ten to one, were fighting a losing battle. The leather-tough little sergeant, who stood about five feet six inches in his cavalry boots, immediately ordered a charge, and for eight miles or more the troopers engaged the Indians in a running battle. Sergeant Stance, already a veteran of five similar encounters with the redmen, led the left flank as his troopers sought to overhaul the Kickapoos. Pulling far ahead of his men, he repeatedly emptied his sidearm and reloaded without breaking stride. Although no Indians were killed, the fact that a detachment of ten black troopers had driven off a band of almost thirty Kickapoos was not lost on the Indians nor on Stance's superiors.

The following day, Stance and his patrol rode back into McKavett with twenty-five horses taken during the two-day patrol. The sergeant made a typically laconic report and turned in for some well-deserved rest. But Captain Carroll, himself one of the most capable Indian fighters on the western frontier, was less blasé about the sergeant's escapade. The following day he commended his redoubtable sergeant for conspicuous courage and devotion to duty and, unknown to Stance, recommended him for the Medal of Honor. On July 24, 1870, the crusty little Indian fighter openly wept as he received the highest military honor his country could bestow.

In 1875, eight long and unbelievably difficult years after the Ninth and its buffalo soldiers had been ordered to duty along the Texas frontier, General Sheridan wrote his superiors that the time had come to give the men and officers of the regiment some respite. As a result, Hatch received orders in September transferring the regiment to the District of New Mexico. The Eighth Cavalry took its place along the Rio Grande—still, and for many years thereafter, a hotbed of murder, malfeasance, and intrigue.

During the time Colonel Grierson had been on temporary duty with the Mounted Recruiting Service, major elements of the Tenth Cavalry had been transferred from Fort Sill to Texas posts to link their activities more closely with those of the Ninth and later the Eighth. When Grierson resumed command at Fort Concho (across the river from the present city of San Angelo) on April 30, 1875, he found his regiment badly scattered. Six companies were garrisoned at Concho, two at Fort McKavett, and one each at Forts Davis and Stockton. In addition, the Tenth was terribly undermanned and, as usual, poorly mounted. Grierson immediately sent an urgent request to General E. O. C. Ord, the commanding officer of the Department of Texas, for two hundred more troopers, and horses with which to mount his men properly. In the mysterious way of the army, the response was not spectacular.

At about the time that Grierson resumed command, General Ord decided that minor raids by renegade Comanches, attacking from their reservations and from the fastnesses of the Staked Plain of West Texas and New Mexico, were causing the army too much trouble. He determined to sweep the Staked Plain clear of these bothersome and destructive raiders and, because Grierson was totally unfamiliar with the area, he ordered Lieutenant Colonel William R. Shafter from Fort Duncan to Concho to take command of the expedition. Shafter's orders also required that he "show in detail the resources of the country, looking to its adaptability for cultivation and stock-raising," and pay special attention to the location of available water.

Black soldiers were the backbone of Shafter's historically significant expedition. The long column that left Fort Concho in July of 1875 consisted of six companies of the Tenth, two companies of the Twenty-fourth Infantry, and one company of the Twenty-fifth Infantry, which were also black units. Sixty-five wagons drawn by six-mule teams and a pack train of seven hundred animals carried supplies for the four-month campaign, and a cattle herd was driven with the command to provide fresh beef.

During his detailed crisscrossing of the huge area over the next several months, Shafter mapped, and in some instances discovered, such well-known landmarks as Monument Spring, Casas Amarillas, Cedar Lake, and the Palo Duro Canyon. Although the expedition, slow and ponderous as it was, killed but a single Indian and captured five others, it did "sweep the plains clear of Indians" and, more important, provided the first careful look at the Staked Plain, dispelling forever the myths that had surrounded the area since Coronado's day. Shafter's report was widely circulated and read, and occasioned a rapid movement of cattlemen and homesteaders to claim and settle the last great home of the Indians of the southern plains.

The movement of the Ninth to New Mexico Territory immediately plunged that stalwart cavalry unit into the troubles that had beset the region for centuries. The respite Hatch had wanted proved to be little better than a trip out of the frying pan into the fire. Although an uneasy peace prevailed, food was scarce at the Chiricahua Agency at Apache Pass, and the agent, Tom Jeffords, had told the Apaches that they would have to supplement their meager diet by hunting.

The peace-keeping Cochise had died the previous year, and Taza, his successor, lacked Cochise's magic at keeping his people under control. On April 6, a small band of renegade warriors under Skinya attacked a station of the Overland Mail, killing the agent and later a rancher along the San Pedro River. The "uprising" was put down a few weeks later when Skinya and his followers returned to the agency and were killed or wounded by peaceful Indians who feared reprisal.

Even though no government reprisal was warranted, the Indian Bureau issued orders that the Chiricahuas were to be removed from their reservation in the mountains and placed on the San Carlos Reservation in the inhospitable Arizona desert.

Juh and Geronimo, holed up for many months in the mountains of Mexico, had been unable to find willing ears before this. Now they would. General John Pope, well aware of the explosive situation, angrily wrote Sheridan that no human, red, black or white, could live for long on the San Carlos Reservation and that the Ninth had been placed in the intolerable position of forcing the Indians to starve to death on the reservation or killing them if they left.

As 1876 became history and the new year began, renegade Chiracahuas stepped up their raids, and the more restless young bucks among the Ojo Caliente, or Warm Springs, and Mescalero tribes slipped away from their reservations with increasing frequency. Late in January, word reached Fort Bayard that a band of half a hundred Chiricahuas had fought a detachment of Sixth Cavalry troopers in Arizona and were likely to be en route to New Mexico. Lieutenant Henry H. Wright, with six troopers of Company C and three Navaho scouts, was dispatched to intercept the Indians and relieve them of their weapons before they reached the San Carlos Reservation.

The buffalo soldiers found the renegades camped in the Florida Mountains and, rather than attempt to take them by force, called for a powwow. Half an hour of talk proved to be fruitless. The Indians, with considerable justification, argued

Courtesy of New York Public Library

Among the black soldiers at the Battle of Bunker Hill was Minuteman Peter Salem, pictured at left firing his musket at British Major John Pitcairn.

Courtesy of Montana Highway Department

York, at left in this diorama from the Montana State Capitol, played a major role in the Lewis and Clark expedition of 1804-06 into the Northwest.

Courtesy of California Historical Society
James Beckwourth, mountain man, found pass through Sierra Nevada.

Courtesy of California Historical Society
Monroe Meadows was named after stagecoach driver George Monroe.

Print, courtesy of Library of Congress
The all-black 54th Massachusetts, led by white officers, assaulted Fort Wagner, July 18, 1863. Sgt. William Carney won Medal of Honor in the action.

From painting, courtesy of National Archives

Lt. Powhattan Clarke won Medal of Honor for rescuing black cavalryman.

Courtesy of New York Public Library

Black cowboy Bill Pickett thrilled rodeo fans bulldogging with his teeth.

Courtesy of Library of Congress

Trumpeter of the Ninth Cavalry. It and Tenth Cavalry, both all-black units known as buffalo soldiers, fought the Apache, Comanche, Kiowa, and Sioux.

Dismounted troopers of the Ninth and Tenth Cavalry pierced Spanish lines fc

Print, courtesy of Library of Congress

ddy Roosevelt's Rough Riders at Las Guásimas, Cuba, June 24, 1898.

Courtesy of National Archives

The 369th, first black regiment to fight in World War I, adopted French helmet. It was under fire 191 days without relief, longest of any U.S. unit.

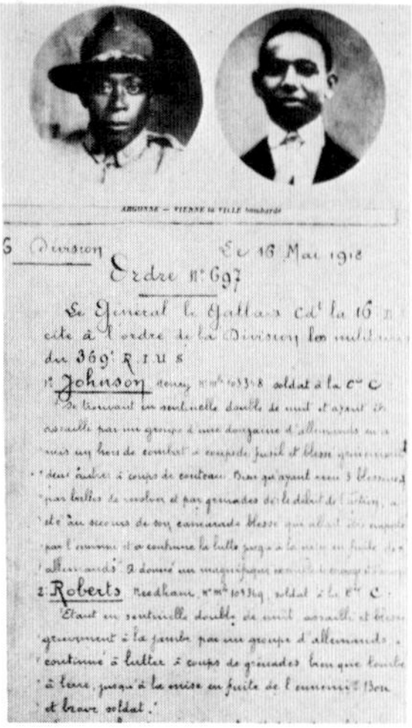

Courtesy of New York Public Library

French cited Henry Johnson and Needham Roberts for bravery.

Courtesy of National Archives

Messman Dorie Miller won Navy Cross for bravery in Pearl Harbor attack.

Courtesy of U.S. Army

Brig. Gen. Benjamin O. Davis, Sr., was the first black general in the U.S. armed forces. He is shown addressing men of his command in France after D-Day.

Courtesy of U.S. Air Force

Davis' son, Benjamin O., Jr., first black Air Force general, was awarded Distinguished Service Medal by Chief of Staff Gen. Nathan F. Twining in 1957.

Courtesy of U.S. Army

Frederic E. Davison, third black general, earned promotion in Vietnam.

Courtesy of Milton Olive, Jr.

Milton L. Olive III died on Vietcong grenade, won Medal of Honor.

Courtesy of U.S. Army

Black weapons squad leader with machine gun crew of 2nd Infantry in Korea.

that without their rifles they would have no means of defense should the white men, most of whom were black, change their minds. As the council dragged on, the troopers and their Indian scouts noted that a number of armed Apaches were surrounding their position.

Seconds later, a rifle shot ended the talk as the troopers scrambled for what little cover they could find. With no real alternative, the troopers returned the fire and then, led by Corporal Clifton Greaves, broke through the ring of hostiles in hand-to-hand combat. For the calm courage he showed that day, Corporal Greaves later received the Medal of Honor, and Privates Richard Epps, Richard Mackadoo, and John Adams were commended for their bravery in the action.

Victorio and his Warm Springs Apaches, incensed by the Indian Bureau's insistence that all the Apache tribes be concentrated at San Carlos, bolted the reservation in August, 1879, with a fervent vow never to return. General Pope, who deplored the concentration policy as a tragic blunder, wrote that "capture is not very probable, but I suppose the killing—cruel as it will be—can be done in time." It fell to the lot of the Ninth and Tenth Cavalry Regiments to be the prime instruments in bringing to a successful conclusion the Victorio War.

The Ninth's first major engagement with the wily Apache chieftain ended in near disaster for the troopers. Under the command of Lieutenant Colonel N. A. M. Dudley, who for months had been a thorn in Hatch's side, the buffalo soldiers were led into an Indian ambush and caught in a withering crossfire. The ambush would have been a massacre had not two other troops in the vicinity heard the rifle fire and come to the rescue. Shortly thereafter, Major Albert P. Morrow, a far abler soldier, took command of operations in southern New Mexico.

Morrow, with detachments from B, C, and G Companies, found Victorio's trail and followed it doggedly for eleven days. Finally, on the Cuchillo Negro River, the Indians turned to fight and were attacked immediately by Morrow's command. The battle raged from noon until late that night, when it was broken off by mutual consent. The Apaches were the first to strike early the next morning, when they gunned down an army sentinel. The running battle resumed, with intermittent engagements between the buffalo soldiers and the Apaches over the next three weeks. Finally Morrow was forced to abandon his pursuit when Victorio holed up in Mexico's rugged Candelaria Mountains.

In the months that followed, several major battles and countless skirmishes were fought between Victorio's renegades and elements of the United States and Mexican armies, the Texas Rangers, and even citizens' posses. Drawing on the San Carlos Reservation for supplies and on Mexico for sanctuary when hard-pressed by American troops, Victorio proved to be unbeatable.

Finally, Victorio's depredations became of such concern on both sides of the Rio Grande that the United States and Mexican governments agreed on a cooperative campaign to destroy him. It seems incredible that it should take the might of two nations to overcome one starving Indian chief, but that was precisely the case with the irrepressible Victorio. A potent concentration of troops under the command of Colonels George Buell and Eugene Carr was assembled on the American side of the Rio Grande, and a comparable concentration of Mexican soldiers under Colonel Joaquin Terrazas assembled on the Mexican side. Ten companies of Grierson's buffalo soldiers were posted along the Rio Grande to prevent any breakthrough into Texas.

During early October the troops of Buell, Carr, and Terrazas converged on Victorio. Scouts' reports indicated that he had taken refuge in the Tres Castillos Mountains. All possible escape routes were systematically sealed off and final plans made for the assault. Then, on October 9, Terrazas showed that he was as capable of duplicity as the Apaches; he informed his American allies that the presence of their troops in Mexico was objectionable and demanded that they withdraw north of the Rio Grande.

On October 14, Mexican troops, attacking from all sides, killed Victorio and most of his warriors, took numerous captives, and brought the war to an end. Although the Mexicans made the kill, credit for the victory—if there was really any credit save courage in it—belonged to the buffalo soldiers of the

Ninth and Tenth and the white American cavalrymen who had fought at their side. Victorio, beaten, dispirited, and constantly harassed by the troopers, was an easy target for the final thrust.

The death of Victorio broke the back of the Apache uprising, but scattered elements remained that were quite capable of creating havoc in small measure. Isolated tribes of Lipans, Kickapoos, and Apaches continued to make telling raids against lonely outposts and unprotected settlements. Still, by 1885 the services of the Tenth were no longer required on the Texas frontier, partly because a reasonable level of law and order had been attained and partly because the stalwart troopers were desperately needed farther west. Orders came in March assigning the regiment to the Department of Arizona, and on April 1 —for the first time in the regiment's history—all twelve of its companies marched together to the tracks of the Southern Pacific for the trip to Arizona.

Arriving at Bowie Station, the troops were split up once again, with Grierson establishing his headquarters command at Whipple Barracks and the other companies taking stations at Forts Grant, Thomas, Apache, and Verde. Their first assignment: to control Geronimo and his marauding Chiricahua Apaches. This task was finally accomplished through dogged pursuit and gradual attrition. In September, 1886, the ubiquitous Geronimo finally surrendered to members of the Sixth Cavalry, and a few weeks later Chief Mangus and his small band were run down by buffalo soldiers and captured. The Arizona Territory was at peace.

To a considerable extent, the same Indians who had made Arizona a battleground were those who had rampaged through New Mexico. With Geronimo, Mangus, and others confined to faraway reservations, General Pope looked for a fitting assignment for the pony soldiers of the Ninth. The situation back in Indian Territory, where David L. Payne alone had made no fewer than nine attempts to colonize Indian lands, seemed a likely choice, and in May of 1881 the Ninth Cavalry Regiment was transferred from New Mexico to Forts Sill, Reno, and Supply. After fifteen years of protecting white men from red men, the black soldiers were now charged with protecting the red men from white men. Hatch, keenly aware of the unpopularity of such an assignment, counseled his men to use as little force as possible in expelling the "boomers" from Indian lands.

Persuasion did succeed at first, but in January of 1883 Payne was back again, this time with nine hundred settlers, some of them heavily armed. The long wagon train was first sighted by Lieutenant Stevens and his patrol near the North Canadian River. The officer attempted to place Payne under arrest, but the man refused even to slow his pace. Mindful of the admonition to use minimum force, Stevens sent a dispatch rider to Captain Carroll at Fort Reno and fell in beside the lumbering wagons. By midafternoon the following day, Payne and his "boomers" had reached the North Canadian and immediately began to set up "Camp Alice."

Within two hours, however, Payne had far more to contend with than an uncertain young lieutenant. Captain Carroll arrived with ninety tough-as-nails veterans of F and I Troops and immediately got down to business: Payne and his followers could move out under their own power, or they could be "helped" out. Payne was arrested and taken to Fort Reno, while the others were escorted to the Kansas line. Payne was later taken to Caldwell, Kansas, and held for trial.

Gentle treatment, however, could not long deter the determined "boomers," who greatly coveted what little land the Indians had been allowed to retain. William Couch, Payne's principal lieutenant, was escorted from the territory three times during the last months of 1883, and in the spring of 1884 he showed up again near the present site of Oklahoma City with more than a thousand would-be settlers. This time, force was required to subdue Couch and some of his henchmen, who were summarily bound and tossed into wagons. Bloodshed was narrowly averted when the cool-headed buffalo soldiers hesitated in responding to a hasty command to fire by one of their officers, and the officer countermanded the order moments later. The narrow escape had its effect, and the sobered settlers quietly submitted to arrest and were escorted out of the territory.

The disagreeable task of driving hopeful settlers off Indian lands came to an end for Hatch and the Ninth in June of 1885 with an order transferring the regiment to Fort McKinney, Wyoming Territory. The long-promised rest had come to the buffalo soldiers, after eighteen years of distinguished service on the wildest frontier this nation has ever known. With the Indian wars behind them and settlers substituting their "civilized ways," the frontier army was faced with little more than the routine of garrison life. Colonel Hatch died peacefully at Fort Robinson, Nebraska, after having guided his buffalo soldiers for twenty-three years.

One final call awaited the Ninth, however. In 1890, the strange and mysterious "ghost dance" religion swept across the northern plains, promising that ghosts would return in the spring, bringing with them the buffalo that had once roamed the plains. The promises of the ghost dancers found no more eager adherents than the once proud Sioux, now reduced to poverty and near-starvation on barren reservations in the Dakotas. Led by Sitting Bull, the Sioux followed the call for religious war on the hated "white eyes" and left their reservations in droves.

This time it was the Indians, not the valiant troopers, who were outnumbered in every engagement they fought. On December 29, the uprising drew to a close with the slaughter of 156 Indian men, women, and children and the wounding of half as many at the Battle of Wounded Knee. Modern warfare, in the form of an early type of machine gun invented by Benjamin Hotchkiss, had been introduced to the frontier.

The following morning, sentinels at the Pine Ridge Agency saw columns of smoke rising from the direction of Drexel Mission, four miles south. Eight companies of the Seventh Cavalry rode out to investigate, only to find themselves pinned down by Sioux sharpshooters commanding the bluffs above.

The sound of the rifle fire alerted Major Henry and his buffalo soldiers of the Ninth. Although they had managed only two hours of sleep, they quickly saddled and forced their mounts to the battle scene. Taking in the situation at a glance, Henry detailed Captain Wright, with I and K Companies, to charge the east slope while D and F, under Loud and Stedman, dismounted and swept the bluffs to the west. The warriors were thrown back and driven off, and the grateful troopers of the all-white Seventh rushed out to embrace their black rescuers.

Corporal William O. Wilson of I Company received the Medal of Honor for conspicuous gallantry during the battle. The uprising was broken, and within two weeks more than four thousand Sioux had returned to Pine Ridge in the final surrender of the American Indian to the ways the victors called civilization.

It would be easy to embellish the trials and glorify the achievements of the men of the Ninth and Tenth Cavalry Regiments, but they need no gilding. The troopers were, above all, men of the lusty frontier; they drank, gambled, wenched, and swore with the best and the worst of them. To picture these men of the raw frontier as saints would be to submerge their more vigorous identity, yet their deeds stand forth among the proudest in military annals.

The buffalo soldiers fought well, it is true. But they also established many army posts that survive today, strung thousands of miles of telegraph wire, provided escort for stages, wagon trains, railroad crews, and surveying parties, and subdued an outlaw if the occasion required. Their patrols discovered and mapped new land and identified water holes that saved countless lives as the wagon trains moved west.

The buffalo soldiers themselves would have wanted no sobriquet other than that of "first-class regiments." That they were.

CHAPTER VII

NEW LOOK AT THE OLD COWHAND

Up the dusty cattle trails from Texas they came—to St. Louis, Abilene, Dodge, the Dakota Territory, and beyond. They rode through Wyoming blizzards and New Mexico sandstorms, across parched deserts and swollen rivers, to bring ten million head of bawling longhorns across the plains to feed a growing, hungry nation moving west. Some of their names—Bill Pickett, Bose Ikard, Henry Beckwith, and a few score more—are remembered by history. But for the most part, the black cowboys, like their white contemporaries, added their feats anonymously to the few decades of American history subsequently glamorized in song and verse as the "golden West."

The annexation of Texas to the Union preceded by only sixteen years the outbreak of the Civil War and the state's subsequent decision to cast its lot with the Confederacy. While that sad conflict left Texas impoverished, its cattle stolen and scattered, and its manpower depleted, it did serve as the focal point for one unheralded and largely unrecorded event: the rise of the black cowboy.

With most of the white men off at war, what little cattle raising was done in Texas during the period from 1861 to 1865 was handled by the women, the children, and the slaves who were left behind. The slaves, many of whom remained steadfastly on the home front during the war years, learned of necessity how to carry forward the multiple requirements of ranch life. Given responsibilities that had been denied them in normal times, the black men soon demonstrated how greatly their capacity had been underestimated, and by the end of the war many were numbered among the most skillful cowhands on the western ranges. It is, perhaps, one of the real ironies of Texas history that the men over whom the Civil War was fought did as much as any others, and perhaps more, to hold the state together during the years of conflict.

At the outset of the Civil War, there were more than four hundred thousand white settlers in Texas and better than four million cattle. Despite the untiring efforts of the black cowhands who stayed behind, the majority of the cattle strayed and ran wild during the war. They also multiplied prodigiously; by 1865 there were probably six million cattle in the state. In marked contrast to the beef surplus that was holding Texas prices to from three to five dollars a head, there was a marked shortage of beef in the North and the East. In the largely agricultural northern states, which lacked Texas' millions of acres of unfenced grassland, the war had reduced the supply of beef cattle to the vanishing point. As a consequence, a high-grade beef animal worth five dollars in the cow country would easily bring ten times that price in the cattle markets of the East. Yet, with a wry humor belieing the seriousness of their predicament, Texans said that you "could tell how broke a man was by the number of cattle he owned—the fewer the cows the wealthier the man."

The problem confronting the cattle ranchers of the Southwest was how to get Texas beeves to northern consumers. In the answer lay the plots of almost as many dime novels and "horse opera" movies as there were longhorns moving up the trails.

In the thirty years following the Civil War, more than ten million bawling longhorns were driven over four famous cattle trails to Kansas railheads or to Dakota-Wyoming-Montana pastures for fattening. These trails, known as the Chisholm, the Western, the Shawnee, and the Goodnight-Loving, all had a part in honing to a fine edge the expertise of the black cowhands who traveled over them.

Relatively few of the white men, and none of the black, who rode these trails kept accurate journals. Texans, as a rule, wrote history with their horses and punctuated it with six-guns. The record was buried in legend and perpetuated by word of mouth, the writing of it left to later generations. Yet, from passing references to "Nigger Jeff," "Black Sam," or simply "a colored man named Charlie," it is clear that no fewer than three thousand and possibly as many as five thousand black cowboys went up the trails from Texas.

One of the legendary cowboy names was "Deadwood Dick." That South Dakota city recalls three cowboys who claimed to be the original holder of this colorful nickname, but there was also a fourth. He was Nat Love, a black cowboy who not only claimed the title but under it wrote an autobiography about his exploits at the turn of the century. In the book, Love declared that he won the name with an exhibition of riding and marksmanship in 1876, at the Deadwood Fourth of July celebration. An examination of historical records and newspaper files does not support the claim, but then the files also fail to support many legends about other Deadwood characters, such as "Wild Bill" Hickock and "Calamity Jane."

The black men who rode the open ranges of Texas, who drove the cattle north, who busted broncs, branded calves, and manned chuck wagons, were no better and no worse than their white contemporaries. All endured the bitter cold of "blue northers" sweeping across the plains, drank "gyp water" from infrequent water holes, and battled Indians to have the herds. The real history of the West records heroism and cowardice, sobriety and drunkenness, fighting and dying among white and black cowboys with utter impartiality. Newspapers of the day reveal more blacks as gunhands and rustlers than as church deacons and sheriffs, not because they were black, but because violence and strife—then as now—were what piqued curiosities and sold newspapers.

Reconstruction days in Texas were as divisive for blacks and whites as they were anywhere in the defeated Confederacy. The slaves had been freed, but most of them—particularly in East Texas—were ill-prepared for freedom. The exceptions were the skilled artisans, cooks, blacksmiths, and a few thousand black cowboys. Also, a few blacks who had gained an education despite all the efforts of a slave society to prevent them held responsible posts in Reconstruction and post-Reconstruction governments. Nine blacks served in the convention of 1875–76 that wrote the present constitution of Texas, joining their white colleagues in drafting a clause that made illegal the concealed carrying of fence-cutting pliers but made no mention of pistols or other weapons.

The social, economic, and legal sanctions imposed on blacks fell less heavily on the cowboys than on others of their race. This had nothing to do with the inherent goodness or badness of the cowboy, but resulted instead from the almost feudal structure of the large cattle ranches. The ranch owner of the early West often controlled a million acres; some ranches, like the famous XIT, contained more than three million acres. Within such a domain, larger than some eastern states, the rancher's word was law.

Cowboys, particularly on the larger spreads, were organized with military precision, with foremen in the role of captains or lieutenants and top hands corresponding to noncommissioned officers. In such a unit, the black cowboy was welcomed as a hand and even as a top hand, though seldom as a foreman. Jim Perry, one of the great ropers and riders, who worked for more than two decades on the XIT, once said, "If it wasn't for my damned old black face, I'd of been bossing one of these divisions long ago." Most of the top hands who rode with him agreed.

Except on the plantations of East Texas, with the slavery that their maximum profit demanded, the Confederate cause in Texas was never a popular one. Charles Goodnight, one of the greatest and most successful ranchers the West has ever known, served for several years as a scout for the Texas Rangers. "I thoroughly believe," he said, "that fully half of Jack Cureton's rangers were in fact Union sympathizers. I know positively that

Captain Cureton believed the war to be cruel, wrong, and uncalled for." Because of this feeling the Reconstruction Era, perhaps in retrospect a necessary cathartic, was for many at the time a branding iron held to an open wound.

The life of the cowboy, glamorized though it has been, had precious little to recommend it by way of creature comforts. Particularly on the long cattle drives north, the cowboy spent most of his waking hours—and a good many of his sleeping ones—in the saddle. The famous cowboy artist, Charles M. Russell, himself a veteran cowboy, once wrote that the old-time cowboy reminded him of the eastern girl who asked her mother, "Ma, do cowboys eat grass?" "No, dear," the mother replied, "they're part human."

Russell, who wrote under the pen name of "Rawhide Rawlins," allowed that the mother had "sized 'em up right," but he believed that, although human, cowboys belonged to a separate species.

"I'm talking about the old-time ones," Russell wrote, "before the country was strung with wire 'n nesters had grabbed all the water, 'n cowpuncher's home was big. It wasn't where he took his hat off, but where he spread his blankets. He ranged from Mexico to the Big Bow river of the north, 'n from where the trees get scarce in the east to the old Pacific. He don't need no iron hoss, but the tools he needed was saddle, bridle, quirt, hackamore 'n rawhide riatta or seagrass rope.

"The puncher himself was rigged, starting at the top, with a good hat—not the floppy kind you see in pictures with the rim turned up in front. The top cover he wore holds its shape 'n was made to protect his face from the weather; maybe to hold it on, he wore a buckskin thong under the chin or back of the head. Round his neck was a big handkerchief; tied loose 'n in the drag of a trail herd it was drawn over the face to the eyes to protect the nose and throat from dust. His feet were covered with good high-heel boots, finished off with steel spurs of the Spanish pattern."

The earliest of the drives that the black and white cowboys made up the trails from Texas knew not even the comforts of the now famous chuck wagon. Every cowhand carried his own food and tin utensils, and cooked his meals over a cow-chip fire. The versatile Charles Goodnight put together the first chuck wagon, complete with the familiar hinged lid on the back that swung down to form a working space for the cook. Goodnight's wagon, and the hundreds that followed it, had iron axles in place of wood and carried a can of tallow for axle grease. The early chuck wagons were mostly pulled by oxen, but these were later replaced by mules and horses.

With the chuck wagons came the demand for trail cooks, the earliest of which were simply ranchhands who exhibited some degree of culinary skill. Because their duties included not only the preparation of meals but also such diverse assignments as being barber, dentist, physician, and often arbiter of disputes, the best of the trail cooks came to rank along with ramrods and top hands in seniority and pay. Not surprisingly, some of the most famous cooks—men whose reputations with Dutch oven and sourdough often persuaded top hands to sign on—had complexions as black as the bottoms of their sand-scoured skillets.

One such man, recalled years later by cattleman John Young while reminiscing with J. Frank Dobie, the famed western writer, was named Sam.

"The one man in our oufit that I recall most often and most vividly was Sam, the Negro cook," Young told Dobie. "He always had a cheerful word or a cheerful song, and he seemed to have an affection for every one of us. When we camped in the vicinity of brush every cowboy before coming in would rope a chunk of wood and snake it to the chuck wagon. The wood always made Sam grinning happy whether he needed it or not."

In keeping with the multifarious activities demanded of all trail cooks, Sam was an entertainer. Young recalled that he played a banjo until one of the cowhands accidentally stepped on it. The crew later chipped in and bought Sam a fiddle, which he played with equal skill. Carrying about two hundred and thirty-five pounds on his six-foot frame, Sam had become a bit too heavy and a few years too old for the active life of a cowboy, but he was still a good rider. He often did double duty as a bronc buster when one of the crew had trouble with an unruly horse, and he was always part of the general hell-raising that was part of life for a happy trail crew.

One evening around the campfire one of the hands looked at Sam's great bulk and said he was "too damn big for a man but not quite big enough to be a horse."

The remark was made in a friendly spirit, and Sam took it so, but he was not one to let a challenge pass. Grinning broadly, Sam said he *was* a horse, and to prove it he would give a dollar to any man who could ride him. Unable to resist what looked like easy money, several hands immediately offered to take him on.

Sam stripped to the waist and tied a bandanna around his neck for the rider to hold on to. One after another the cowboys pulled off their boots and spurs and mounted his back. One by one they picked themselves up from the soft sand into which they were thrown by the human "horse," whose agile mind anticipated and frustrated their every action. Not a man collected from Sam that night.

Whenever camp was established in one place long enough for the men to do a bit of hunting, Sam would provide them with some of the best eating known on the plains. If the black cook had time to barbecue antelope ribs, roast buffalo steaks, or prepare a wild turkey, the crew would enjoy what he called a "wedding feast"—a wedding, that is, of lunch and dinner. Then all the crew except a nighthawk or two would splash a handful of water on their faces, wet down their hair, and wait eagerly for Sam to sing out in his deep voice, "Come an' git 'er while she's hot 'n juicy."

Tales such as these make life on the trail sound pleasant and placid, when actually it was hard, and always dangerous, work. If the cowboys weren't plagued by blizzards, dust storms, wild animals, stampeding herds, or rattlesnakes, there were always the Indians.

J. L. McCaleb, a cowboy with a crew on the Chisholm Trail

in 1868, recalled the day he found a five-dollar gold piece along the trail. The black cook coveted the find and challenged McCaleb to a shooting match, the cook's two-year-old heifer against the gold piece.

"I was good with a pistol," McCaleb said, "but I knew the cook was hard to beat. But I wasn't too nervous, as I knew the two-year-old was about six to one if I won. One of the boys got a little piece of board, took a coal out of the fire, made a black spot about the size of a 25-cent piece, stepped off fifteen steps, and yelled, 'all ready, shoot.'

"I was to shoot first, so I jerked my old cap-and-ball Navy out and just about a second before I pulled the trigger I saw the heads of six Indians just over a little rise in the ground, and coming toward camp. This excited me so that I did not hit the spot, only about half my bullet touched the board just to the right of the target. I yelled to the Negro, 'Shoot quick! Look at the Indians.' By that time we could see them plainly on top of the rise. He fired, but never touched the board. So six big Osage Indians saved my valuable find. . . ."

As was typical of the old-time cowboys, McCaleb was delighted with the humor of the situation but so accustomed to danger that he didn't bother to tell what happened to the Indians.

About two years later, another case of careless shooting won another black cook a place in the history of the West: he became the first man to be locked up in the Abilene, Kansas, jail.

Abilene, northern terminus of the Chisholm Trail and the first of the Kansas railheads, also was the first Kansas town to achieve notoriety. Some measure of the character of the town may be had from the description of John M. Hunter in his book, *The Trail Drivers of Texas*. Abilene, he wrote, was the "wickedest and most God-forsaken place on this continent."

In 1870, seeking to restore a modicum of peace and respectability to the community, the town trustees commissioned the building of a stone jail. No sooner had construction begun than Texas cowboys pulled down the walls. The trustees then hired a strong guard and under its protection the jail was completed.

Soon thereafter a Texas outfit camped on Mud Creek, about twelve miles out of town, grazing its herd as the cattle awaited sale and shipment. Into town one evening rode the outfit's black cook whose name history has failed to record. Quickly drowning with Abilene red-eye his memories of cow-chip cook fires and hungry cowpokes, he began shooting up the town. No real damage was done, but the cook made a lot of noise. The town marshal came running and, as one contemporary account has it, "managed by some unaccountable good luck" to arrest the cook and throw him into jail.

There the cook stayed until his hungry trail crew discovered his whereabouts. Leaving a couple of men to guard the herd, the cowhands mounted and rode into town, drove the marshal into hiding, shot the lock off the jail door, and freed the cook. So, not only was a black man the first to occupy Abilene's new jail; he was also the first to break out!

Life in the railhead towns of Kansas could be cruel as well as humorous, and not always did vignettes have happy endings. Henry Hilton was one of the first of the black cowboys to take the trail to Dodge City. Finding Kansas to his liking, he used his trail money to buy and stock a small ranch a few miles outside of Dodge. One day, as he was riding into town, a group of white cowboys began to torment him. One tried to rope him off his horse, and Hilton warned that he didn't plan to stand for any more hazing, "even if he was a nigger."

When another cowhand persisted, throwing a loop and almost pulling Hilton from his mount, the black rancher pulled his six-gun and shot the cowboy dead. Even though most local citizens and "about half the cowboys" thought Hilton justified in killing his man (many were shot for less in those days), he was bound over for murder and released on his own recognizance. He never stood trial, however.

Before Hilton's case was called, he was found in a barroom, dead as stone and locked in the arms of another black identified as Bill Smith. The men were discovered in the morning in front of the bar, their empty six-shooters lying on the floor beside them. With incredible gullibility, Coroner's Jury ruled that two "justifiable homicides" had been committed, each man shooting the other in self-defense.

Because most of the white drovers who made their way up the trails from Texas were "unreconstructed rebels," many of whom had been subjected to the indignities of the carpetbag regime, it was inevitable that racial strife should walk the streets of Dodge and other frontier settlements. Yet stronger even than his allegiance to a fallen cause was the cowboy's loyalty to other members of his trail crew, be they black or white. An example of this comradeship, recorded by Ross Santee, involved a white cowboy named Bill Sparks and a black trail mate.

Bill and his friend, who had ridden up the trail together only a day or so earlier, were walking toward the Long Branch Saloon in Dodge when they were stopped by a man who had overindulged in the refreshments offered by that famous establishment. The drunk, according to Sparks, "began abusing the Negro for no apparent reason other than he appeared to be colored." Wanting a drink more than he did trouble, the black did nothing, but Sparks took up the quarrel and "beat hell" out of the drunk.

No sooner was that accomplished than Sparks was accosted by a cattleman who berated him for "siding with a nigger." Bill didn't take kindly to this remark, either, and was about to win his second fight of the day when the cattleman slugged him with a loaded quirt. Sparks retaliated by pulling the coupling pin from the yoke of a nearby wagon and returning the favor. Having thus won each other's attention, the two combatants then discussed the issue in forthright western style and became fast friends.

Hundreds of black cowhands remained on the Texas ranches, never seeing the cattle trails, while others rode the trails to the railroad and then continued on to the Dakota Territory, to Wyoming, Montana, and beyond. One famous black cowboy who "won his spurs" in the shin oak and huisache thickets of South Texas was Henry Beckwith, acknowledged by some western historians as one of the finest cow handlers who ever lived.

Little is known of Beckwith's early life, but he probably was a fugitive slave who "took to the brush" to avoid recapture. When the Emancipation Proclamation made him legally free, he went into business for himself, hunting down stray cattle that, in the same pattern he had followed, had found a home in South Texas' *brasada* ("brush") country. During more than four years of war, hundreds of thousands of calves had grown up there, unbranded, unclaimed, and untamed.

These cattle, extremely dangerous to a man on foot, were rounded up in the years just after the war and slaughtered just for their hides and tallow. Big factories grew up at such places as Brazoria and Quintana, where workmen stripped off the hides, boiled down the tallow, and skidded the carcasses down chutes into the river. A report in a Texas newspaper of the late 1860's reports Brazos River catfish of "gigantic size" as a result of gorging themselves on the wasted meat. An establishment at Quintana, at the mouth of the Brazos, attracted so many sharks that people were afraid to go swimming.

It was to satisfy the insatiable appetites of the hide and tallow factories that Henry Beckwith hunted cattle in thickets so dense that neither man nor horse nor cattle could see more than a few paces. Much of the *brasada* has now been cleared by modern methods such as chaining and chemical control, but even today there are places in South Texas that a man on horseback can enter only if he rides up the dry creek beds, or arroyos, that crisscross the area.

Beckwith carried neither bedroll nor blanket, but slept with his horse blanket spread over sticks. He drank black coffee mixed with chili juice to sustain life when his meager supply of jerked beef and cornbread ran low. Riding much of the time at night, he used his nose and his ears to guide him to the man-killer cattle he sought. His nocturnal habits led Mexican cowboys to call him *el coyete* because, like the coyote, he needed little sleep. If the night was extremely cold, he might build a tiny fire and hunker over it throughout the night. When he had twenty or thirty head of longhorn cattle inside a brush corral, he would drive them to the factory, spend perhaps a day in civilization, and return again to his beloved *brasada*.

One black cowboy who rode up the trail from Texas and never returned was Bill Williams, who ended his days as a drover by hiring on as bronc buster on the Lang Ranch in South Dakota. His methods were much admired by Theodore Roosevelt, who settled in the Badlands in 1884. Roosevelt built a ranch on the Little Missouri, served as a deputy sheriff, and became a cattleman. His spread was "next door" to the Langs', and Lincoln Lang, in his book, *Ranching with Roosevelt*, describes the horsebreaking methods employed by Williams.

The black cowboy, according to Lang, was a "past-master of the art—cool, collected and apparently fearless. If there was anything he did not know about handling horses, we never found it out. Moreover, if there was a horse in the range country that could throw him nobody ever produced it."

Williams broke wild mustangs by gradually winning their confidence, not by the conspicuous cruelty that was usually employed. The cowboy spent many hours, first with saddle blanket and hackamore, later with saddle and bridle, getting the horse accustomed to being handled and mounted. By the time Williams was ready to ride the unbroken horse, he had so won its devotion that no real bronc busting—in the accepted sense of the word—was required. Roosevelt was an interested observer of this technique and later adopted it to his own operation.

Roosevelt became a close friend of the Langs. He once complimented the senior Lang on naming his son after the Great Emancipator, and this in turn led to a discussion of relationships between the black and white races.

"It became impressed on me," Lincoln Lang later wrote, "that the color of a man's skin is no voucher for the qualifications lying beneath. I learned that the devil is just as likely to be found masquerading beneath a white as a dark skin, so it would seem just as well to go slow in drawing conclusions."

Men such as Lang and cowboy Bill Sparks were typical of a breed of westerners who elected to ignore color and seek more critical qualities in forming their friendships and loyalties. But the friendship that developed between the pioneer cowman and trailblazer Charles Goodnight and his trusted cowboy, Bose

Ikard, is perhaps unequaled in all the true tales of the frontier West.

Bose Ikard, described by Colonel Goodnight as "one of the best night hands I ever had," was born to slavery in Noxubee County, Mississippi, in June, 1847. Owned by Dr. M. Ikard, whose family name he adopted when Lincoln's proclamation set him free, Bose was brought to Texas along with Ikard's family when he was five years old. He grew up on the beautiful Cross Timber frontier, not far from Goodnight's original Black Springs Ranch. There he learned to farm, hunt cattle, and fight Indians, all accepted as necessary adjuncts to life on the Texas frontier in the years just prior to the Civil War.

When war came, Bose was among those who remained on the homestead, struggling valiantly to hold their owners' belongings together until their return. After the war, he remained with the Ikard family until 1866, when Oliver Loving—one of Goodnight's early partners and a famed pioneer cattleman in his own right—took him on the trail.

Ikard helped break the Goodnight-Loving Trail and rode it for four years, finally returning to Texas with Goodnight in 1889. Then forty-two years of age, Bose had wanted to remain in Colorado to homestead, but Goodnight—by that time his close friend and trusted counselor—persuaded him to return to Texas and buy a farm. In their declining years the two old friends kept in close touch, Goodnight assisting Ikard in the years before his death at eighty-three. J. Evetts Haley, whose first hand account of Colonel Goodnight's life is a frontier classic, reported that Goodnight was "tremendously affected" by the death of Bose Ikard in 1929. Goodnight himself died less than a year later, at the age of ninety-three.

Cowboy Bose Ikard was a good bronc rider, an exceptional nighthawk, a fine cook, and, according to Goodnight, "surpassed any man I had in endurance and stamina. There was a dignity, a cleanliness, and a reliability about him that was wonderful. He paid no attention to women. His behavior was very good in a fight, and he was probably the most devoted man to me that I ever had."

"I have trusted him farther than any living man," Goodnight

also said of Ikard. "He was my detective, banker, and everything else in Colorado, New Mexico, and the other wild country we traveled together. The nearest and only bank was at Denver, and when we carried money I gave it to Bose. . . .

"We went through some terrible trials during those four years on the trail. While I had a good constitution and endurance, after being in the saddle for several days and nights at a time, on various occasions, and finding I could stand it no longer, I would ask Bose if he would take my place, and he never failed to answer me in the most cheerful and willing manner. He was the most skilled and the most trustworthy man I ever knew."

One story told by Goodnight, and contained in Haley's biography of the pioneer cattleman, demonstrates the kind of man Ikard was, and the trust Goodnight placed in him. Although there were many events involving the two men, this one covered four almost unbelievable days and nights during Goodnight's second drive up the Goodnight-Loving Trail in 1867. The drovers were barely beyond the settlements, on the Clear Fork of the Brazos, when Indians attacked during the night and stampeded their herd. After the main herd had been turned, Loving and most of the hands held them in a broad valley while Goodnight and one hand went out to round up a second bunch that had strayed. Returning with the strays, the two men topped the Clear Fork hills near midnight and saw Loving's campfire burning brightly in the valley below.

"If the Indians needed any notice of our whereabouts," Goodnight later recalled, "Loving had surely given it plainly. As soon as I reached camp, I extinguished the fire, but failed to saddle a fresh horse, which I should have done. I had had no sleep the night before, so I told Mr. Loving to let me sleep about an hour and wake me, because we would probably have trouble. I did not take the time to unroll my bed; just threw my buffalo robe down, fell on it, and was asleep in an instant.

"One edge of the robe caught on the high grass, which held it up about a foot from the ground. Mr. Loving was out with the boys to keep them encouraged and to their places, but did not awaken me, saying the next morning he was afraid I would give out for want of rest and sleep. Just before day about a dozen Indians got in the gully, only a few feet away from where I lay, and opened fire. One of the arrows would have hit my body about midway had it not struck the lower edge of my buffalo robe, which, held up by the grass, turned the arrow beneath me and saved my life."

After shooting up the camp, in which only Goodnight and two or three other cowhands remained, the Indians managed to stampede the horses. While Goodnight was saving the horses, the cattle again stampeded and scattered. The oufit put in the day rounding them up, but the herd tallied out about 160 head short. The Indians were still in the area, so Goodnight decided to move the herd that night without the missing cattle.

"We had not moved far," Goodnight continued, "until about half the herd began to run. I had placed two first-class men (Bose Ikard and another top hand) in the rear, on what we called the 'corners,' and took 'One-Armed' Wilson and went on point myself. As the stampeders came up one side of the herd, Wilson and I caught them and turned them back. As they raced to the rear of the herd, the corner men caught them and turned them back up the opposite side toward the pointers. The strange part of it is that over half the herd moved along quietly in the dark, while the others ran around them as described.

"Late in the night it commenced to storm fearfully, and became very dark. At times the lightning was intense, and during flashes we could see clearly. It looked as though the bellies of the steers were touching the ground–they were going so fast. By ten or eleven o'clock they seemed to be entirely run down. By one o'clock the storm became so dense and the wind came at such a velocity we had to stop. We could see nothing but the electricity on our horses' ears. . . ."

While working his horse alongside the herd, Goodnight came to Ikard and another night rider named Bill Taylor. Together they managed to stop the herd on high and rocky ground. The cattle, nearly dead from fatigue, soon went to sleep, and the cowboys, after three days and nights in the saddle, dozed on their horses as they circled the herd. But the worst was not yet over: once cattle start to stampede, they become "spooked," and their fright spreads like a disease throughout the herd.

"The cattle had been so shot to pieces and so badly spoiled," said Goodnight, "that they continued stampeding, and after we passed Buffalo Gap [near the present city of Abilene, Texas] we had a run which I shall never forget. They had been quiet all night, and at daybreak I told Bose, who was on guard with me, to watch them and I would wake the cook. I reached camp and tied my horse to the wagon wheel, giving him some rope so he could get a little grass. Then I commenced to wake the men who were asleep around the wagon on the side of the herd. Something happened, in an instant the herd stampeded right down on the camp, and it looked as though the men would be trampled to death. There certainly was some scrambling, as most of them had not got out of bed.

"I jerked a blanket off one of the beds, jumped in front of the cattle that were coming at full speed, and by waving the blanket and doing all the yelling I could, succeeded in splitting the herd around the wagon and beds. By this time it was light enough to see. I mounted and rode up the side of the cattle as fast as possible, wondering why Bose had not turned the front. When I had almost caught up with him, he looked back and saw me, and immediately his horse shot out like lightning, and he threw the leaders around. After we got them circled, I asked him why he had not turned them sooner.

" 'Well, I'll tell you sir,' he grinned, 'I wasn't certain who had the herd until I saw you. I thought maybe the Indians had 'em, and I sure wasn't going to help the damn Indians round up our cattle.' "

Such was the life of a cattle drover on the Goodnight-Loving Trail, and such the measure of a man who could retain his sense of humor after four desperate days and nights in the saddle. Bose Ikard is buried today at Weatherford, Texas, under a marker that reads:

> Bose Ikard
>
> Served with me four years on the Goodnight-Loving Trail, never shirked a duty or disobeyed an order, rode with me in many stampedes, par-

ticipated in three engagements with Comanches, splendid behavior.

C. Goodnight

If Bose Ikard was the greatest trail hand who ever lived, and there are those who say he was, then certainly another black cowboy named Bill Pickett has to rank as one of the greatest cowboy showmen. Although Pickett attained fame as a hand on northeastern Oklahoma's famous 101 Ranch, he was himself a Texan, one of the rare breed typified by Henry Beckwith and other South Texas "brush-poppers."

The 101 for many years was one of the nation's great cattle ranches. For a time, during the early 1900's, it also was home ground for one of the most successful Wild West and rodeo shows the world has ever seen. Bill Pickett was one of the show's stellar attractions.

The story of Bill Pickett, the 101, and the Miller Brothers show had its beginnings one spring day in 1871 when G. W. Miller, father of the brothers, left Missouri for Texas on a cattle-buying expedition. Driving his cattle north from Texas, he crossed the Cherokee Strip and was immediately struck by its cattle-raising potential. Here was square mile upon square mile of rich grazing land within a few days' drive of the Kansas markets. Technically, the land belonged to the Indians, so it was with the tribal chieftains that Miller reached an agreement to lease sixty thousand acres, an adequate spread in Oklahoma's long grass country, along the Salt Fork of the Arkansas River. There he founded his 101 Ranch, which grew and prospered until 1892. In that year, the federal government forced the Indian owners to accept a token payment for their land so that it could be opened for settlement, and Miller's lease became worthless.

The federal "purchase" forced Miller to move before an onslaught of homesteaders–the "sooners" from which Oklahoma drew its nickname. Fortunately, he didn't have to go far. Several years earlier he had befriended the Ponca Indians, on the eastern edge of the Strip, and this tribe was permitted to keep its tribal lands. Miller negotiated a lease on one hundred thousand acres for an annual rental of one cent an acre.

By now G. W. Miller's three sons—Joe, Zack, and George—had grown to men and entered the cattle business with their father. Despite some ups and downs, the ranch became one of the most prosperous in the Southwest, and during the late nineties acquired some of the best hands in the business. This, of course, was after the days of the great trail drives, and hands were known for their specialties—roping, riding, cutting, bronc busting, or whatever.

The hands at the 101 were so capable that whenever they competed in local contests, the forerunners of today's rodeos, they invariably won the top prizes. It wasn't long before they were charged with professionalism and barred from amateur rodeos in cow towns like Enid and Wichita. This was the crew with which Bill Pickett signed on at the turn of the century.

Pickett was no ordinary bulldogger. Fred Gipson, in *The Fabulous Empire*, his story of the 101, tells it like this:

"The way Bill went at it, he piled out of his saddle onto the head of a running steer, sometimes jumping five or six feet to tie on. He'd grab a horn in each hand and twist them till the steer's nose came up. Then he'd reach in and grab the steer's upper lip with his strong white teeth, throw up his hands to show he wasn't holding any more, and fall to one side of the steer, dragging along beside him until the animal went down."

Pickett's technique was unique enough to earn him his title as "inventor" of the sport and to win audiences that included the crowned heads of Europe. Whether he invented it or not, Bill's performances certainly earned bulldogging the respected place it has held on the program of every rodeo since. The event is now generally known as steer-wrestling rather than bulldogging, and today's practitioners have abandoned Bill's lip-biting technique in favor of applying leverage until the steer goes down under its own weight.

At the time of G. W. Miller's death in 1903, he had about two hundred ranch hands on his payroll. Big as he had built the 101, his widow and sons set out to make it even bigger, into an empire reminiscent of Goodnight's JA Ranch and the syndicated XIT. The 101 also sought to increase the number of specialists on its payroll. Kurt Reynolds was known as the best all-around cowboy, Johnny Brewer could ride anything on four legs, Jim Hopkins could lay a lariat on any steer, and Bill Pickett and Lon Sealy were unbeatable as bulldoggers. The brothers also hired a cowboy named Tom Mix—a man who, with no lack of humor, took his stage name from his former profession, bartending.

Although Will Rogers was never a regular hand at the 101, for several years, at intervals, he shared the bunkhouse and worked with 101 cowboys. He had once seen Oro Paso, the Mexican trick roper with Buffalo Bill's show, do his tricks, and he vowed he would master the art if he "wore out every lasso on the reservation."

A black cowboy named Henry Clay worked patiently with Rogers to help him perfect his tricks. Together, they worked out a routine in which Clay would ride past on a horse and call out the horse's leg for Rogers to drop his loop over. In later years, with due credit to Clay, Rogers said he learned to "make his ropes do just about anything but sit up and talk."

The 101 put on its first full-scale rodeo in 1905 for the National Editor's Association in Guthrie, Oklahoma. During the next several years, the Miller brothers became famous for the shows they staged in Chicago, New York, London, and Mexico City.

One of the most exciting, by all accounts, was an early performance in New York's Madison Square Garden. Rodeos were something new to New Yorkers, and the troupe performed to a small crowd the first night. As Pickett's steer came out of the chute, it took one look at the crowd and the lights and, clearing a six-foot board fence, went into the grandstand. The black cowboy, on his horse, was in hot pursuit and also cleared the fence. Will Rogers, who was hazing for Pickett, decided he wasn't going to be outdone and took his horse over the hurdle and into the stands. There, amid screaming customers, Pickett rode down his steer and bulldogged it. Rogers threw a loop over its hind legs and, with Pickett still hanging on, dragged the bawling steer back into the arena. Newspaper coverage of the first night was enough to fill the Garden for the rest of the performances.

Good as he was, Pickett almost met his match trying to wrestle a Mexican fighting bull, though the problem wasn't with the bull but with the spectators. With the 1908 season profitably under their belt, the Millers decided to take their show to Mexico. After a so-so reception in Agua Caliente, they moved on to Mexico City, arriving there during a fiesta. The Latin-tempered Mexicans, oriented to bullfighting, were from the outset more than a little resentful toward the brash gringo cowhands.

Knowing little of the importance of bullfighting to the Mexicans, the Millers created added animosity by encouraging newspaper reports that they believed Bill Pickett's bulldogging act was "a greater show than any bullfight." Joe Miller added the final straw by announcing that Pickett could throw two steers in the time it would take for two Mexican bullfighters to throw one. When no bullfighters came forward to accept the challenge, Miller offered to donate a thousand dollars to charity if any Mexican bullfighter could duplicate Pickett's act.

No Mexican was foolish enough to accept the challenge, but the bullfighters did come up with a counteroffer: they bet five thousand pesos that Pickett couldn't hold on to one of their fighting bulls for five minutes. After some hurried consultation with his star performer, Miller accepted the bet. The special act was scheduled as part of the regular 101 show a few days later.

When the day came the stands were filled, but not with fans or friends. The incensed Mexicans roundly booed the opening acts. They had come for one reason: to see the death of a black cowboy who was fool enough to wrestle a fighting bull with his bare hands. From the outset, Pickett was at a disadvantage. The horse he was riding, though a good chaser, refused to work in close. Bill eventually slid off over the horse's rump to grab the bull's horns.

"For the next several minutes," according to Fred Gipson's account, "the bull made a whipcracker out of Bill Pickett. He slammed the Negro's body against the arena wall. He thew up his head to sling the man right and left, trying to dislodge him. He whipped him against another wall. He reached with his forefeet and tried to pry him loose. Finally, he got down on his knees and drove his sharp horns into the ground, time and again, trying to run Bill through."

Pickett gradually began to wear down the bull's strength, but then the enraged Mexicans began throwing a variety of objects at the determined bulldogger. When he was hit in the ribs with a beer bottle, Bill loosened his grip, and thereafter he could do nothing but hang on for his life as the bull threw him violently around the ring. After six minutes had gone by and it became evident that the Mexican officials had no intention of ringing the bell, 101 hands rode into the arena and roped the bull. The crowd threw every object within reach, and only the intervention of a troop of Mexican soldiers kept them from invading the ring.

Bill and his horse survived, although the animal had been severely gored in the rump. Joe Miller collected his five thousand pesos. Pickett, in fact, survived for many years, although his career, and the Miller Brothers show, ended abruptly in London in August, 1914. War had come to England, and under a national emergency order the Crown commandeered all the troupe's stock except six horses and a wagon.

Like most other southwestern ranches, the 101 was hard hit by the combined drought and depression of the thirties. In 1932, Zack Miller–the last of the brothers remaining alive–became ill, and Pickett was the only one of the old 101 hands still with him. To please Miller, Pickett, who was then in his seventies, went out to the corral one day to cut out some horses. A big sorrel gave Bill some trouble; at his age he couldn't move quickly enough. A hoof grazed his head, knocking him to the ground. The sorrel then stomped and kicked him, fracturing his skull.

Bill Pickett died eleven days later and was buried on a high knoll near old White Eagle's monument. The fabulous cowhand, one of the last of his breed, did have an uncanny ability to please a crowd. Fred Gipson said it this way:

"And when old Bill Pickett tied onto a runaway steer's nose

with his teeth and busted him against the ground, the crowd reared up on its hind legs screaming. Right down to the last puff of dust kicked up in the arena, that show was wilder than a wolf."

So were they all—wilder than wolves—the strange breed of cowboys, black and white, who helped tame the western wilderness. Although most of them will remain forever nameless, the battles they fought, the cattle they drove, the lives they led have become a glamorous part of our nation's history.

CHAPTER VIII

HEROES OF SAN JUAN HILL

Now and then, in the weeks preceding his arrival in the steaming jungle, Major General Joseph Wheeler could not escape the feeling that life had given him a second chance. Well over three decades had slipped by since the aging commander had mingled with troops preparing for battle. He was overjoyed to be back in action thirty-three years after he had unwillingly surrendered a promising military career, but the pleasure was tinged with a sense of rankling irony.

This time Wheeler was fighting *for* the United States government, not against it. His uniform had changed color, from gray to blue, and some of the officers who were sailing with him across the Caribbean had faced him from opposing breastworks during those four bloody years of the Civil War. Strangest of all were the faces of the men in his command—most of them were black.

General Wheeler, one of the Confederacy's leading cavalry leaders, was not without misgivings when he accepted orders to lead a squadron consisting of four experienced troops from the Ninth and Tenth Cavalry, U. S. Regulars. All these veterans were of African descent and virtually all were the sons and grandsons of slaves.

In the dawn of that morning in Cuba on July 1, 1898, General Wheeler watched closely as the black soldiers prepared themselves for battle. He passed a quiet command. An officer shouted, "Move out!" and platoon by platoon the black cavalrymen, obviously uncomfortable without their horses, but in order and on line, moved quickly to the assault. In the oppressive heat of the Caribbean, the sweating regiments of black troopers, marching side by side with inexperienced Caucasian volunteers, began to grope their way up the San Juan foothills, toward the circle of muzzle flashes popping from the enemy's Mauser rifles in the wooden blockhouses on top of the hill ahead.

The assault of San Juan Hill proved to be the decisive land battle of the short-lived and utterly ridiculous Spanish-American War. Its success rejuvenated Joseph Wheeler's military career and sent younger soldiers, such as Colonel Leonard Wood and Lieutenant Jack Pershing, on to international fame. More important, it propelled another soldier who participated in the charge up San Juan's barren slope, Colonel Theodore Roosevelt, toward the path that eventually led to the White House.

Ultimately, little would be remembered of the Spanish-American conflict except the highly publicized charge of the Rough Riders up San Juan Hill. The role of Wheeler's black troopers throughout the event would be forgotten.

Roosevelt remembered on occasion, but even he was ambivalent about the black man's role. His best description came in a speech delivered in New York in October, 1898, when he was trying to win election as governor of New York:

"We went up absolutely intermingled, so that no one could tell whether it was the Rough Riders or the men of the 9th who came forward with the greater courage to offer their lives in the service of their country. . . . When you've been under fire with a man and fought side by side with him, and eaten with him when you had anything to eat, and hungered with him when you hadn't, you felt sort of a comradeship that you don't feel for any man that you have been associated with in other ways. I don't think that any Rough Rider will ever forget the tie that binds us to the 9th and 10th Cavalry."

The unexpected presence of Americans in Cuba was the result of a series of events that had steadily worsened Spanish-American relations during most of the years since the Civil War. As a once mighty world power, Spain had entered the second half of the nineteenth century reeling from the revolutions that had spread like smallpox through her colonies.

The sole remnants of what had been a powerful Spanish western empire were the islands of Cuba and Puerto Rico. But revolt in their colonial family had taught the Spanish leaders nothing; they continued to exploit the natives of Cuba and Puerto Rico by exercising heavy-handed autocratic rule. The Spanish Crown permitted corrupt and high-salaried officials to levy exorbitant taxes while passing few civic improvements on to the people. In Cuba, in addition, the Crown imposed discriminatory duties on American imports, and in so doing alienated buyers in the best market for the island's chief source of revenue, sugarcane.

Discontent among the Cubans was also aggravated by Spain's refusal to follow the example of every other modern nation and put an end to slavery. Insurrection had a special appeal to the black slaves who made up about one-third of the island's population. In 1868, revolt had finally broken out and escalated into war. The fighting flared in eastern Cuba off and on until 1878. The Spaniards had then regained control of the government and immediately undertook to retrieve the cost of ten years of war from the people in the form of taxes.

Throughout this period, many in America were watching the course of events with keen interest. The Cuban thirst for independence persisted, and a second rebellion erupted in 1895. This time, however, substantial American holdings that had been developed on the island were threatened. Americans owned plantations, mines, and railways that were valued at fifty million dollars, and they conducted commerce with the island that amounted to one hundred million dollars a year.

Spain was under constant attack in the American press, and the United States government responded by putting increasing pressure on the Spanish government. A series of incidents, some magnified out of proportion by the "yellow" press of the day, outraged many Americans. This was the mood in the nation on

February 15, 1898, when the battleship "Maine" exploded in Havana Harbor. Two hundred and sixty-six American sailors—twenty-two of them black—lost their lives.

The incident further inflamed the American public, and, although abject apologies were made by Spain, Americans expressed their rage and their verdict in the slogan, "Remember the Maine, to hell with Spain." On April 11, President McKinley sent a war message to Congress, and within two weeks that body had demanded that Spain withdraw from Cuba and authorized the president to use military and naval forces to drive the Spanish from the island if that became necessary.

The war of 1898 may have been one of the most popular conflicts ever fought by the United States. Many Americans wanted it, some for economic, others for political and humanitarian reasons. To bolster the consensus, the president appointed Wheeler, Fitzhugh Lee, and Matthew C. Butler, all southerners, as major generals in the volunteer army. His purpose was to relieve the lingering bitterness over the Civil War still remaining in the South, and to encourage southern senators and representatives to join their northern colleagues in approval of a fifty-million-dollar war credit for national defense.

The army, with only about thirty thousand officers and men scattered throughout the nation in small garrisons and frontier outposts, was ill-prepared for war. Congress voted to expand the regular army to sixty thousand men. In April the President issued a call for a volunteer army of one hundred and twenty-five thousand soldiers, and in May he asked for seventy-five thousand more.

Black Americans readily identified with a call to arms that sought independence for a populace heavily sprinkled with Afro-Cubans. In 1898, nearly one-third of the 1,600,000 Cubans were nonwhite. Much of the island's leadership, developed during three decades of insurrection against the Spaniards, was also nonwhite. Antonio Maceo, the daring leader of the Cuban black infantry, died in the war, as did eight brothers before him. Quíntin Banderas, the "Black Thunderbolt," commanded the Cuban black cavalry.

The emotional patriotism that swept black Americans is reflected in the comments of W. T. Goode, who served in the all-black Eighth Illinois Volunteer Regiment:

"He [the black soldier] was going to do vengeance against the treacherous murderers of those 266 brave seamen who met their fate right under the frowning guns of Morro Castle in Havana Bay, and within a hundred miles of their home shore. Such a daring and dastardly deed will never be obliterated nor blotted from the annals of America, nor will it die out in the hearts of the young patriotic sons of America."

The army had no problem in securing volunteers. But, under the conditions of the first call for volunteers, only organized state militia were acceptable. This excluded the black American from the contest, because very few Afro-American soldiers served in the northern militia and southern units barred them from enlisting.

Because of the black man's clamor to help in the fight, Congress passed an act authorizing the formation of ten black regiments. Only four were actually organized, but a number of other black volunteer outfits were eventually mustered in Alabama, Kansas, Virginia, Ohio, North Carolina, and Illinois. Some of them served as occupation troops, but none of these regiments had an opportunity to fight in the war.

The black soldiers who did see action in Cuba more than made up for the absence of those who were left out. They were members of four units already in the regular army, the regiments that had already displayed such great skill and courage in pacifying the Indians of the West.

When the War Department issued its call to arms, the Ninth Cavalry was in the Department of the Platte and the Tenth Cavalry at Assiniboine, Montana. The two black infantry regiments were also in the West—the Twenty-fourth at Fort Douglas, near Salt Lake City, Utah, and the Twenty-fifth at Missoula, Montana. The black soldiers were sent off to war with appropriate fanfare; the patriotic citizens of Missoula even delayed Easter Sunday church services so that the entire town could see the black soldiers off on their train.

The scene at Tampa, when six thousand regular army troops arrived there for embarkation, was one of indescribable confusion. Few of the men were properly equipped; the black units, for example, were still carrying gear suited for the frigid Great Plains where they had spent the previous winter. The cavalrymen of the Ninth and Tenth were without their accustomed mounts, because of all the men gathered in Tampa—including the highly touted Rough Riders—only Colonel Theodore Roosevelt was permitted to take his horse, apparently a splendid animal, if one believes the many wartime accounts of "spirited mounted charges."

Roosevelt, who later became the best-known individual hero of the war, was serving as assistant secretary of the navy when war began to threaten in 1897. The brash young man did all in his power to bolster the strength of the nation's sea power. Ten days after the "Maine" went down, he took advantage of his superior's absence from Washington to put the entire navy on war footing.

Roosevelt's planning put Commodore George Dewey in command of an American Asiatic squadron in striking distance of the Spanish fleet in Manila Bay when war broke out. The North Atlantic squadron, built around the battleships "Indiana," "Iowa," "Massachusetts," and "Oregon," was prepared to sail into the Caribbean at a moment's notice. Thus, the navy was prepared to strike at the Spanish fleet both in the Philippines and off the coast of Cuba, and was thoroughly ready for war.

Roosevelt himself did not intend to play a passive role, and, despite his careful planning of the naval role, he did not plan to act out his own at sea. Instead, as soon as war was declared, he organized a volunteer cavalry regiment with the imaginative title "Rough Riders" and began recruiting a band of amateur heroes—cowboys, ranchers, Indians, and college athletes—to serve. It became one of the most highly publicized military units, if not one of the most effective, in the annals of military history. Roosevelt's sole, and rather surprising, concession to modesty was the acceptance, because he had no military experience, of a post as second in command. He allowed Colonel Leonard Wood, an officer in the medical corps, to lead the regiment.

To the credit of Roosevelt, because of his careful preparations it was the United States Navy that struck the first blow of the war. It came on May 1, and not in Cuba but the Philippines. Commodore Dewey, seizing the initiative, led his squadron into Manila Bay just before dawn and methodically obliterated the Spanish fleet that was anchored there. Admiral Montojo's losses in the one-sided bombardment included more than three hundred and eighty killed and many more wounded. Not a single American lost his life, and only seven sustained wounds.

Ten days later, one of the navy's two thousand black sailors was cited for heroism when he lost his life, along with three white shipmates, on board the torpedo boat "Winslow" in the harbor of Cárdenas, Cuba. Elijah B. Tunnell, cabin cook on the vessel, was in his galley when the boat began to draw heavy fire from the Spanish batteries on shore. Tunnell ran to the deck to help rig up a tow for the stricken vessel, but before the job was finished a shell burst on the deck, killing Tunnell and the others.

Events were moving more slowly in the Atlantic theater than in the Philippines, but the outcome was equally decisive. The first concern of the American fleet was to intercept and destroy a Spanish squadron that had set sail from the Cape Verde Islands on April 29. A hasty blockade was established, but the Spanish commander, Pasqual Cervera, succeeded in reaching the port of Santiago de Cuba on May 19 without being detected.

When the fleet's presence there was discovered, Santiago's harbor was effectively blockaded by American warships under the command of Rear Admiral William T. Sampson. Sampson was confident of victory but did not want to risk losing his ships to the mines and gun batteries that protected the harbor entrance. He asked for a land expedition to come to his aid.

The United States Army's land forces were already on the move toward Santiago when Sampson's message reached General William R. Shafter, who was in command of the expeditionary force. The black soldiers of the Twenty-fifth Infantry had disembarked on June 22 at Daiquiri, near Guantánamo Bay, and during the next day were followed ashore by a force of six thousand black and white soldiers, including the Twenty-fifth

Infantry, the Ninth and Tenth Cavalry, and the Rough Riders—more formally known as the First Volunteer Cavalry. On June 24, two battalions of the Rough Riders moved up the Santiago Road three miles, from Siboney to Las Guásimas, followed by the footslogging horsemen of the Ninth and Tenth Cavalry units.

Las Guásimas was an outpost the Spaniards expected to abandon, but not without a fight. The fort was manned by four thousand infantry troops who were determined to delay the Americans as long as possible. Roosevelt's Rough Riders were in the lead of a force of nearly one thousand Americans when the fort was sighted and rifles began to fire. The Tenth Cavalry, armed with semiautomatic weapons, moved up to positions in the line on the left and right of the Rough Riders as the combined units—some white, some black—charged toward the enemy's fortifications.

Stephen Bonal, who watched the battle, later said that the combined American force would have overrun the Spaniards on the initial charge had the First Volunteers not been without their machine guns. Typical of the course of events in this incredibly haphazard war, "the mules carrying them could not be found."

When it became apparent to the black cavalrymen that the Rough Riders were going nowhere, and were in danger of annihilation, the battle-experienced troopers quickly moved to the front of the American lines and began to pin down the Spaniards with deadly accurate fire. Several of the men rushed forward, knocked down an improvised enemy fort, cut a barbed wire barrier, and left an opening for the Volunteers, who then rushed through and routed the Spaniards firing from there.

A battle report from Captain Charles G. Ayers of Troop E, Tenth Cavalry, to Brigadier General B. M. Young described another example of the cool courage of the black troops at Las Guásimas. The cavalrymen were ordered to "support the troops in our front should they need it. The position was in plain view of the Spaniards, who occupied a high ridge and had the exact range; but pursuant to their instruction they held their position one hour and a quarter without firing a shot, for fear of firing upon their own men. Their coolness and fine discipline were superb."

Many insist that the Ninth and Tenth Cavalry Regiments actually saved the Roosevelt force from disaster at Las Guásimas. The testimony of soldiers who witnessed the fight suggests that this was probably true.

"If it had not been for the Negro cavalry the Rough Riders would have been exterminated," said one white officer. "I am not a Negro lover. My father fought with Mosby's Rangers, and I was born in the South, but the Negroes saved that fight, and the day will come when General Shafter will give them credit for their bravery."

Another southerner reported, "I never saw such fighting as those Tenth Cavalry men did. They didn't seem to know what fear was, and their battle hymn was 'There'll be a hot time in the old town tonight.' "

During this battle Private Augustus Walley saved the life of a white cavalry officer. Walley had already earned the Medal of Honor for a similar achievement while fighting Apaches in New Mexico in 1881. At Las Guásimas the private was firing from behind a bush when he saw another soldier struggling to carry a wounded man away from the action. It was Captain Ayers trying to save Major B. F. Bell of the First Cavalry, who had been shot through the leg. Walley left his cover and, crouching as low as he could, ran forward through a hail of Spanish bullets to help the officers. Spanish riflemen, concealed in a nearby trench, directed their fire at the three Americans, and it appeared that they were doomed until the black private stood straight up and leveled a burst of gunfire at the trench. The enemy firing stopped, and Walley helped carry Bell to safety. The official army report commended Walley's gallantry, along with that of Second Lieutenant George Vidmer and Privates Burr Neal, W. R. Nelson, and A. C. White for their support in the episode.

Within two hours after the fighting started, the Spanish had been driven from their trenches and the American force took control of Las Guásimas. During the week-long lull before the next encounter with the Spanish, Teddy Roosevelt paid the first of many tributes to the black fighters. "No troops could behave better than the colored soldiers," he remarked.

At daybreak on June 30, the American forces pressed on to El Caney, a small village northeast of Santiago, for their second major battle with the Spaniards. The El Caney garrison was a key target, for it stood in the way of the principal objective of the U. S. forces, the top of San Juan Hill, overlooking the city of Santiago. El Caney rested on a foothill that was well fortified and was also protected by a tangle of bushes, fences, and stunted trees on slopes that had been reinforced with strands of barbed wire. Approaches to the slopes were marshy, and from blockhouses on the hillside and concealed trenches in the jungle underbrush Spanish sharpshooters could look down the throats of the Americans attacking from below.

Once again, as at Las Guásimas, Roosevelt gave his gray-uniformed volunteers the honor of leading the assault. They fared even worse than they had the week before, because the Americans had underestimated the enemy's strategic position and firepower. This time, also, the black regulars were not immediately at hand to help. They had been held back, off the hill and away from the village, with orders not to fire. The day's fighting left the Riders with heavy casualties and in an untenable position that was vulnerable to enemy fire from all sides.

What happened the following day was reported by First Sergeant M. W. Sadler, Company D, Twenty-fifth Infantry:

"On the morning of July 1 our regiment, after having slept a part of the night with stones for pillows . . . arose at dawn without a morsel to eat, formed line and after a half day of hard marching succeeded in reaching the bloody battleground of El Caney. As we were marching up we met regiments of our comrades in white retreating from the Spanish stronghold. As we pressed forward all the reply that came from the retreating soldiers was: 'There is no use to advance further! The Spaniards are entrenched and in blockhouses. You are running to sudden death.' But without falter did our brave men continue to press to the front. . . .

"The first battalion of the 25th, composed of Companies C,

D, G, and H, were ordered to form a firing line. At 1,000 yards distance to the north the enemy, 2,000 strong, was in entrenchments hewn of solid stone. On each end of the breastwork there were stone blockhouses. Our regiment, 507 men all told, advanced 200 yards under the cover of jungles and ravines. . . . The enemy began showering down on us volleys from their strong fortifications and sharpshooters hid away in palm trees. Our men began to fall, many of them never to rise again. But so steady was the advance and so effective was our fire that the Spaniards became unnerved and began shooting over us. They were afraid to put their heads above the brink of the entrenchments. . . .

"The advance was continued until we were within about 150 yards of the entrenchments. And then came the solemn command, 'Charge.' Every man was up and rushing forward at headlong speed over the barbed wire and into the entrenchments. The 25th carried the much coveted position."

Private T. C. Butler of the Twenty-fifth was the first to penetrate the stone walls of the main Spanish blockhouse. He captured the enemy flag and was proudly starting off to deliver it to his commanding officer when a late arrival, an officer from another command, ordered him to hand it over. Butler did so, but, to prove that the flag had been in his possession, tore off a piece of it to show to his comrades.

One of the more courageous soldiers during the charge on El Caney was Sergeant Edward L. Baker, Jr., of the Tenth Cavalry. This black soldier probably had a greater right to call himself an American pioneer than any man in Cuba. He was born in a wagon train near the North Platte River in Laramie County, Wyoming, and in 1879 joined the Ninth Cavalry as a trumpeter. During five years of service Baker fought Indians all over the West, including one deadly contest with the Apaches at Gaballon Canyon, New Mexico, in 1881.

Baker was a man of great ambition. In 1887 he enlisted in the Tenth Cavalry and advanced rapidly from private to sergeant major. The determined young black constantly sought ways to advance his military career. He spoke Spanish fluently and had some knowledge of Russian, Chinese, and French. Just before the

Spanish-American War began, he had asked for an extended furlough in order to attend a cavalry school at Saumur, France. He agreed to pay his own expenses, and his application was enthusiastically endorsed by his white superiors. Then the war in Cuba broke out, dashing Baker's plans.

At El Caney the frontier sergeant found himself dodging bullets in an action hotter than any he had ever experienced against the Apaches. Many of his fellow cavalrymen were pinned down by Spanish fire on the sandbank of a river near the Cuban village when Colonel T. A. Baldwin, rallying the men for another charge, was knocked down by an enemy shell. In spite of the rifle fire and exploding shells, Baker ran to the wounded officer to try to help.

"I'm all right, Ed," Colonel Baldwin said. "Go back and rally the men."

As Baker ran to carry out the wounded officer's orders, he saw a soldier in the river struggling frantically to keep his head above water. Barker dropped his weapon, waded through the waist-deep water, and dragged wounded Private Marshall to safety.

Baker had saved the life of a fellow soldier at the most perilous moment in the battle. He later recalled that one shell "passed so close I could feel the heat." The citation given Baker when he was later awarded the Medal of Honor said that he "gallantly assisted in the rescue of the wounded from in front of the lines and under heavy fire of the enemy."

In a newspaper report on the siege, the *New York Mail and Express* published the eyewitness account of one of its reporters:

"No more striking example of bravery and coolness has been shown since the destruction of the 'Maine' than by the colored veterans of the Tenth Cavalry during the attack upon Caney on Saturday. By the side of the Rough Riders they followed their leader up the terrible hill from whose crest the desperate Spaniards poured down a deadly fire of shell and musketry. They never faltered . . . firing as they marched, their aim was splendid, their coolness was superb, and their courage aroused the admiration of their comrades. Their advance was greeted by loud cheers from the white regiments. . . . The war has not shown greater heroism."

With El Caney under control, the troopers pushed on to nearby San Juan Hill, the last line of defense under Spanish control. It was still daylight on the first of July when the disorganized American soldiers began their second rush of the day toward this uphill objective. The enemy had fortified the ridges of San Juan Hill with blockhouses and trenches, but few natural obstacles either obstructed or offered cover for Roosevelt's volunteers and the four black regiments as they stormed up the rocky San Juan slopes.

"When we reached the enemy's works on San Juan Hill our organization was badly mixed," recalled Sergeant Presley Holliday of the Tenth Cavalry's Troop B. "Captain Watson, my troop commander, reached the crest of the hill with about eight or ten men of his troop. . . . We kept up the forward movement and finally halted on the heights overlooking Santiago, where Colonel Roosevelt, with a very thin line, had preceded us and was holding the hill. . . . The greater part of Troop B was separated from its commanding officer by the accidents of battle and was led to the front by its first sergeant."

Holliday said that the group of soldiers that had gathered on the peak of the hill included Rough Riders as well as black soldiers from the Ninth and Tenth Cavalry.

In the confusion and disorder of that final charge, Frank Knox, a white soldier, became separated from his regiment. "I joined a troop of the 10th Cavalry, colored, and for a time fought with them shoulder to shoulder, and in justice to the colored race I must say I never saw braver men anywhere. Some of those who rushed up the hill will live in my memory forever."

John J. Pershing, a first lieutenant in the Tenth, said he felt that the storming of San Juan Hill had forged a deeper bond of unity among the victors. The man who would later attain fame as "Black Jack" Pershing said that black and white soldiers had joined their fighting skills in an effort that was "unmindful of race or color" to gain a victory for America.

Sergeant Major Benjamin F. Sayre, Company C, Twenty-fourth Infantry, described the attack in a letter to a friend:

"It was our regiment that took the fortified ridge of San Juan, the last stronghold of the enemy before Santiago. Seven of our officers were laid low and thirteen of our non-commissioned officers, before we had gone one hundred yards after fording the river. But we went right at them with a yell, every man shooting straight to kill. The steady advance of the black troops under the withering fire nonplused the enemy. They became panic stricken and leaping out of their entrenchment fled shamefully. In a few minutes we were on the heights firing down on them as they ran and dodged about among the trees. The hill top, blockhouse and trenches were literally filled with their dead and wounded, some of them shot to pieces."

On the day that the hilltops around Santiago were secured, another heroic episode occurred at Tayabacoe, in the province of Puerto Príncipe. It began when two transport ships, the "Florida" and the "Funita," with 50 black cavalrymen and 375 Cubans aboard, eased into the harbor. Their mission was to deliver ammunition and food to Cuban insurgents at Tunes, near Cienfuegos. A small detachment of Cubans and white Americans rowed ashore to survey a Spanish blockhouse, but the enemy leveled a deadly fire at them, wounding and killing several men and destroying their small boats with artillery fire.

Lieutenant C. P. Johnson sent a Cuban rescue detachment from the "Florida" to bring the stranded men back to safety. They started rowing to shore but turned back when enemy shells began bracketing their boats. Three more attempts were made by Cuban rescue parties, each without success. In desperation, Johnson turned to the men of the Tenth Cavalry for volunteers who would make another attempt to rescue the stranded men.

Without hesitation, Privates Dennis Bell, Fitz Lee, William H. Thompkins, and George H. Wanton stepped forward and offered to try. Although darkness had fallen, artillery fire still zeroed in on their boat as the four rowed frantically toward the menacing beach. Finally the quartet made it and began creeping through the underbrush, searching for the stranded men.

"Hey, over here!" a voice called.

Suspecting a trick, Thompkins moved cautiously forward and asked, "Who's there?" The voice answered, "Chandler," and the private remembered hearing the name Winthrop Chandler back on the boat. Suddenly out of the dark staggered two white soldiers. "Thank God, you found us," one of them said.

By this time the activity had alerted the Spanish, and rifle fire began to stream toward the shadowy figures. The men had to fight their way back to the boats. Even as they rowed toward the lights of the "Florida," bullets splashed in the water around them. By three o'clock that morning, all were safely back aboard the transport ship.

For their gallantry, each of the four cavalrymen was awarded the Medal of Honor. They were the first Afro-Americans to win this distinction in the Spanish-American War.

With the Spanish defeated on the fringe of Santiago, the American troopers next had to cope with another kind of enemy that, in many respects, was more dangerous than their Spanish adversaries. The men called it "yellow jack," the yellow fever that struck down so many men not accustomed to the tropics. A sergeant from the Twenty-fourth Infantry described this threat, more perilous than battle, shortly after the Americans had taken San Juan Hill:

"The first report was two hundred killed on our side and thirteen hundred wounded or missing. The death rate has increased by an average of six or eight each day. Men are dying off like sheep, for the fever has broken out among them, and if they do not get our troops away pretty quick hundreds will die. Every precaution has been taken. Every building has been burned to the ground, our drinking water is boiled, and every article of bedding and wearing apparel thoroughly aired and sunned. . . . Men are falling down as if struck on the head with a sledge hammer. The spread of canvas for our hospitals alone covers the area of a small city."

The Twenty-fourth Infantry spent forty days in the trenches and then was ordered back to Siboney. When the regiment of 450 men and 15 officers arrived at the port, it discovered that the fever had broken out among the volunteer ranks and was spreading to men in every company. Officers were immediately asked to supply 65 volunteers to work in the pest camp where "yellow jack" patients were being treated.

"This was the crucial test of the mettle of the men and an anxious moment indeed," recalled Major A. C. Markley, commander of the Twenty-fourth. The black troops were equal to the challenge. More volunteered than were needed, to spend several weeks burying the dead and nursing the dying in the hospital, and only twenty-four in the entire regiment escaped illness from the fever.

At a peace jubilee held three months later, Major General Nelson A. Miles, ranking officer in the United States Army and a man who had enjoyed long experience with black troops in the West, referred to the effort made in Siboney by the black soldiers of the Twenty-fourth:

"The white race was accompanied by the gallantry of the black as they swept over entrenched lines and later volunteered to succor the sick, nurse the dying, and bury the dead in the hospitals and Cuban camps."

In one of the postwar articles Roosevelt wrote for *Scribners' Magazine*, it was hinted that the black soldier had weakened in the thick of battle in Cuba. The article caused some bad feeling until Roosevelt denied the conclusion. The number of favorable comments Roosevelt made about the Afro-American soldiers who fought with him during the war are so numerous that it is likely the misunderstanding was an honest one. During his campaign for governor of New York in October, 1898, the future president said:

"Now a word as to the colored man in military life. I'm glad to see here one or two men in uniform. In fact, I rather think that however any other colored man may vote, you won't get a trooper of the 9th or 10th Cavalry to vote against a Rough Rider. And the feeling is reciprocated. As I heard one of the Rough Riders say after the charge at San Juan, 'Well, the 9th and 10th men are all right. They can drink out of our canteens.' "

Roosevelt also said that "the Spaniards called them 'smoked Yankees,' but we found them to be an excellent breed of Yankees. I am sure that I speak the sentiments of officers and men in the assemblage when I say that between you and the other cavalry regiments there exists a tie which we trust will never be broken."

The expeditionary force had accomplished its mission, to squeeze the land and sea forces of the Spanish at Santiago between the might of America's army and navy. But, although the infantry and cavalry had won the battle, they were too weak to seize complete control of the enemy's central headquarters. The American fighting force was nearly spent, and the officers in command scarcely knew whether to advance or retreat. Roosevelt even commented that the situation was approaching "a terrible military disaster."

Fortunately, the Spanish were even more thoroughly disheartened than the Americans. Their army was short of ammunition, and the city of Santiago was on the verge of famine. It seemed to the Spanish that nothing could halt the American advance and that surrender was inevitable. Under orders from Madrid, Admiral Cervera made a brave attempt to escape with his squadron on July 3. Admiral Sampson's big battleships opened up on the older, wooden-decked Spanish ships as they tried to slip out of the harbor.

What happened that day was still visibly evident to Corporal W. T. Goode, of the black Eighth Illinois Infantry, when he viewed the scene of the naval battle a month later:

"On the right of the entrance stood old Morro Castle, grim, sullen, and dismantled, her natural stone having been perforated by the solid shot from American battleships. . . . About 400 yards from the entrance, in about 90 feet of water, lay the slower of Cervera's squadron, the Viscaya. . . . The Cristobol Colon, being a little more fortunate, had succeeded in getting some 40 miles down the Windward Passage, before a shell from the Oregon sealed her fate. The Almeranto Oquenda met the same fate. We could see the smoke stacks of another Spanish cruiser, which was also sunk near the entrance of the bay; she did not get the chance to get out of the bay before she likewise was doomed. This was the Maria Teresa. The half-sunken hull of the Reina Mercedes was further up the bay. . . ."

When the fight was over, Cervera had lost every ship, and the Spanish casualties were nearly five hundred killed or wounded. The American fleet was virtually untouched, with one man reported killed and another wounded.

Two weeks later General Toral, in command of the Spanish forces at Santiago, signed the articles of capitulation with General Shafter. Shortly thereafter, an army commanded by General Miles began the occupation of the nearby island of Puerto Rico.

With Cuba's naval protection gone and its communications with Spain severed, there was nothing left for the Spanish government to do but sue for peace. This was accomplished through the French Embassy in Washington, which opened negotiations for an armistice on July 26.

Just before peace talks started, Fireman Second Class Robert Penn became the only black sailor to win the Medal of Honor during the war. Penn was working in a compartment next to the number two boiler room on the U.S.S. "Iowa" early in the morning of July 20 when an explosion was heard in the boiler room. Penn ran to the compartment and found the room filled with steam. Boiling water, released at 120 pounds of pressure, covered the floor. Despite the scalding water, Penn entered the room just in time to save an injured coal passer from falling. He hoisted the 140-pound man over his shoulders and carried him to safety.

Penn then returned to the boiler room. By now the fire had begun to seep out of the furnace, presenting the danger of another explosion. Disregarding the heat and the danger, the black seaman built a makeshift bridge by throwing a plank across two ash buckets. He then cautiously inched his way along the board, which sagged almost into the boiling water.

Penn made trip after trip across his fragile bridge, carrying shovels of flaming coals from the furnace to a safer location. When the last coals were removed, it was evident that a single man had prevented an explosion that could have taken the lives of many aboard the battleship. Commodore Perry said he believed that the seaman had proved himself "insensible to danger."

When the armistice was signed on August 12, the status in the world community of both Spain and the United States had changed dramatically. Spain agreed to withdraw entirely from the Western Hemisphere. Spanish sovereignty over Cuba was relinquished, and all the rest of the Spanish West Indies, including Puerto Rico, was ceded to the United States. On the other side of the world, the American government gained possession of Guam, and of the city, harbor and bay of Manila until the government of the Philippines could be organized. A payment of twenty billion dollars was made to Spain for the transfer of her Philippine possessions.

The greatest significance of the Spanish-American War was that Spain no longer wielded power or influence in the Western Hemisphere and that the war marked a turning point in foreign policy for the United States. America emerged as a world empire, committed to a new policy of overseas dominion and imperialism. The war also stimulated enthusiasm for the power of the United States Navy, pointed out the weaknesses in an army that was still organized under Civil War standards and needed modernization, and established the career of the nation's first internationalist president, Theodore Roosevelt.

The war of 1898 enabled the black fighting man to prove once again his valor on the field of battle. However, despite his sacrifice and courage, the new century found him still a second-class citizen on the field of peace.

CHAPTER IX

SAVING THE WORLD FOR DEMOCRACY

Private Henry Johnson was lying on his belly in the mud, craning his neck toward the barbed wire that stretched across the battlefield a few yards ahead of the ambuscade. It was two-thirty in the morning of May 14, 1918, and for the second night in a row there had been no sign of the enemy. Johnson lay there, tense, his eyes and ears alert for any sign of a German patrol.

Not long before, his corporal and two others of his five-man combat unit had crawled into the dugout for some much needed rest. The bright moon that had passed over them during the long night faded below the horizon as Johnson and his friend, Private Needham Roberts, kept their watchful guard.

Suddenly, Johnson sensed that Roberts was at his side. Motioning for silence, the other soldier gestured toward the blackness ahead. Together the two men slipped back to the east side of the enclosure, peering into the night and straining their ears for the faint noise that had brought Roberts to the alert.

There it was again: a faint click, perhaps that of a wire cutter in the hands of a stealthy German. In unison the two soldiers screamed, "Corporal of the guard! Corporal of the guard!"

One of the men fired a rocket to illuminate the battlefield so that the suspected attackers might be revealed, but even as he did a barrage of hand grenades fell into the pit. Roberts was thrown back against the dugout by the blast and, wounded severely, could not rise. The explosion trapped the three other soldiers sleeping in the dugout, leaving none but Henry Johnson, also wounded, to meet the enemy soldiers who were charging at a dead run toward the American outpost.

While the immobilized Roberts lobbed grenades into the darkness beyond them, Johnson grabbed his Labelle rifle and met the first of the attackers as they leaped into the enclosure. His heart sank at their numbers, for the French weapon held only three shots. He fired twice, and the weapon's muzzle was almost touching the chest of the German that the third–and last –bullet killed.

As the enemy soldier fell, another leaped over his body toward Johnson, a pistol in his hand. There was no time to reload the rifle. Johnson grabbed it by the muzzle and brought it crashing down on the German's head. As the victim's legs crumpled under him, the German gasped, in perfect English, "This black bastard has got me!"

"Yes, and this little black bastard'll git ya agin if ya git up," Johnson exulted, as he looked about to see what threat he must dispose of next.

Glancing over his shoulder toward his black comrade, Johnson saw two Germans attempting to carry Roberts off as a prisoner. Without hesitation, the tough little soldier, bleeding from several wounds, unsheathed his bolo knife and leaped on the nearest German. His knife sank to its hilt into the soldier's head.

As Johnson ripped the knife free, the soldier he had clubbed regained consciousness and charged toward him, his Luger automatic spitting bullets. Johnson was hit again and fell to his knees, but as the German closed in he met him with a vicious thrust of the bolo that put nine inches of cold steel through his adversary's stomach.

The sight of their disembowled comrade was too much for the attackers. They wanted no more of a "one-man army," and turned and fled. Johnson, however, was not yet ready to let them off; as the fleeing enemy struggled through the gap they had cut in the wire, he kept up a barrage of grenades until the last of them had disappeared from sight. When a relief party arrived, the half-conscious private was still muttering, "Corporal of the guard!"

Johnson's commander, Major Arthur W. Little, in his account of the event, which was emblazoned across America's front pages as "Henry Johnson's War," provided some gory details about the black soldier's feat:

"When daylight came, we trailed the course of the enemy retreat (a roundabout course of at least a half mile through the woods) to the bank of the river, where they crossed. We trailed the course with the greatest of ease, by pools of blood, blood-soaked handkerchiefs and first aid bandages, and blood-smeared logs, where the routed party had rested."

The major noted that in their haste the Germans had abandoned a great deal of property, either because of panic or in order to carry their dead and wounded. Included were about forty potato-masher grenades, seven long-arm wire cutters, and three Luger pistols.

"We found marks in the clay, outside the wire of the combat group, to show where two hospital stretchers had been set down during the fight," Little continued. "From our knowledge that it was customary to equip no more than one man of every four with the heavy long-arm wire clippers, we made the deduction that there were certainly no less than 24 men in the German patrol. . . . Also, the fact that none of the dead or wounded was left in our hands, coupled with our knowledge that of the dead alone there were at least four, contributed convincingly to the conclusion that the enemy was of a minimum of 24 men."

Who was this intrepid warrior who single-handedly had killed, wounded, or put to flight a force of at least twenty-four enemy troops? Not a professional soldier, to be sure–it was his first time in combat–but no stranger to a uniform, nonetheless. Before he sailed to France to fight for his country, he had worn one daily as a redcap in the New York Central Railroad Station in Albany, New York.

Irvin Cobb, then a war correspondent for the *New York Evening World*, arrived at Major Little's headquarters a few hours after Johnson and Roberts were carried from the battlefield. When he had heard the story of Johnson's heroism and viewed the site of the encounter, Cobb asked Little how much combat training the soldier had been given before his first encounter with the enemy.

Little replied that the official total was three weeks, but because of time lost changing stations it had really only amounted to one week. Cobb was astonished. "Why," he said, "if he had had the normal training that our young men at home are getting today, I believe that by tomorrow night Henry Johnson would have been storming Potsdam!"

Johnson, who was later promoted to sergeant, was only one of more than 370,000 black Americans who served with the United States forces in World War I. Of all of them—black or white—he was the first to win the cherished French Croix de Guerre.

The advent of World War I found black Americans existing in the most discriminatory environment since the end of the Civil War. In the late nineteenth and early twentieth centuries, "Jim Crow laws" had spread like crabgrass throughout the South, becoming a substitute for slavery to keep the blacks "in their place." Those who fled the South to escape poverty and persecution found similar treatment awaiting them in northern cities at the hands of workers, particularly recent immigrants, who felt that the black presence threatened their own opportunities.

In 1912, their leaders had urged black voters to desert the Republican party that they had so long supported because of its role in the demise of slavery. They had lost confidence in President William Howard Taft and in another candidate they had once supported, Theodore Roosevelt, who had recently joined the new Progressive party. More attractive was Democratic candidate Woodrow Wilson, who had assured blacks that if he was elected president they could count on him "for absolute fair dealing, for everything by which I could assist in advancing the interests of their race in the United States."

Wilson, early in his term, brought black Americans to a sad

awakening. Although elected with their help because of his pledge of greater equality, he kept his promise by further diminishing the status of the black. By executive order, he extended segregation to the restaurant and rest room facilities maintained for federal employees. When black leaders protested that this form of discrimination had not prevailed even under slavery, the President dismissed them in a fit of pique. Meanwhile, his first Congress was considering a flood of discriminatory legislation greater than any other in the history of the United States.

As a consequence, black Americans were concerned mainly with their own problems when, on June 28, 1914, Archduke Ferdinand was assassinated at Sarajevo. Neither they nor most other Americans, for that matter, foresaw that the event would lead to a four-year world conflict. No one imagined that the approaching military holocaust would engulf the world, redraw the boundary lines of Europe, spawn the Russian Revolution, jolt the United States out of a century of isolationism, set the stage for the rise and fall of fascist Germany and imperialist Japan, and lead to the ultimate polarization of the East and West.

As the war in Europe ground on, American bitterness increased, particularly among first- and second-generation Europeans whose native lands were being ravaged. With the sinking of four unarmed American merchant vessels in early 1917, accompanied by heavy loss of life, President Wilson asked Congress for a declaration of war. On April 6 he signed the joint resolution declaring a state of war with Germany.

The declaration won widespread support from a nation that was eager to "save the world for democracy," although for black Americans there was precious little democracy to save, and the last place to find it was in the armed forces of the United States.

On the day war was declared, there were about 750,000 men in the regular army and the National Guard, but only 20,000 of these were black. Half of the trained black soldiers were in the segregated units that had already demonstrated their skill and valor during the Indian wars and in Cuba in 1898–the

Ninth and Tenth Cavalry Regiments and the Twenty-fourth and Twenty-fifth Infantry units. The remainder were in segregated National Guard units in New York, Illinois, Ohio, the District of Columbia, Maryland, Connecticut, Massachusetts, and Tennessee.

Yet, despite the discriminatory treatment the blacks knew they would receive, the military services found them clamoring to serve. More than 2,250,000 registered for the draft and about 31 percent were accepted for service, compared with 26 percent of the registered whites. More than 140,000 black soldiers were sent to France, but the vast majority were confined to menial duties and only 40,000 actually got to fight. For the most part, the combat soldiers were in units assigned to the French command.

Although their numbers were limited, the black combat troops made an impressive showing on the battlefront. They were feared by the Germans who faced them across no-man's land and respected by the Frenchmen who fought in the trenches at their side.

Ironically, the first black regiment to reach France—Henry Johnson's outfit—was shipped overseas ahead of schedule because of discrimination against them by white civilians at home. In October, 1917, the Fifteenth New York Infantry, which had been activated in the spring, was ordered to training at Spartanburg, South Carolina. When news of the assignment became public, officials of the southern town protested to Washington. Mayor J. F. Floyd expressed the fears of the community when he told *The New York Times:*

"I was sorry to learn that the Fifteenth Regiment has been ordered here, for, with their northern ideas about race equality, they will probably expect to be treated like white men. I can say right here that they will not be treated as anything except Negroes. We shall treat them exactly as we treat our resident Negroes."

That ominous warning prompted the commanding officer of the Fifteenth New York, Colonel William Hayward, to call the entire regiment together immediately after its arrival and warn the men of the treatment they might expect in the community. He secured, by a show of hands, the pledge of the men to refrain from retaliation against any affront, physical or otherwise, to which local residents might subject them.

It was not long before the black New Yorkers learned what it meant to be treated like "resident Negroes," and the lessons were not pleasant, but they endured them stoically, as they had promised their colonel they would. This did not, however, forestall violence in Spartanburg. The black troops were under wraps, but their white comrades weren't. On several occasions, when black soldiers were attacked on the streets of Spartanburg and silently took their punishment without striking back, white soldiers from other regiments retaliated for them.

Major Little, in his history of the Fifteenth, *From Harlem to the Rhine*, recalled one such incident:

"One evening, in Spartanburg, a colored soldier was thrown off the sidewalk of the main street and into the gutter. He was attacked by two men. There had been no words or altercation of any kind. The colored soldier's sole offense was in being on the sidewalk. The boy picked himself up. Then he picked up his hat. By that time a crowd had gathered to see the fight."

The black soldier faced the crowd, announced contemptuously that he had promised his colonel he would not strike back, turned on his heel, and walked away. Meanwhile, two white soldiers from the Seventh Regiment who had observed the incident walked up to the crowd. "I didn't promise my colonel to keep my hands off you bullies," one of them announced. "Neither did I," agreed his friend, and with that the two men leaped on their black comrade's tormentors and knocked *them* into the gutter.

Incidents such as this continued throughout October, but the encounter that decided the regiment's fate came one evening when Lieutenant James Reese Europe, the much admired regimental bandmaster, and Drum Major Noble Sissle, a talented artist who was very popular with the men, were walking by a local hotel.

Lieutenant Europe wanted to buy a newspaper and asked

a hotel employee who was standing at the door whether anyone would take offense if he bought one in the hotel. He was assured that no one would, and Sissle volunteered to go in and get the newspaper for him. Sissle bought the paper and was on his way out when the proprietor rushed across the lobby and knocked the drum major's hat off his head. As Sissle bent to pick it up, the man cursed, struck, and kicked him, and threw him into the street. Major Little describes the reaction inside the hotel:

"The action was over, of course, in shorter time than that in which it can be described. Within a few seconds, however, the lobby of that hotel was in an uproar. Forty or fifty white soldiers, lounging there, had witnessed the outrage. Somebody yelled:–'Let's kill the so and so, and pull his dirty old hotel down about his ears!' A rush was started, and Sergeant Sissle's assailant was in a fair way to find himself in more trouble than most men ever live through; when suddenly, a voice of command was heard above all other voices.

" 'ATTEN . . . TION!'

"It was an officer who spoke; and those men, of subconscious spirit of obedience, stood fast.

" 'Get your hats and coats and leave this place, quietly, and walk out, separately or in twos, to Main Street,' the officer continued.

"And again the men obeyed. . . .

"The officer who had quelled that riot by the power and majesty of command was a black man, a full blooded Negro, 1st Lieutenant James Reese Europe."

The officers of the regiment knew that the attack on the two popular musicians was more than they could expect the men to bear. Not only were the two men personal favorites of the regiment, but the Fifteenth Regimental Band was considered the best in the army and a source of great pride to the others in the unit.

Colonel Hayward consulted with his Washington superiors, who agreed that they dare not leave the black troops in Spartanburg. If the black soldiers didn't start a riot soon, their white comrades would. Army officials, however, were unwilling to set a precedent by moving the black soldiers to another camp and giving the biased town a victory, so they chose the only remaining course. The Fifteenth New York was redesignated the 369th Infantry Regiment and, without ever joining the Ninety-third Division of which it was a part, was sent to France.

The men of the 369th left for Europe on December 14, 1917, after three false starts. Their transport ship, the "Pocahontas," first had engine trouble 150 miles out of New York Harbor and had to return. As they were about to depart a second time, fire broke out in a coal bunker, and another delay ensued. Several days later, after this damage had been repaired, the ship again left the pier, in the midst of a blinding snowstorm, and was forced to anchor inside Sandy Hook. During the night she was rammed by an oil tanker.

When the men finally arrived at Brest on New Year's Day, 1918, the regiment was assigned to the French command, and many of the men were sent to a French training camp to learn the use of French weapons. By April, a year after American entry into the war, they were at the front.

The black soldiers who had been forbidden to fight in Spartanburg got their chance in France, and the Germans, who soon named them the "Hell Fighters," were the victims of their pent-up wrath. The 369th, one of the first American units to face the Germans, compiled an incredible record. It remained under enemy fire for 191 days without relief, longer than any other United States regiment. It suffered more than 1,500 men killed and wounded.

With the exception of one engagement in which their artillery support failed, the rugged black soldiers of the 369th took every objective to which they were assigned. The unit never lost a foot of ground in defensive operations, nor was any member captured by the Germans. And, as victory neared, the 369th was the first of all Allied units to reach the Rhine.

Before the regiment left Europe, the French expressed their gratitude and admiration by awarding the entire regiment the Croix de Guerre. During the war the outfit had been cited 11 times for bravery. In addition, individual gallantry in action by

171 officers and enlisted men of the 369th had been recognized by award of the Legion of Honor or the Croix de Guerre.

Although the 369th was the first black regiment in combat, its performance was not unique. Other black regiments, attached to the 92nd and 93rd Divisions but serving with the French, fought with comparable valor and distinction. They were at St. Mihiel and Champagne, Château-Thierry and Belleau Wood, in the Argonne Forest and at Vosges and Metz. The black troops were never brought together as a unit—the 92nd was sent overseas from seven different camps, and only four regiments of the 93rd were actually formed—yet all the individual units displayed remarkable *esprit de corps.*

Two additional regiments of the 93rd Division, the 371st and the 372nd, followed the 369th to France, arriving in April of 1918. The 371st Infantry, which had trained at Camp Jackson, South Carolina, was attached to the 157th French Division—the renowned "Red Hand Division"—and soon began to distinguish itself in the front lines.

The black soldiers of this regiment went into action first at Avocourt and Verriers, northwest of Verdun, and in the offensive of September, 1918, they were heroes at Monthois. General Goybet, the commanding officer of the "Red Hand Division," said of them:

"Never will the 157th Division forget the indomitable dash, the heroic rush of the American regiments (Negro) up the observatory ridge and into the plains of Monthois. . . . These crack regiments overcame every obstacle with a most complete contempt for danger. Through their steady devotion, the 'Red Hand Division' for nine whole days of severe struggle was constantly leading the way for the victorious advance of the French army."

One hundred and thirteen men of the 371st Infantry were killed in action and twenty-five died of wounds. More than eight hundred and fifty of its black soldiers were wounded. In the process they won the distinction of being the only American infantry regiment to shoot down three enemy planes with rifle fire.

Marshall Pétain was among those who praised the men of the

regiment for their courage, and the entire unit was awarded the Croix de Guerre with Palm. The French citation read:

"Under the command of General Miles, this regiment, with superb spirit and admirable disregard for danger rushed to the assault of a strongly defended enemy position which it captured after a hard struggle under violent machine-gun fire. It then continued its advance, in spite of the enemy artillery fire and heavy losses, taking numerous prisoners, capturing cannon, machine guns, and important material."

In addition to the regimental citation, the French awarded the Legion of Honor to three officers of the 371st, and the Croix de Guerre to eighty-nine of its enlisted men. Twelve enlisted men won the U. S. Army's Distinguished Service Cross.

The other regiment singled out for praise by General Goybet for its service with the "Red Hand Division" was the 372nd Infantry, a unit made up of National Guardsmen from Ohio, Maryland, Massachusetts, and the District of Columbia, plus about 250 draftees. Beginning in late May, it held a section of the front lines near Argonne, and then went on to endure the massive German bombardment at Verdun.

In the September offensive, the 372nd Infantry went "over the top" with the French, so distinguishing itself that this regiment, too, won the Croix de Guerre. French Vice Admiral Moreau said the regiment had shown "the finest qualities of bravery and daring exploits."

Two individual heroes of this action were black soldiers from Massachusetts, Corporals Clifton Merimon and Clarence R. Van Alen. Merimon and his platoon were in action near Bussey Farm when they were pinned down by an enemy machine gun that killed and wounded several of them. Flinging hand grenades, Merimon rushed the gun emplacement and killed the gunner. Then, reorganizing what was left of the unit, he led the men south of the farm where, according to War Department records, "in spite of being gassed, he single-handedly knocked out another machine gun emplacement."

The day after Merimon's fight with the Germans, Van Alen encountered a similar situation, in which automatic weapons fire was decimating his platoon. The black soldier attacked the enemy position alone, killed four gunners, and captured three others. Later the same day he launched another one-man attack on a trench mortar battery that was harassing the French and put it out of action.

Both Merimon and Van Alen were awarded the Croix de Guerre with Palm and the Médaille Militaire by the French, as well as the American Distinguished Service Cross.

The last of the 93rd Division regiments to reach France was the 370th Infantry, which arrived in June, 1918. Like its sister regiments, this unit, in peacetime the 8th Illinois Infantry, was equipped by and served with the French.

The 370th went into action at St. Mihiel, fought in the Argonne Forest during July and August, and stayed in action with the French 59th Division until after the signing of the Armistice on November 11, 1918. In the interim, the regiment held a section of the line around Mont des Tombes and Les Tueries, and its men were the first Americans to enter the fortress of Laon when it was taken from the Germans, who had held it for four years. The regiment finally pursued the Germans into Belgium, where it captured a fifty-wagon German supply train in the last battle of the war, fought half an hour after the Armistice was signed.

One man of the 370th Regiment was awarded the Distinguished Service Medal, twenty-one received the Distinguished Service Cross, and sixty-eight were decorated with the French Croix de Guerre.

Like the 370th Infantry, the black regiments of the 92nd Division arrived in France in June, 1917, and after eight weeks of combat training began moving toward the front, where they relieved several French and American regiments in late August. The unit arrived in the trenches in the midst of a German offensive and promptly was subjected to a barrage of shells, gas, and propaganda. Taking advantage of the discriminatory conditions to which the black troops had been subjected, the Germans attempted to persuade them that they enjoyed no freedom worth fighting for. A circular scattered among them asked:

"What is Democracy? Personal freedom, all citizens enjoying the same rights socially and before the law. Do you enjoy the same rights as the white people do in America, the land of Freedom and Democracy, or are you rather not treated over there as second-class citizens? Can you go into a restaurant where white people dine? Can you get a seat in the theater where white people sit? . . . Is lynching and the most horrible crimes connected therewith a lawful proceeding in a democratic country? . . .

"Why, then, fight the Germans only for the benefit of the Wall Street Robbers and to protect the millions they have loaned to the British, French, and Italians?"

Despite repeated invitations to join their "friends" in the opposing trenches, and the constant reminders of the inequities to which they were exposed, the black soldiers fought like tigers for the remainder of the war. The company commanders had so many volunteers for hazardous patrols that they maintained waiting lists of men who wanted a priority on the opportunity to risk death. Prowess and courage were not limited to the infantry; the divisional artillery brigade was one of the most accurate to be found among the American forces.

An outstanding regiment of the 92nd Division was the 367th, which was cited for bravery in the drive toward Metz. The regiment's first battalion was awarded the Croix de Guerre. Fifty-seven black enlisted men and officers of the 92nd Division were awarded the Distinguished Service Cross. Among them was Corporal Ed Merrifield, who also won the Croix de Guerre for a display of extraordinary courage near Lesseay. The citation said that Merrifield, "although severely wounded, remained at his post and continued to fight a superior enemy force, beating off a raid."

The superb performance of the black divisions was acknowledged by General "Black Jack" Pershing, commander of the American Expeditionary Forces, when the 92nd Regiment passed in review prior to its departure from France in January, 1919:

"I want you officers and soldiers of the 92nd Division to know that the 92nd Division stands second to none in the record you have made since your arrival in France. I am proud of the part you have played in the great conflict which ended on the 11th of November. Yet you have only done what the American people expected you to do and you have measured up to every expectation of the Commander in Chief."

When the black troops returned to the United States, they were greeted enthusiastically during the traditional triumphal marches up Fifth Avenue in New York. An estimated one million New Yorkers turned out in February, 1919, when their own black regiment, the 369th, came home. Business came to a near standstill in Chicago when that city's 370th Regiment—once the 8th Illinois—paraded through the black neighborhoods and the city's bustling Loop.

The black soldiers had helped to save the world for democracy, but they soon discovered that it was only the white world they had saved. When they removed their khaki uniforms, the skin beneath them was still black, and the full fruits of democracy were not yet for them.

CHAPTER X

THE REVENGE OF PEARL HARBOR

It was a quiet Sunday morning in Honolulu. Diamond Head stood out sharp and clear in the morning light, and the beach at Waikiki was already bathed in sunshine. In Pearl Harbor, at the north end of Battleship Row, the bandsmen of the U.S.S. "Nevada" were lined up on the fantail, waiting for eight o'clock and the signal to play the morning colors.

As bandleader Oden McMillan raised his hand and the twenty-three musicians sounded the first notes of the national anthem, an unfamiliar aircraft streaked in low and then swept back skyward only a few feet over their heads, the bright red circle plainly visible on its tail. Without faltering, the band played on, reaching the phrase "the rocket's red glare" as a column of flame and smoke mushroomed upward from the battleship "Arizona" moored nearby.

Farther down Battleship Row, directly opposite the Southeast Loch, only those who had duty were stirring aboard the "West Virginia" and the battleship "Tennessee," which was moored alongside. Most of the officers and crewmen of the "West Virginia," and of the other eight battlewagons that were moored in the harbor, were spending the weekend ashore or were sleeping peacefully aboard.

Dorie Miller, the huge black mess attendant from Waco, Texas, was not enjoying the luxury of extra sleep, but it was a pleasant and relaxing morning for him, nonetheless. Only two officers were on hand in the junior officers' wardroom to claim his attention, and it was his added good fortune to escape the usual chore of arousing Ensign Edmond Jacoby from his slumbers, because the officer was off duty today.

Awakening Jacoby was always an onerous task for Miller, even though the powerful mess attendant was the star heavyweight boxer of the "West Virginia's"* crew. Jacoby, a reservist from the University of Wichita, always slept as though he had been drugged, and for a time Miller had been able to rouse him only by jerking the young ensign out of his bed. That expedient, although Jacoby approved, had gone by the boards when one of the more meticulous officers, an Annapolis man, had reminded Miller that navy regulations frowned on enlisted men who laid hands on officers—even officers who were only reservists. This posed a dilemma for Miller, because Jacoby was not the sort who could be roused with a polite, "Good morning, sir." The messman's solution, which also defied the traditions of the Naval Academy, was to bend over the sleeping officer, his mouth three inches from Jacoby's ear, scream, "Hey, Jake!" and then dash from the room.

On the morning of December 7, 1941, with Jacoby "sleeping in," this dubious informality on Miller's part wasn't required, but Ensign Jacoby got up early anyway. His alarm clock—even as the "Nevada's" band sounded the last notes of "The Star-Spangled Banner"—was the first of six torpedoes that slammed into the "West Virginia's" hull, jolting him awake. He was soon knocked out again by another blast that toppled a steel locker over on his head.

It was several minutes before either Jacoby or Miller knew what had happened, but it was not long before they and the entire world knew that the Japanese sneak attack on the huge American naval base in Hawaii had begun.

General quarters was sounded as the "West Virginia" reeled from the impact of the torpedoes that streaked through the

* Most historians and reference sources place Dorie Miller on the U. S. S. "Arizona" during the Pearl Harbor attack. Official navy records reveal no service by Miller on this ship.

water from a squadron of Japanese torpedo bombers that came straight at her, up the Southeast Loch. Five torpedoes ripped into the "Oklahoma," also moored on the outside and next in line. The "Arizona," shattered by torpedoes, also took a bomb near its second turret that crashed through the forecastle and exploded in the forward magazine. As the great ship blew up, fire streaked five hundred feet into the sky, and the force of the blast reached the other ships, lifting Ensign Vance Fowler off the "West Virginia's" deck into the sea.

The "Tennessee," protected from the torpedoes by the "West Virginia," did not escape the enemy's bombs. A splinter from a bomb that hit the "Tennessee" raked the "West Virginia's" bridge, and Captain Mervyn Bennion slumped to the deck. Ensign Victor Delano rushed to his skipper's side, took one look at the gaping wound in his stomach, and knew that medical attention would do no good. He looked for morphine to ease the captain's pain and, finding none, tried anesthetizing him with a can of ether he found in a first-aid kit. It made Bennion drowsy, but he remained conscious to the end.

Miller and Jacoby, meanwhile, were making their way to the deck. The black mess attendant encountered Lieutenant Commander Doir Johnson, who was on his way to the bridge from the forecastle, and the officer asked him to come along. Arriving on the bridge, where Captain Bennion still lay in an exposed position, Johnson and Miller lifted their skipper and carried him to a sheltered spot behind the conning tower.

Having done all he could for the wounded captain, Ensign Delano spotted two inactive machine guns forward of the conning tower. He recruited another officer and a seaman to turn them on the attacking enemy planes, and Mess Attendant Second Class Miller to supply them with ammunition. Delano's attention was then attracted elsewhere, and the next time he checked the machine guns he saw Miller at one of them, pouring a stream of bullets at the Japanese planes that roared in over the deck.

Miller was in his glory, doing what the rigidly segregated navy would not officially allow black sailors to do. Although he had never been trained in its operation, he kept the machine gun chattering steadily away. Before the heat of the flames on the "West Virginia" and the "Tennessee" forced their crews to leap into the sea, Dorie Miller had become a legendary figure in a day about which there was little good to remember. In the confusion of the battle, an accurate assessment of his astonishing marksmanship was impossible, but he was officially credited with downing two Japanese planes, and some witnesses insisted that his deadly machine gun had disposed of as many as six.

Miller was honored as one of the first heroes of World War II. Six months later, Admiral Chester W. Nimitz, commander in chief of the Pacific Fleet, pinned the Navy Cross on the twenty-two-year-old black's chest, and the sailor returned to America to tour the nation in a War Bond drive. Then he went back to sea in the Pacific and served until Thanksgiving Day of 1943, when he went down with most of his ship's seven-hundred-man crew in the torpedoing of the aircraft carrier "Liscome Bay."

Miller was only one of many noncombatant blacks who deserted the galleys and wardrooms to engage the enemy during World War II. At least three others were also decorated for courage in combat. Leonard Roy Harmon, of the U.S.S. "San Francisco" and William Pinckney, of the U.S.S. "Enterprise," were awarded the Navy Cross, and Elbert H. Oliver, of the U.S.S. "Intrepid," won the Silver Star.

Although it finally cost him his life, Dorie Miller's courage won more than the navy's highest award for himself. His example helped trigger a drive for greater opportunity in the military services for others of his race. How, after all, could the navy continue to restrict blacks to service in the galley and wardroom when, without the benefit of any training, one of them had demonstrated in the first battle of the war the skill and courage to man a machine gun under heavy strafing from enemy planes, and to drive two or more of them into the sea?

The navy's discrimination against blacks had been extremely harsh. Although officially eligible for enlistment as mess attendants, blacks had been denied even this opportunity between 1919 and 1932, when only Filipinos were recruited for the

Steward's Branch. Active recruiting of blacks as messmen was resumed in 1932, but there were only about four thousand of them in the navy in June, 1940.

Even with war clouds on the horizon, the navy steadfastly refused to accept blacks for service other than as messmen, proclaiming that it would lead to "disruptive and undermining conditions." An official navy statement explained that "the policy of not enlisting men of the colored race for any branch of service but the messman's branch was adopted to meet the best interest of general ship efficiency. . . . This policy not only serves the best interest of the Navy and the country, but serves as well the best interests of [Negroes] themselves."

Many Americans, white as well as black, disagreed vociferously with the policy and with its conclusions. During the first half of 1942, pressure for more constructive participation by blacks in naval operations caused Secretary of the Navy Frank Knox to announce that the navy would alter its policy on June 1 and begin recruiting blacks for general duty, although in separate units and only at shore installations and on harbor craft. Within a year and a half, however, so many had enlisted that utilizing them effectively became a problem, and the navy established a special unit that manned two seagoing craft with black personnel and white officers.

On June 18, 1942, a Howard University medical student, Ensign Bernard W. Robinson, became the first black to win a commission in the United States Naval Reserve. In April, 1944, twenty-two blacks were commissioned as naval officers, and by August of that year the new navy secretary, James V. Forrestal, had approved the assignment of blacks to twenty-five auxiliary craft on which they would do general duty alongside white personnel. This experiment proved so successful that blacks were soon assigned to all the auxiliary vessels of the fleet. By the summer of 1945, segregation had been abolished in all navy camps and schools, and there were 58,000 black seamen, compared to 57,000 steward's mates.

By February of 1946, it would become clear that the performance of the navy's black fighting men had erased the specious arguments that had once limited their duty, and Forrestal would lift all restrictions on the types of duty to which blacks could be assigned. The navy would thus become the first of the military services to reestablish integrated fighting forces such as those that had won independence for America more than a century and a half earlier.

It was during the war, in May, 1942, that the U.S. Coast Guard began accepting blacks for general duty, and in April of that year the Marine Corps admitted its first black volunteers in 167 years. Only the merchant marine found such action unnecessary: it had been integrated from the start. Before the war ended, fourteen Liberty ships had been named after outstanding blacks, four after Negro colleges, and four after black heroes who died in service. When the merchant ship "Booker T. Washington" was launched in September, 1942, a black captain, Hugh Mulzac, was at the wheel. He was the first of four blacks assigned to the command of Liberty ships.

The opportunities available to black Americans serving their country in the army and the air force were far more restricted. In the two decades that followed World War I, the Army had dwindled to 230,444 men, and fewer than 4,000 of them were black. Even with the buildup during the many months before Pearl Harbor, mid-1940 found the army with barely 9,000 blacks in its ranks.

With the passage of the Selective Service Act in September of 1940, the War Department announced that blacks would be enlisted in proportion to their percentage of the population. Their service, however, would continue to be in segregated units. Only in the training of officers was the segregation barrier broken, with a decision that all officer candidate schools would train black candidates in the same classes as whites. By the end of 1942, studying side by side with white candidates, more than one thousand blacks had won their bars as second lieutenants in the United States Army.

The army, however, did not alter its policy of limiting blacks to service in segregated units. Moreover, a disproportionately high percentage of black recruits was assigned to the service branches. Thus, blacks were engaged in cargo handling at ports throughout the world and made up about half of the transportation corps in Europe. Black soldiers had a major role in some of the most dramatic engineering feats of the war. Nearly ten thousand of them fought the Japanese while building the Ledo Road between India, Burma, and China. Blacks also helped build the Alcan Highway and constructed airports at scores of locations, from the steaming jungles of New Guinea to the frozen tundra of the Arctic.

Of the more than 1,500,000 blacks who entered the armed forces, many did see combat in every theater of the war. The first black unit ashore in the North African invasion was the 450th Anti-Aircraft Artillery Battalion, which later was also the first to enter combat in Europe. General Mark W. Clark cited the battalion for "outstanding performance of duty." Twenty-two black combat units served in Europe, among them the 969th Field Artillery Battalion, which won the Distinguished Unit Citation for "outstanding courage and resourcefulness and undaunted determination."

When the first Negro Tank Battalion arrived in the combat zone in 1944, General George S. Patton gave its men a typically hard-boiled welcome, pointing out that all Americans had their eyes on them.

"Don't let them down, and damn you, don't let me down," Patton told the black troops of the 761st Battalion. Never a diplomat and always explicit, Patton told the men that as long as they killed Germans "I don't care what color you are."

One hundred and eighty-three days later, after fighting their way through six European countries and distinguishing themselves in the Battle of the Bulge, the men of the 761st had lived up to the tough but popular general's expectations. They had knocked out more than 300 enemy machine-gun nests, captured 7 enemy towns and a radio station at Salz, inflicted nearly 130,000 casualties on the enemy, and won 391 decorations for extraordinary heroism in combat. Their gallant service had been cited by four major generals and the under secretary of war.

Despite the zeal and courage they demonstrated, the black combat units remained segregated until the near disaster of the Battle of the Bulge. When the Germans cracked through the American lines in this offensive, a frantic call went out in

January of 1945 for volunteers from the service units. Fifty-five hundred black soldiers stepped forward, eager to go to the front. About twenty-five hundred men in black platoons were sent to join the United States First Army in the combat zone, where they were integrated into companies with white platoons to repel the determined Nazi attack. They won the praise of General Lanham, who told them: "I have never seen any soldiers who have performed better in combat than you."

Alan Morrison, reporting for *Stars and Stripes* on the efforts of black and white units during the Battle of the Bulge, noted that the integration of the black platoons into previously all-white companies was accomplished without any problems. He quoted the commanding officer of one such company, Captain Wesley J. Simons, of Snow Hill, Maryland, as saying, "I was damned glad to get those boys. They fit into our company like any other platoon, and they fight like hell. Maybe that's because they were all volunteers and wanted to get into this."

The War Department, in April, 1945, commended the black volunteers, asserting that they had "established themselves as fighting men no less courageous or aggressive than their white comrades." General Dwight D. Eisenhower, asked to comment on the performance of black troops, said that he did not differentiate among soldiers:

"I do not say white soldiers or Negro soldiers and I do not say American soldiers or British soldiers. To my mind, I have a task in this war that makes me look on soldiers as soldiers. Now, I have seen Negro soldiers in this war and I have many reports on their work where they have rendered very valuable contributions and some of them with the greatest enthusiasm."

The irony of these comments lies in the fact that some did still feel the need to question the courage of black soldiers, and others the need to rise to their defense. It was paradoxical that black soldiers, after having served with distinction in every war since the American Revolution—over more than one and one-half centuries—were still having to prove that they were willing and able to fight. Yet prove it they must, and prove it they did, with the same incredible courage that had enabled their race to endure more than three hundred years of slavery, prejudice, and discrimination in the very land they fought to defend.

Only in the Mediterranean theater was any question ever raised about the courage and determination of black units. The Negro 92nd Division which had already served in Africa, entered its first offensive action in Italy in the crossing of the Arno River, and quickly took several towns. When it subsequently lost them, critics seized on the reverses as evidence that black soldiers were inadequate. In February, 1945, the division came under even sharper criticism for weakening in the face of the enemy in the Cinqualle region of Italy.

The adequacy of the 92nd is best demonstrated by its overall record in World War II. The black men of the 92nd were awarded more than twelve thousand decorations and citations, including two Distinguished Service Crosses, sixteen Legion of Merit awards, ninety-five Silver Stars for gallantry, and nearly eleven hundred Purple Heart medals. In the Rome campaign, more than three thousand men were reported killed, wounded, or missing in action.

The Silver Star was awarded to Captain Charles F. Gandy of the 92nd Division, who "led his company out in broad daylight and . . . by personal example and leadership, succeeded in getting his entire company across a canal, with an abrupt twelve-foot wall. This was accomplished in rain and under extremely heavy fire. . . . Captain Gandy went forward alone to reconnoiter [and while] engaged in this activity, he was mortally wounded by enemy machine-gun fire. His outstanding gallantry and leadership in combat exemplified the heroic traditions of the United States Army."

The Distinguished Service Cross was awarded to another black officer, First Lieutenant Vernon L. Baker of Cheyenne, Wyoming, for the "extraordinary heroism" he displayed near Viareggio, Italy, when he silenced three German machine-gun nests and killed or wounded nine of the enemy.

The "extraordinary heroism in action" of a twenty-four-year-old tank commander of the 614th Tank Destroyer Battalion earned the Distinguished Service Cross near Climbach, France. The black officer literally shot his way through the Siegfried

Line "in a blaze of fire from enemy rockets, artillery and machine guns." The hero, Captain Charles L. Thomas of Detroit, was wounded in the chest, legs, and arms.

Other blacks who were decorated for heroism in ground combat with the enemy included four who won the Silver Star: Lieutenants Reuben Horner, John Madison, and Kenneth W. Coleman and Private Ernest Jenkins. The last, a native of New York City, knocked out a German gun position and captured fifteen enemy soldiers.

Of all the service branches, on the day Pearl Harbor was attacked only the U. S. Army Air Corps was all white. It took the protest resignation of Judge William H. Hastie, a distinguished black who was serving as civilian aide to the secretary of war, to force the glamour branch of the service to reconsider its policy. In July of 1941, the air corps established a flying school for blacks at Tuskegee Institute but, unlike the army, it segregated the officer candidates even during their instruction period.

Eight months later the air corps commissioned its first five black pilots, and before the war ended six hundred had been trained at Tuskegee. They fought in Africa, France, Italy, Poland, Romania, and Germany. Eighty-eight of them won the Distinguished Flying Cross.

The first men to win their wings at Tuskegee formed the nucleus of the 99th Pursuit Squadron, and by January, 1943, forty-three black pilots had been assigned to fight duty with this new unit. The squadron was sent to North Africa, where it became part of the four-squadron 79th Pursuit Group. This outfit, flying low-altitude P-40's in hazardous dive-bombing attacks on the enemy, became known as the "Falcon Desert Fighter Group" and was widely acclaimed for its heroics.

Leading the 99th when it arrived in North Africa was Captain Benjamin O. Davis, Jr., a black career officer who had been graduated from the United States Military Academy at West Point in 1936. The officer's father, whose own army career spanned half a century, had been promoted to brigadier general in October, 1940, the first black to achieve this rank.

After combat training under experienced pilots in French

Morocco, the squadron saw its first action in an attack on Panelleria, in the Mediterranean theater, and quickly established itself as a superb fighting unit. On the 99th's first mission, Lieutenant Charles B. Hall, of Brazil, Indiana, won the Distinguished Flying Cross for shooting down a German Focke-Wulf 190. He was the first black pilot to gain official credit for destroying an enemy plane in combat.

Although nearly half the pilots in the all-white squadrons of the 79th Pursuit Group were from the South, it soon became apparent that none of the officers was concerned about the color of the fellow pilot who might one day rescue him when an enemy fighter zeroed in on his tail. Walter White, a black war correspondent who visited the 79th after the group had moved to a base in Italy, found an exceptional camaraderie among the airmen. In his book *The Rising Wind*, he wrote:

"Whatever prejudice, created by race or environment, existed on either side when the group was activated began to seem a bit superfluous and even silly in the face of death and danger. The experience gained in North Africa, Sicily, and now in Italy had earned them the reputation of being 'the hottest fighting unit in Italy.' "

White described a visit he made to the operations building of the 79th Group at Capodichino Airport:

"A huge map covered one side of the square, flat-topped, box-like building. A Negro sergeant was marking on the map the bomb runs for the mission about to start—not only for the 99th but for the other squadrons of the 79th Group. Across the way, a second Negro sergeant and a white one worked with heads close together on another technical preparation for the flight. Inside and outside, in the cold sunlight stood little groups of fighter pilots smoking a last cigaret together before climbing into their ships. . . .

"Democracy seemed more nearly achieved in that moment than it had ever seemed before, though it is tragic that a war of such proportion and destructiveness had apparently been necessary to cause Americans in isolated instances like this one to forego race prejudice."

This message, however, was apparently lost on air corps

officials. After the 99th had been in combat for almost a year, participating in almost five hundred combat missions and nearly four thousand sorties against the enemy, it was transferred in December, 1943, to the newly formed 332nd Fighter Group, an all-black organization.

Under the command of Captain Davis, who later was promoted to major and then to lieutenant colonel in a single day, the 332nd Group won acclaim in many engagements. One of the most conspicuous was its service over the crucial Anizo beachhead in January, 1944. There, in some of the most vicious aerial battles of the Italian campaign, the group shot down sixteen Nazi Messerschmitts and Focke-Wulfs while protecting the Allied invasion forces.

The ground forces at Anzio were in great peril because of the desperate efforts being made by Hitler to prevent the landing of a force that would threaten Rome. Sharing this danger were the men of the quartermaster and port battalions who operated the landing craft that ferried the Allied troops ashore. About 70 percent of these men were black. Although the men of the 332nd Fighter Group subjected the Nazi dive-bombers to unrelenting attack and mercilessly strafed the enemy troops on the ground, the blacks on the LST's sustained heavy casualties. One battalion of black troops had fifty-two men killed and ninety-three wounded in a few days of action at the beachhead.

The three squadrons of the 332nd flew more than 15,500 missions and nearly 11,000 sorties in the Mediterranean theater. Enemy equipment destroyed by the black pilots of the group included 261 aircraft, 51 locomotives, and a destroyer. More than 200 of its missions were as escort during bombing raids and, although the group had no defense against ground fire, no bomber under its protection was lost to an enemy plane.

In March of 1943, while escorting a B-17 bomber flight on a raid over Berlin, the 332nd racked up a victory that led President Franklin D. Roosevelt to award it the Distinguished Unit Citation for "extraordinary heroism in action." Not one of the group's fifty-nine planes was lost in the action, which the citation described in these terms:

"Nearing the target approximately 25 enemy aircraft were

encountered which included ME-252s which launched relentless attacks in a desperate effort to break up and destroy the bomber formation.

"Displaying outstanding courage, aggressiveness, and combat technique, the group immediately engaged the enemy formation in aerial combat. In the ensuing engagement that continued over the large area, the gallant pilots of the 332nd Fighter Group battled against the enemy fighters to prevent the breaking up of the bomber formation. . . . Through their superior skill and determination, the group destroyed three enemy aircraft, probably destroyed three, and damaged three. Among their claims were eight of the highly rated enemy jet-propelled aircraft, with no loss sustained by the 332nd Fighter Group. . . . By the conspicuous gallantry, professional skill, and determination of the pilots, together with the outstanding technical skill and devotion to duty of the ground personnel, the 332nd Fighter Group has reflected great credit on itself and the armed forces of the United States."

The 332nd was credited with sinking an enemy destroyer off the Istrian Peninsula and escorted bomber squadrons on many vital missions, including those against the oil fields of Romania. More than eight hundred Air Medals were awarded to the men of the group. The commanding officer, Colonel Davis, personally flew on sixty missions, winning the Legion of Merit on three occasions, the Distinguished Flying Cross, the Air Medal with four Oak Leaf clusters, and the Silver Star. The last he got for "gallantry in action" while leading a squadron of P-51 fighter planes against airfields in the south of Germany.

After the war, Davis followed in his father's footsteps to become the first black general officer in the United States Air Force on October 27, 1954. He was also the first black to command an air base–Godman Field, in Kentucky. Davis was later promoted to major general and, on April 16, 1965, President Lyndon B. Johnson promoted him to lieutenant general, and he was named chief of staff, U. S. Forces in Korea, and chief of staff, United Nations Command in Korea.

Black Americans also fought valiantly in the Pacific theater. Private Robert Brooks, the son of a Kentucky sharecropper, was the first black American to die in land combat with the Japanese. At Portlock Harbor, New Guinea, in March of 1943, Private George Watson won the Distinguished Service Cross for heroism during an enemy bombing raid. Watson, "after assisting several men to safety on a raft from their sinking boat, which had been attacked by Japanese bombers . . . [was] pulled under and drowned by the suction of the craft."

The 24th Infantry Regiment was among the American units that wrested the New Georgia Islands from the Japanese in May, 1942. The black 93rd Division, which first saw service at Bougainville in the Solomon Islands, subsequently fought in the Treasury Islands, at Morotai in the Dutch East Indies, and in the Philippines. Other black soldiers fought at Guadalcanal and Okinawa, and were with General Douglas MacArthur when he waded ashore on his triumphal return to the Philippines. Black marines participated in the invasion of Saipan.

In September, 1944, when American military strength was at its peak, there were more than 700,000 blacks in the army alone. About 165,000 served in the navy and another 17,000 in the United States Marine Corps. About half a million blacks served overseas.

The contribution of black Americans was not limited to the battlefields in World War II. When President Roosevelt hailed the Lend-Lease Act of March 11, 1941, as a measure to create an "arsenal of democracy," he might more appropriately have called it an arsenal of white supremacy. At that time, blacks were granted little opportunity for employment in the mushrooming defense industries of the United States.

According to historian Dr. Benjamin Quarles, "90 percent of the holders of defense contracts used no Negroes at all or confined them to nonskilled or custodial jobs." Protests by black and white citizens were of no avail until A. Philip Randolph, president of the Brotherhood of Sleeping Car Porters, threatened a national march on Washington and began organizing an effort to bring one hundred thousand blacks to the nation's capital on July 1, 1941. When Roosevelt was unable to persuade him to cancel the march, the President finally issued, on June 25, Executive Order 8802, which required that a nondiscrimination clause be included in defense contracts and established a Committee on Fair Employment Practices to enforce the order.

As a result, blacks gained the opportunity to develop technical and professional skills that they contributed to the war effort in unprecedented numbers. By the summer of 1944, an estimated 100,000 blacks were at work in the aircraft industry—helping in the President's dramatic crash effort to produce 50,000 planes a year. By October of that year, more than 300,000 blacks had received training for work in defense industries. Meanwhile, government agencies had opened their doors to blacks in clerical and professional capacities, with the result that their employment in the federal establishment in Washington rose from 8.5 percent in 1938 to 17 percent at the end of the war.

It is unlikely that the war effort could have been prosecuted with such success had it not been for the contribution of this substantial new pool of trained manpower. And it is certain that American casualties would have been substantially greater had it not been for the contribution of a distinguished black civilian who never fired a shot in anger. This home-front hero was a brilliant young surgeon, Dr. Charles Richard Drew.

Dr. Drew, an Amherst graduate who earned his M.D. at McGill Medical School, wrote a dissertation on "banked blood" while working on a doctor of science degree at Columbia University. Later he developed many of the techniques for separating and preserving blood.

Prior to the war Dr. Drew had established and operated the world's first blood plasma bank, at Presbyterian Hospital in New York City. This pioneering experience led the British to ask him to come to London in October, 1939, to serve as medical director of a blood plasma project that they were trying to establish.

Dr. Drew's knowledge and experience were of inestimable value to the British. While assisting them, the black surgeon further perfected blood plasma techniques, and, when he returned to the United States in 1941, he was put in charge of the American Red Cross project to establish donor stations for the collection of blood for use by American servicemen. The success of the Red Cross effort was due in large measure to the skill and experience Dr. Drew had acquired.

It would be impossible to estimate the number of people throughout the world who owe their lives to the pioneering work begun by Dr. Drew almost thirty years ago. Certainly the number is in the millions in the United States alone. The crushing irony is that, although the black doctor's genius was welcomed to manage the project, his own blood was not considered fit to mingle with that of white donors because it might "taint" the blood of white recipients.

There is no longer any segregation of the blood of donors, but Dr. Drew experienced a far deadlier form of racism that, in some places, is with us yet. In April, 1950, at the age of forty-six, with a brilliant career behind him and a brilliant future still ahead, Dr. Drew was injured in an automobile accident near Burlington, North Carolina. He was bleeding profusely when he was delivered to the nearest "white" hospital, and because he was black the personnel there turned him away. Before he could be taken to another hospital, the great black scientist, desperately in need of the treatment that he had done so much to devise if his own life was to be saved, bled to death.

CHAPTER XI

FIGHTING FOR FREEDOM IN ASIA

On August 14, 1945, a jubilant nation heard President Harry S Truman announce the unconditional surrender of the Japanese. The black servicemen who were on the battlefields came home to greater freedom and opportunity than had been won by any previous generation of black soldiers, with the exception of those who served in the Union Army that broke the chains of slavery in the Civil War. Although the black heroes of World War II still did not enjoy an equal share of the democracy they had helped to preserve, they found that the status of black Americans had improved substantially while they were away at war.

Just as black soldiers had won beachheads on the road to equality in the armed forces, so had their civilian brothers earned a more significant role in the offices and factories at home. The new skills that had enabled black Americans to make a vital contribution to the industrial and military might of America in time of war could not be ignored by a prosperous and powerful nation seeking to rebuild the world in an era of peace.

Perhaps even more significant to the future progress of black Americans were the new attitudes, aspirations, and expectations that had developed during the conflict. Service overseas and the migration of millions of Negroes from southern farms to the industrial cities of the North had exposed black soldier and civilian alike to ways of life that had long been denied them. Moreover, confidence born of achievement had overcome centuries of denigration and revealed to the black that, whether the competition was in the cockpit of an airplane or at the controls of a lathe, no man could claim superiority because of the color of his skin.

With the war behind them, this more assured new generation was not content to retreat to the menial and subservient role that had been the pathetic and shabby reward of black heroes who had fought for freedom in the past. Instead, the leaders of a better educated, more broadly experienced, and far more confident black race sought to hold and extend the gains that had been made.

Recalling that the Armistice ending World War I had been the signal for a return to near-exclusion of blacks from peacetime military service, black leaders won the support of many prominent whites in a determined effort to insure that the achievement of peace in 1945 would not halt progress toward complete equality in the army, navy, and marines. Responding to this insistence, the army adopted a policy providing for the enlistment of blacks in proportion to their percentage of the total population. As a result, although they were still restricted to segregated units, more than 17 percent of those who enlisted in the six months following V-J Day were black.

While Negroes applauded the new enlistment policy, they found the continued segregation intolerable because in the army, as in every other walk of life, the inevitable consequence of segregation was discrimination against the minority that was set apart. In October, 1947, with a former army chaplain, Grant Reynolds, as their leader, a group of black civilians formed a Committee Against Jim Crow in Military Service and Training. Their efforts encouraged President Truman, on July 26, 1948, to issue an executive order directing "equality of treatment and opportunity" in the armed forces. It also created a Committee on Equality of Treatment and Opportunity in the Armed

Services, which Truman directed to devise plans for the achievement of these goals for all servicemen.

The army soon adopted a new policy removing all restrictions on the service of black soldiers. Another hopeful omen was the graduation, in 1949, of Wesley A. Brown from the United States Naval Academy—the first black to be graduated from Annapolis. In the months that followed, the navy and the air force began making more rapid strides toward total integration and equality of opportunity for black sailors and airmen. Despite the dire predictions of segregationists, blacks were introduced into all-white units almost without incident.

The progress of efforts to implement the new integration policies was accelerated after June 25, 1950, when North Korean troops suddenly crossed the thirty-eighth parallel and invaded the Republic of South Korea. Two days later President Truman ordered the United States armed forces to intervene in the conflict, and America was again engaged in a bitter, though undeclared, war.

The consistent impact on racial attitudes of a common threat was demonstrated once again in Korea. With U. S. forces besieged by a determined enemy, the peacetime inclination of many officers to judge men by their color instead of their courage quickly disappeared. Through their valor under fire, the black soldiers in Korea turned rejection into respect, and their services in the foxholes soon were much in demand.

The black soldiers of the famed old Twenty-fourth United States Infantry Regiment provided an inspiring example for their race. The war was less than a month old when this outfit, which had already proved its mettle in the Indian wars, against the Spanish in Cuba, and in World Wars I and II, recaptured Yechon from the communists after a sixteen-hour fight.

When the Ninth United States Infantry Regiment began experiencing heavy losses, the commanding officer began to replace his casualties with men from the all-black Third Battalion. The blacks quickly won a respected place in the white ranks as they met with quiet determination the screaming onslaught of fanatical communist invaders from the north. Few men of the regiment—white or black—would soon forget the courage of men such as First Lieutenant Ellison C. Wynn, the black commander of B Company, who won the Distinguished Service Cross for heroism during an assault on an enemy stronghold near Kuni-ri. Although all of his machine gunners had been killed and he was wounded, Wynn held off the enemy with hand grenades to enable his men to withdraw.

The behavior of men like Lieutenant Wynn, and the grateful response of their white comrades, helped to prove that battlefield integration of army units could be achieved without rancor or loss of efficiency. In fact, the evidence soon mounted that integration actually produced a boost in morale, and an official report of the Defense Department ultimately concluded that "thorough evaluation of the battle-tested results to date indicates a marked increase in the overall combat effectiveness through integration."

When General Matthew B. Ridgway was elevated to command of all the Far Eastern forces, after General Douglas MacArthur's recall, he was already convinced by his observation of black soldiers under fire that total integration of his command would give it added strength. He promptly secured approval of the Department of Defense to eliminate all segregation in the armed forces serving in Korea. On October 1, 1951, the Twenty-fourth Infantry, the last of the army's all-black units, was deactivated. Appropriately, it was one of the regular army's first four black units, formed nearly a century earlier, after the Civil War, that was the last to serve.

It was also fitting that, before the record books were closed on the Twenty-fourth Infantry in Korea, several of its men added new laurels to the already distinguished record of that historic unit. Among these heroes was Second Lieutenant William D. Ware, a black from Texas who won the Distinguished Service Cross for gallantry in a bitter action near Sangju. In July, 1950, less than a month after his arrival in South Korea, Ware and his men were attempting to hold a position in the line that was threatened by the invading enemy. Suddenly, they were attacked by a numerically superior force of North

Korean troops who were armed with automatic weapons and supported by mortar fire. Ware, armed only with a rifle, saw that the wholesale slaughter of his unit was impending and ordered the men to withdraw. They last saw him still standing fast, taking a deadly toll of the charging communist soldiers as his position was overrun.

Two men of the Twenty-fourth Infantry earned the Medal of Honor. Not since the Spanish-American War had the nation seen fit to grant this award to a black soldier, despite many valid opportunities to do so. Both of the black heroes who won it in Korea sacrificed their lives in the effort.

The first Medal of Honor awarded to a black soldier in Korea went to a youngster from Brooklyn who had once been a resident of the New York Home for Homeless Boys. He had been one of the first Americans to arrive in South Korea, landing at Inchon on June 27, 1950. Six weeks later, on August 6, he became one of the first to die.

This courageous infantryman, Private First Class William Thompson, was serving with the First Platoon of the Twenty-fourth's Company M when it was attacked by a much larger force of suicidal communist troops. Thompson turned a machine gun on the enemy as they charged toward him, tossing grenades and attempting to silence his gun with small-arms fire. The black soldier would not yield and poured a deadly stream of bullets at the enemy, slowing their advance enough to enable his comrades to withdraw to stronger defensive positions.

Even then, although badly wounded by shrapnel and rifle fire, Thompson refused to withdraw, continuing to mow down the waves of attacking North Koreans with withering machine-gun fire. His commander ordered him to retire to a safer position, and his comrades attempted to remove him from his machine gun by force, but Thompson held his position until an enemy grenade burst near him, killing him.

On June 21, 1951, General of the Army Omar N. Bradley, chairman of the Joint Chiefs of Staff, awarded the Medal of Honor posthumously to Private First Class Thompson, citing him for "conspicuous gallantry and intrepidity above and beyond the call of duty in action against the enemy."

Less than four months before the Twenty-fourth was deactivated, another of its men, Sergeant Cornelius H. Charlton, won the Medal of Honor in action against the enemy near Chipo-ri. Charlton, born in East Gulf, West Virginia, to a family of seventeen children, was living in the Bronx when he enlisted in the regular army in November, 1946. He was a veteran of more than four and one-half years of service and leader of his platoon when it began an assault on Hill 542 in late May of 1951.

On June 2, the fourth day of the assault, C Company was attacking a strong enemy position when automatic weapons fire cut down several of its men, including the white officer who was in command. The twenty-one-year-old black sergeant immediately assumed command of the unit and led the survivors in another assault. Although the enemy held a commanding position at the top of a steep slope, Charlton personally accounted for six communist soldiers in a relentless charge that wiped out their stronghold. The remainder of the battle was described graphically in the citation read when Secretary of the Army Frank Pace, Jr., presented the Medal of Honor to Charlton's parents at the Pentagon on March 12, 1952:

"Sergeant Charlton . . . continued up the slope until the unit suffered heavy casualties and became pinned down. Regrouping the men, he led them foward only to be again hurled back by a shower of grenades. Despite a severe chest wound, Sergeant Charlton refused medical attention and led a third daring charge which carried the crest of the ridge. Observing that the remaining emplacement which had retarded the advance was situated on the reverse slope, he charged it alone, was again hit by a grenade, but raked the position with devastating fire which eliminated it and routed the defenders. The wounds received during Sergeant Charlton's daring exploits resulted in his death, but his indomitable courage, superb leadership and gallant self-sacrifice reflect the highest credit on himself, the Infantry, and the military service."

Charlton earned the nation's highest military award for relieving a wounded white officer under combat conditions in which the participants became color-blind. As the armed forces became increasingly integrated, this interaction of black and white heroes became almost commonplace, and as often as not the roles of the black and white soldiers were reversed.

One such episode, in which a white American earned the Medal of Honor for a heroic effort to save the life of a black comrade, occurred in December, 1950, when Ensign Jesse L. Brown was shot down near the Chosin Reservoir in North Korea. Brown, a Mississippian who was the first black commissioned as a navy pilot, was flying off the aircraft carrier "Leyte" when his plane crashed in the snow-covered mountains and he was trapped alive in the burning wreckage.

A fellow white pilot from Massachusetts, Lieutenant (j.g.) Thomas J. Hudner, Jr., immediately went to Brown's aid. The terrain was so rough that a normal landing was impossible, and Hudner eased his ship in on its belly along the rock-strewn mountain slope. Disregarding the possibility that the burning plane might explode at any minute, Hudner rushed to Brown's side but found that he could not pull him free. The temperature was below zero, and Hudner was without gloves, but with bare hands he packed snow around the fuselage in an effort to keep the flames from reaching the trapped pilot.

Hudner returned to his own plane and radioed for help, and then continued his efforts to pull Brown free. It was a race with time, as an enemy plane advanced toward him while he waited for a helicopter to arrive. The rescue pilot finally landed, too late to save Brown's life, but Lieutenant Hudner was awarded the Medal of Honor for the courage he displayed in the attempt.

The valor of black Americans in Korea, and the demonstrable advantages of desegregation of the military services, encouraged the continuation of those efforts when the truce finally brought the Korean conflict to an end. Thus, when American involvement escalated into a full-scale war in Vietnam, a fully integrated American military establishment was prepared to take a hand. Discrimination still existed, but it was no longer necessary for black Americans to fight for the right to fight. If anything, they were permitted to carry a disproportionate share of the hazardous action in the jungles of South Vietnam.

Black Americans were also encouraged to enter the armed

forces by the progress that had been made in elevating blacks beyond the enlisted ranks. Benjamin O. Davis, Jr., the West Point officer who had distinguished himself as a fighter pilot in Italy during World War II, ascended to the rank of lieutenant general, the highest yet achieved by a black in the United States military services. He gained added stature in 1965 when he was appointed chief of staff of the United States Forces in Korea and of the United Nations Commission there. Subsequently, Davis served as commander of the Thirteenth Air Force, with headquarters at Clark Field in the Philippines, and in 1968 was assigned to McDill Air Force Base, Florida, as deputy commander of the United States Strike Command.

Meanwhile, the navy had elevated Samuel L. Gravely, Jr., to the rank of lieutenant commander in 1962, and given him command of the U. S. S. "Falgout," a destroyer escort. He was the first black to command an American warship since the Civil War. Later, he was made captain of a navy destroyer, the U. S. S. "Taussig."

The black American's greatest progress into positions of command, however, was seen on the battlefields of Vietnam, where he at last had the opportunity to be judged solely for the skill and courage he displayed under conditions identical to those experienced by the white soldiers with whom he served. Outstanding among the black military leaders in South Vietnam was Colonel Frederic E. Davison, a rugged professional soldier who won the respect of black and white servicemen alike as commander of the 196th Light Artillery Brigade. Davison, a career officer who had led an all-black infantry company in Italy and North Africa during World War II, had struggled with great determination up the military ladder of a rigidly segregated army. There were only six white soldiers in his World War II regiment and, typically, they were the top officers in the command.

Davison served in the army during a period when he could be personally acquainted with every black field-grade officer in its ranks, and over the years he saw a great deal of progress made. He finally won his own promotion to brigadier general in 1968, and was placed in command of the 199th Light Infantry Brigade. According to war correspondents who were on hand for the event, most soldiers in Vietnam shared the opinion expressed by General Creighton W. Abrams, Jr., the U. S. commander in Vietnam, when he pinned the silver star of a general officer on Davison's collar: "In my judgment I know of no soldier more deserving."

Davison, known to his men as a fair but exacting commander, had earlier enhanced his reputation during the Vietcong's Tet offensive in February, 1968, when he assumed command of the brigade in the absence of Brigadier General Franklin Davis, Jr. Davis was hospitalized, and Davison, his deputy commander, performed admirably in his absence. Even after General Davis returned, the men of the command still found themselves referring to Davison as "the old man," and this he became again on August 6, when Davis was seriously wounded and sent back to the United States.

General Abrams' predecessor as United States commander in Vietnam also had evidenced a healthy respect for the qualities of black fighting men and the contributions they made in the struggle with the Vietcong. Nineteen black officers occupied significant posts on General William C. Westmoreland's headquarters staff, and this close association with black soldiers may have influenced the general in what he described as his "intuitive feeling that the Negro serviceman has a better understanding than the white of what the war is all about." Speaking to a group of fellow South Carolinians in 1967, Westmoreland commented that "the performance of the Negro serviceman has been particularly inspirational to me. They have served with distinction. He has been courageous on the battlefield, proficient, and a possessor of technical skills."

At the close of 1967, slightly more than 300,000 Afro-American's were on active duty with the United States armed forces, and nearly 56,000 of them were in Southeast Asia. They constituted nearly 9 percent of the nation's active servicemen, and nearly 10 percent of those serving in Vietnam. These overall figures, however, do not reveal the full extent to which the black soldier participated in the fighting zones. Nearly 20 percent of American troops in actual combat were blacks, and black men made up more than 25 percent of the paratroops and other volunteer elite units.

The evident preference of black soldiers for the most hazardous combat duty can be attributed in part to their often greater need for the extra pay that accompanies these assignments. Even more important, to men who had frequently been relegated to menial roles in civilian life, was the added stature that came with perilous duty, and the opportunity it gave them to demonstrate their capacity as fighting men. Moreover, true equality was most nearly achieved among the soldiers who faced the most awesome peril.

Correspondents who covered the war in Vietnam were quick to note the impact of combat service under trying and dangerous conditions on relationships between black and white soldiers. In one dispatch to The New York Times News Service, Thomas A. Johnson, a black reporter, noted that "it is in the front lines that commonly shared adversity has always sprouted quickly into group loyalty and brotherhood. And whether between white and white, Negro and Negro, or Negro and white, Vietnam is no exception."

Captain Richard Traegerman, a twenty-five-year-old Philadelphian who wore a West Point ring, explained the phenomenon to Johnson with great and telling simplicity. "The stereotypes they had believed just sort of melt away," he said.

Correspondent Johnson was on hand for the battle of Hue in February, 1968, and during a lull in the bitter fighting he stood knee-deep in red mud with a group of black and white marines as a bottle of "liberated" Scotch was passed around. One after another, each of the exhausted marines took a swig from the bottle.

One of them sighed contentedly as he took his turn at the bottle and said, "Integration whisky."

"That's just what's going to win this . . . war," a black sergeant added. "Integration."

A white lance corporal, using the black verbal shorthand for "soul brother" without realizing it, agreed. "You're damn straight, Bro," he nodded soberly.

A black specialist four in General Davison's brigade made a similar observation in conversation with Raymond R. Coffey, a correspondent for the *Chicago Daily News*.

"The [white] guys in the field are O. K.," he said. "You drink out of the same canteen, share your C-rations and everything, sleep in the same foxholes." Then, with great concern, he added:

"But at home it seems to me things are getting worse instead of better. If everyone had to come over here and live the way an infantry soldier does, I think it would be a better world."

Reservations such as this were typical of the attitude of many black soldiers in Vietnam. Navy Hospital Corpsman James E. DuPuy, thirty, of Goldsboro, North Carolina, who served with the marines at Khe Sanh, confessed to Coffey that he was puzzled over the fact that black and white men who formed fast friendships in the foxholes seemed unable to carry them over into civilian life.

"Some of the people I've served with and gotten along well with, they get out of service and they change," DuPuy observed. "I guess they're afraid of what society is going to say if they have any dealings with Negroes."

Unfortunately, this concern was often real. Inherent racial attitudes that have conditioned most Americans during more than three centuries of prejudice and discrimination often reappeared all too quickly once the soldiers were removed from the combat zone. Black and white soldiers who had shared their C rations in a foxhole in the Vietnam jungles often found themselves worlds apart when they returned to Saigon for rest and rehabilitation. This certainly accounted, at least in part, for the fact that military service that seemed onerous to the white soldier was regarded as a more rewarding and comfortable environment by many blacks, and this distinction showed up in the first-term reenlistment rates. During 1966, 66.5 per cent of the eligible blacks reenlisted, compared with only 20 percent of the whites. Although the percentages fell in 1967, the ratio remained relatively unchanged, with 31.7 per cent of the black soldiers reenlisting, compared to only 12.8 percent of the whites.

The inclination of black soldiers to grasp a rare and welcome opportunity to prove their manhood by serving in the frontlines also showed up with great clarity in the casualty rates. At the end of 1967, black soldiers constituted little more than 11 percent of the army troops engaged in Vietnam, but they had sustained more than 16 percent of the combat deaths. More than 12 percent of the marines who died in Vietnam in 1967 were black, although blacks made up only 8 percent of the leatherneck combat force.

Inevitably, the degree of involvement and self-sacrifice of black servicemen in Vietnam produced some outstanding black officers, and some incredible examples of heroism among black enlisted men. The First Air Cavalry Division yielded more than its share of both. This outfit, which accounted for more Vietcong dead than any American division in Vietnam, numbered some tough black officers among its battalion commanders. One was Lieutenant Colonel James Frank Hamlet, a forty-five-year-old officer from Buffalo, New York, who enlisted as a private in 1943. He unfailingly boarded a helicopter to join his troops even on the most hazardous missions. Another tough black battalion commander from the same division was Lieutenant Colonel Roscoe Robinson. It was he who commanded the unit that relieved the besieged marines at Khe Sanh.

Major James T. Boddie, Jr., a thirty-six-year-old black pilot from Baltimore, Maryland, flew more than 150 missions during his first seven months in Vietnam, winning nine Air Medals and recommendations for the Silver Star and the Distinguished Flying Cross. He apparently took a more generous view of the anti-war demonstrators at home than they took of his efforts over North Vietnam. "I'm here to protect their right to dissent," he told a *Time* magazine reporter.

For many black men in Vietnam, protecting that right to dissent demanded efforts beyond the call of ordinary duty. Platoon Sergeant Elija Fields, of Quincy, Florida, crawled through enemy machine-gun fire on February 9, 1967, and was shot twice as he pulled a badly wounded comrade to safety. He was awarded the Distinguished Service Cross.

An army medic, Specialist 6 Lawrence Joel of Winston-Salem, North Carolina, was also shot twice as he treated the wounded men of a platoon that had been ambushed by Vietcong near Bien Hoa in November, 1965. Joel, a high school dropout, had been raised by a foster family from the age of eight, and already had a long military career behind him when he went to Vietnam at the age of thirty-nine. He was the first black in Vietnam to win the Medal of Honor for an action that he survived.

Joel acknowledged, as any honest soldier would, that he was "afraid" when his platoon of the 503rd Infantry, 173rd Airborne Brigade, was pinned down by the enemy on a routine search-and-destroy mission. When the firing began, he wasn't even sure who the targets were, but, taking no chances, he ducked behind a small rock.

"Soon it got real quiet," Joel said. "I could hear men holler 'Medic!' all around. I was afraid to go out there and some other men said, 'We'll go out and get them for you.' But I knew that was my job. I made a dash to reach one man and got shot in the leg."

During the twenty-four hours that followed his initial wound, he was shot a second time and saw twelve men of his forty-man unit killed and fifteen others wounded. Throughout the long and deadly night Joel crawled over the battlefield, patching up wounds, administering plasma and morphine, and applying mouth-to-mouth resuscitation without ever being quite sure whether his patient was dead or alive. His legs swelled as his own wounds went unattended, and, although his pain was almost more than he could bear, he gave himself only one shot of morphine for fear that any more of the drug would render him incapable of caring for his buddies. He was among the last to be evacuated the following day.

Joel was embarrassed when the president presented him with the Medal of Honor and called him "a very brave soldier" with "a special kind of courage." Back home in Winston-Salem, the entire town–black and white–turned out for an unprecedented parade and luncheon in his honor. Joel, then one of only four black men in this century to have won the nation's highest military honor, responded modestly to all the attention he had received, saying, "I do not wear this medal for Lawrence Joel. I wear it for every American and for all the soldiers who died."

One of the most ironic episodes of the Vietnam war led to the posthumous award of the Medal of Honor to a black infantry commander—the first officer of his race to win the nation's highest military award.

On October 31, 1967, Captain Riley Leroy Pitts was leading his company in an assault on a strongly entrenched enemy unit. They were under enemy fire from three sides when Pitts picked up a grenade taken from a captured Vietcong and threw it at a machine gun bunker. The grenade rebounded into the midst of Pitts and his men.

Without hesitation, Pitts threw himself on the grenade, but miraculously it did not explode. His respite from death was brief, however. A short time later, Pitts moved from the cover of the dense jungle foliage in order to direct the attack more effectively, and in this exposed position he was fatally wounded.

President Johnson commented, when he awarded the medal to Pitts's widow, Mrs. Eula M. Pitts of Oklahoma City, that "what this man did in an hour of incredible courage will live in the story of America as long as America endures—as he will live in the hearts and memories of those who loved him."

Captain Pitts's fearless effort to save his men came two years after a similar episode in which a slim, handsome young black named Milton L. Olive III had also won the Medal of Honor for heroic action. Olive was only seventeen years old in August, 1964, with a year of high school still ahead of him, when he said good-bye to his parents and their pleasant bungalow on Chicago's South Side and went off to enlist in the regular army.

His father, a perceptive man whose life revolved around his only son, never knew what secret compulsion prompted his son to enlist. Certainly, unlike many black soldiers, it wasn't the need to escape any problems at home. Young Milton was doing well in Saints Junior College High. He and his father, Milton B. Olive, Jr., an employee of a city youth agency, had much in common; their mutual interest in photography was supported by enough equipment to stock a small camera store. The draft board wasn't breathing down his neck, so there was no immediate need for young Olive to go.

Whatever his motivation, Olive left on August 17 for the United States Army Training Center at Fort Knox, Kentucky, where he received basic combat training until October, 1964. He celebrated his eighteenth birthday at the Artillery and Missile School at Fort Sill, Oklahoma, once the home of the black cavalrymen who fought in the Indian wars. Then, in rapid succession, between February and May of 1965, he underwent further training at Fort Polk, Louisiana, and Fort Benning, Georgia, where he received the basic airborne training course. With that behind him, he was assigned to the 173rd Airborne Brigade in Vietnam.

Still only eighteen years old, and now a private first-class, Olive joined Company B, 3rd Battalion (Airborne), of the 503rd Infantry Regiment.

He had been in Vietnam for less than six months when, on October 22, he and the other men of the Third Platoon moved into the jungle near Phu Cuong on a search-and-destroy mission against Vietcong who were operating in the area. Before long the American soldiers encountered heavy enemy rifle fire. They were pinned down momentarily, but soon leaped up to assault the Vietcong positions, causing the enemy to flee.

"As the platoon pursued the insurgents," the official army record reports, "Private Olive and four other soldiers were moving through the jungle together when a grenade was thrown into their midst. Private Olive saw the grenade, and then saved the lives of his fellow soldiers at the sacrifice of his own by grabbing the grenade in his hand and falling on it to absorb the blast with his body."

Six months later, the young black soldier's parents joined two of the men whose lives he had saved—one of them black and the other white—in the White House Rose Garden. There, President Johnson awarded the Medal of Honor posthumously for "Private Olive's conspicuous gallantry, extra-ordinary heroism, and intrepidity at the risk of his own life above and beyond the call of duty. . . .

"Through his bravery, unhesitating actions, and complete

disregard for his own safety, he prevented additional loss of life or injury to the members of his platoon."

Even as Olive's father remained puzzled over the motives that had impelled his son to enlist, so was President Johnson at a loss to account for the extraordinary courage that enabled the young soldier to choose certain death to save the lives of others.

"Who can say," the President asked, "what words Private Olive might have chosen to explain what he did. Jimmy Stanford and John Foster, two of the men whose lives he saved that day on that lonely trail in that hostile jungle, 10,000 miles from here, are standing on the White House steps today because this man chose to die. I doubt that even they knew what was on his mind as he jumped and fell across that grenade.

"But I think I do know this: On the sacrifices of men who died for their country and their comrades our freedom has been built. Whatever it is that we call civilization rests upon the merciless and seemingly irrational fact of history that some have died for others to live, and every one of us who enjoys freedom at this moment should be a witness to that fact."

Milton L. Olive's father, on learning that his only son would receive the nation's highest military award, expressed his gratitude to the president in a letter written on March 10, 1966. With the quiet eloquence that was also present when you met him face-to-face, he wrote:

"Many people and news reporters have asked why he did it. How do you feel? Across six thousand years of recorded history, man has pondered the inevitable. The conclusion is, it is too profound for mortal understanding. Perhaps, you too, Mr. President, and the American people would like to know how I feel. I have had to use strength, taken from the courage of a brave soldier to be able to bear a heavy cross. I suppose that Divine Providence willed it and that nothing could be more glorious than laying down your life for your fellowman in the defense of your country.

"Our only child and only grandchild, gave his last full measure of devotion on an international battlefield 10,000 miles from home. It is our dream and our prayer, that some day the Asiatics, the Europeans, the Israelites, the Africans, the Australians, the

Latins, and the Americans can all live in One-World. It is our hope that in our own country, the Klansmen, the Negroes, the Hebrews, and the Catholics, will sit down together in the common purpose of good will and dedication; that the moral and creative intelligence of our united people will pick up the chalice of wisdom and place it upon the mountain of human integrity; that all mankind, from all the earth, shall resolve 'to study war no more.' That, Mr. President, is how I feel and that is my eternal hope for our Great American Society."

As President Johnson said when he quoted Mr. Olive's letter at the conclusion of his own remarks at the Rose Garden ceremony:

"I have no words to add to that."

CHAPTER XII

THE LONG STRUGGLE FOR FREEDOM

Each chapter in the story of our nation's efforts to achieve freedom, and to defend the principles of democracy against repeated challenges from those who would destroy it, is a tribute to the noble spirit and enduring courage of Americans whose color did not limit the part they played in victory. It is a record that every American, black as well as white, can recall with pride.

Courage in the quest for freedom is a quality that we, as a nation, have long honored and revered. This virtue, however, is not one to be admired only in those who have defended the United States against its external enemies. Equally laudable is the continuing struggle of others, unabated since the first black men and women reached these shores, to make freedom and equality a reality within America, for all Americans.

The white American, in his quest for freedom, has had respite between the wars. The black American, having risked his life to preserve freedom for the nation, has always returned home to the unremitting endeavor to gain a piece of freedom for himself. His ability to endure a struggle that, in three and a half centuries, has seen few victories and countless defeats is an example of physical and emotional endurance unparalleled in human history. What reservoirs of physical and spiritual strength a race must have to survive and persist in the face of the indescribable oppression, the brutal violence, the unceasing denigration, and the long denial of opportunity and achievement that have been the lot of the black in the United States. There is a heroism in this unceasing display of courage and tenacity that makes a black face its own badge of courage, a symbol of valor that all Afro-Americans can proudly share.

It was Hegel who wrote, in his *Philosophy of History*, that "peoples and governments have never learned anything from history, or acted on the principles deduced from it." Certainly the historical record of the black in our country suggests that this is true, that each generation of Americans, instead of profiting from what history could teach it, has condemned itself to learn the same lessons anew.

Why has it been necessary, in every war in which our nation has engaged, for blacks to prove once more their fitness to serve? Why the blind adherence to cultural stereotypes that our own senses must tell us are unreal? Why the apparent surprise and concern over the *methods* employed in the present fight for equality, and the lack of concern over the *injustices* that they seek to correct, when the entire course of history reveals that all men of every color will employ any means necessary in the struggle against injustice, as long as it continues to exist?

Today, as it views the continuing efforts of black people to gain an equitable share of the American dream, the nation cannot afford to neglect the lessons of history. It must understand that there is nothing new in the aspirations of today's generation of black Americans, that they seek no more than what they have always sought—the opportunities and privileges that most Americans already enjoy. If there is a difference, it is only in the level of black expectations, in the more sophisticated intellectual armament that increasing numbers of educated and experienced black people can bring to bear in the contest, and in the evolution of a legal structure that, for the first time in United States history, is designed to assist the Afro-American in his struggle rather than to perpetuate denial, repression, and misery.

Certainly the nation today is more aware of the efforts of black spokesmen such as W. E. B. Du Bois, Rev. Dr. Martin Luther

King, Jr., James Meredith, Whitney M. Young, Jr., Stokely Carmichael, Roy Wilkins, and Malcolm X than it ever was of the civil rights leaders of the previous centuries. Modern mass communications have focused so much attention on the efforts of such men as these that no attempt will be made to discuss them in this book. But to fully understand them, the nation needs the perspective of history as it listens to what they are trying to say.

Those who hear the protests of contemporary black leaders, who witness the marches and the sit-ins, who are shocked by the violence in the streets, as though it were something new, are prone to ask, "What do *they* want?" For the answer they need only ask themselves what blacks have wanted since the first slave was put ashore in Jamestown in 1619. Or, better still, what *they* would want if *they* were black.

What did Joseph Cinque want, in 1839, when he found himself chained in the stinking hold of a Spanish slave ship, his back bleeding from the lash? Freedom was what he wanted, and it was freedom that he was willing to die for.

Cinque, a tall, powerful, handsome black with the proud demeanor that marked him as the son of a tribal chief, had been kidnapped with forty-nine other men and four women at Lemboko, which was in the Mendi country of West Africa. He and the others were whipped aboard the "Amistad," a small sailing ship, driven below decks, and chained in quarters so cramped that they could scarcely move for the long voyage to Cuba.

The apprehensions of the African captives were magnified by total uncertainty as to their fate. Their only language was their native Mendian tongue, which none of the crew understood. Cinque, attempting to determine what was in store for them, resorted to crude sign language in an effort to communicate with the cook. The cook understood, and with subtle cruelty replied by gesturing toward the cooking pot that was boiling on his stove. To men and women from a continent that knew cannibalism, the wordless threat was unmistakably clear.

Cinque, believing that he and his friends were to be boiled alive, was determined to avoid so repelling a fate. During the night he worked loose a nail from a nearby board, and with this crude tool he managed to unlock his chains. Then, working as quickly and quietly as he could, he set the other captives free. Whispering to avoid alarming the crew, he made a desperate appeal to the other blacks:

"I would not see you serve the white men. You had better be killed than live many moons in misery. . . . I could die happy, if by dying I could save so many of my brothers from the bondage of the white men."

The others also preferred death to servitude or the cooking pot, and at about three o'clock in the morning, having armed themselves from a shipment of machetes destined for the Cuban sugar plantations, the blacks silently crawled up the ladder to the deck. Cinque, in the lead, quickly disposed of the cook and then the captain, and the remainder of the terrified crew leaped over the rail and into the sea.

Only two of the white captors, the Spanish owners, remained aboard the ship. One had been wounded, and he pleaded with Cinque to spare them and to save the crew, arguing that only thus could Cinque and the other blacks sail back to Africa. The leader of the rebellious prisoners, who knew nothing of seamanship or navigation, was compelled to consent.

The Spaniards, however, had no intention of returning to Africa. Knowing that Cinque could establish the direction they were traveling from the position of the sun, they sailed east by day. At night, however, the crew put on extra sail, reversed the ship's course, and raced to the west. In this fashion, with each daytime voyage canceling part of the westward progress made the night before, the ship moved slowly toward North America. As the supply of rations and water dwindled, seven of Cinque's men became ill and died.

Weeks later, with crew and captives alike thirsty and half-starved, the ship came in sight of land. The blacks knew at once that it was not their native land, but they knew there was nothing they could do. There, off Montauk Point in the waters of Long Island sound, an American naval frigate, the "Washington," seized the "Amistad" and imprisoned the mutineers.

Through his audacious action Joseph Cinque, destined to become a slave, became instead the leading character in an international drama. The Spanish government, although it prohibited trading in slaves, demanded the return of Cinque and the others because they were the "property" of subjects of the Spanish crown. President Martin Van Buren, concerned over the international consequences if he failed to grant the Spanish request, was ready to accede, but he encountered such a storm of protest from white citizens that the case of the Africans was taken to court.

The Africans lost the initial court action and were ordered returned to their captors, but the case was appealed. The residents of Farmington, Connecticut, a stronghold of abolitionist activity, invited the prisoners to live in their community while they awaited trial, and their prospects also brightened when John Quincy Adams, the former president, agreed to represent them before the Supreme Court of the United States.

While awaiting their final trial, the Mendians attended a school in Farmington set up for them in some rooms over Edward Deming's store on Main Street. With the aid of Professor Josiah W. Gibbs, a linguistic expert at the Yale School of Divinity, they learned to speak, read, and write English. They were converted to Christianity and on Sunday attended the historic old First Congregational Church. One of the Africans, Foone, was buried in the churchyard after drowning in a river in which the Africans loved to swim.

Cinque and his followers lived in Farmington for two years, until the Supreme Court set them free. Then, to their great joy, the community collected funds and supplied them with equipment, and they returned to Africa in 1842. They established a mission near Sierra Leone and named it Mendi, after their native land.

Most of the party remained at the mission, and one of their descendants, more than forty years later, came to the United States, won a degree from Fisk University, and studied theology at Yale Divinity School and the Chicago Theological Seminary. Cinque himself found only bitter disappointment on his return to Africa. During his absence, his wife and three children had been captured by rival tribes and sold into slavery. Disheartened and defeated, he left his friends at the mission and returned to his pagan ways. A Grand Rapids missionary, Rev. Albert P.

Miller, served at the Mendi mission and saw Cinque there in 1879, just before the tragic black hero died.

The exploits of Joseph Cinque are remarkable because the revolt he led is one of only two recorded instances in the history of the slave trade in which the captives broke their bonds and seized the ship. The other occurred two years later, in 1841, when a slave named Madison Washington spurred a rebellion on the slaver "Creole" to free the other prisoners, including his own wife. When the other captives wanted to execute the ship's crew, from which they had received such cruel and inhuman treatment, Washington dissuaded them.

"We have got our liberty, and that is all we have been fighting for," he said, as he prepared to sail the ship to the West Indies. "Let no more blood be shed."

Although Cinque's successful revolt at sea was almost unique, resistance by black slaves to their captors was commonplace on American soil. Much of the literature about the antebellum South portrays the slaves as smiling and servile, happy with his lot. Yet behind the smiles lurked a fierce determination to be free. The contemporary press gave such efforts little notice, but the resistance of slaves was so contant a threat that many plantation owners slept with pistols under their pillows because they lived in unending fear for their lives.

The revolt of Nat Turner, featured in William Styron's brilliant novel, has made that brutal episode well-known, but few present-generation Americans are aware that it was only one of many. Literally hundreds of slave revolts have been documented, enough to make it clear that the story of slavery in America is also the story of persistent black resistance to involuntary servitude. Although the price paid by the slave, because of the existence of "the peculiar institution," was unconscionable, a heavy price was also paid by the enslavers. Today, the nation still carries a heavy burden because of the impact that generations of slavery had on its black population, and because of the insidiously destructive effects slavery had on the economic growth and development of the South.

A Virginia legislator, T. Marshall, warned of the costly effects of the slave system when he attacked it in a speech in 1831:

"Slavery is ruinous to the whites. Our towns are stationary, our villages almost everywhere declining—and the general aspect of the country marks the curse of a waseful, idle, reckless population who have no interest in the soil, and care not how much it is impoverished. Public improvements are neglected, and the entire continent does not present a region, for which nature has done so much and art so little."

Many states in the Deep South are still struggling to overcome the economic lassitude that developed from a social organization that made physical toil the object of scorn and failed to see that even cheap, captive labor could not effectively compete with technological progress.

Although violent reactions to slavery were commonplace, dissatisfaction with servitude was more often expressed in subtler ways. To make life difficult for their masters, slave feigned illness, ruined equipment, deliberately slowed the pace of their efforts, and, when the opportunity offered, tried to escape. Such efforts required great courage, because the penalties were likely to be unbelievably severe for those whose dash for freedom failed. Often, those who succeeded were aided and abetted by increasing numbers of abolitionists in the North. These opponents of slavery not only fought vigorously for legislation to end the vicious practice, but also set up an elaborate system, which came to be known as the Underground Railroad, through which escaping slaves could be assisted on their journey from oppression in the South to freedom in the northern states and Canada.

The abolitionists numbered in the thousands, many of them distinguished and prominent white citizens in the cities of the North. Others were free or fugitive blacks of means and stature or, in many instances, of no stature at all.

Not all these freedom fighters were men. Two of the most vigorous and widely known were women: Sojourner Truth and Harriet Tubman.

Sojourner Truth was born a slave in upstate New York in 1797, but after thirty sordid and bitter years was freed in 1827 under New York's gradual emancipation act. She wasted her first years of freedom, but after a few years she became deeply religious and burned with the desire to help set the rest of her people free. In 1843, changing her slave name, Isabella, to the more striking one of Sojourner Truth, the fiery and compelling black woman left New York, with a bag of clothes and twenty-five cents, to begin a lifetime crusade against slavery. From platforms throughout the North, she raised her battle cry against slavery, so persuasively that she enlisted many to the abolitionist cause.

Harriet Tubman, also deeply religious, was the opposite of Sojourner Truth in all respects but one: she shared the same passionate hatred of slavery and determination to end it. She was short and stocky instead of lean and tall. She was also more a doer than a talker, and her exploits ultimately won her the title "The Moses of Her People."

Harriet Tubman was born about 1820 on a farm near Bucktown, in Dorchester County, Maryland, one of eight children in a slave family owned by Edward Brodas. The large family was typical of an era in which slaveholders insisted on fecundity and punished females who failed to give birth as frequently as nature allowed; babies were one of the plantation's most valuable crops.

Typically, also, Harriet was hired out at the age of six, to begin the first of a succession of situations in which she was whipped almost daily. The punishment came because from the outset she was completely intolerant of slavery. She was only fifteen when she interfered with an overseer in the capture of a runaway slave, and was knocked unconscious by a blow on the forehead with a two-pound weight.

Harriet survived the blow, although she suffered from periodic attacks of dizziness for the rest of her life, and at the age of twenty-nine she finally made the break for freedom. Moving north through the darkness, she reached an Underground Railroad station near Camden, Delaware, and from there was taken to New Castle, Wilmington, and finally north to Philadelphia.

For a year Harriet Tubman worked in Philadelphia and enjoyed her new freedom. But constantly, in the back of her mind, was the nagging realization that, although she was free, her husband, John Tubman, and her many friends and relatives still in the South were not.

With the assistance of white abolitionists whom she had met, she returned to Maryland—risking her own recapture—and was able to bring out her sister, brother-in-law, and their own children. Thus began a long series of expeditions into the slave states —nineteen in all—during which Harriet Tubman repeatedly risked capture and execution in order to liberate more than three hundred slaves. At the height of her career, the rewards offered for her capture totaled more than forty thousand dollars.

When the Civil War began, Harret Tubman knew that she must have a role. Like most blacks, she saw it as a war of liberation that would do in one stroke for all slaves what she had been striving to do for a handful at a time. Armed with a letter from Governor John Andrew of Masschusetts, she went to one of the Sea Islands of South Carolina, Hilton Head, in May, 1862, and reported to the commanding officer, General David Hunter.

She could not have found a more willing advocate. Hunter was an ardent exponent of arming blacks in the Union's cause. Mrs. Tubman was first assigned as a nurse, and for several months worked in one hospital after another, caring for wounded white soldiers and for many of her own people who had escaped into the Union lines.

Early in 1863, after the Emancipation Proclamation had been signed, she was sent south into Georgia and Florida to establish a spy network, and to guide the black regiments commanded by Colonel Wentworth Higginson and Captain James Montgomery on raids up the St. Johns and St. Marys rivers.

When the war ended, Mrs. Tubman caught a train north, but the conductor refused to honor her government pass and ordered her to the baggage car. She refused to go, and he and three white passengers dragged her, fighting every step of the way, out of the passenger coach. The black heroine who had emerged from the battle zones unscathed and with the praise of every commander whose burden she had lightened with her services discovered that her new, legal freedom meant having her arm and shoulder badly wrenched by a bigoted conductor on a civilian railroad train.

The government itself proved to be no more grateful. Despite the efforts of many prominent white friends, Mrs. Tubman was unable to collect the $1,800 to which she was entitled for her wartime services. Back at home, she supported herself selling vegetables door-to-door, and used much of the meager proceeds to travel throughout the nation, lecturing in behalf of equal rights for black Americans.

At the age of seventy-six, Miss Tubman bid $1,400 for a plot of land adjacent to her home, although she had scarcely a dime to her name. Then she raised the money to pay for the land and to build on it the John Brown Home. There, for the rest of her life, she cared for all who came to her in need of food, a bed, money, or simply a friend. Although crippled by arthritis and confined to a wheelchair, she was still a respected leader of her people—among black and white alike—when she died in her home in Auburn, New York, at the age of ninety-three.

There were also white women among the most vigorous foes of slavery. The most notable of these was Harriet Beecher Stowe, whose book *Uncle Tom's Cabin* rallied many to the abolitionist cause. Because women had yet to achieve equality for themselves, however, by far the majority of abolitionists were men.

The early black abolitionists included Paul Cuffe and James Forten, both of whom had served in the American Revolution and gone on to become prosperous businessmen—Cuffe as a shipowner and Forten as a sailmaker who became the wealthiest black in Philadelphia. Another, David Walker, learned to read and write after maturity and in 1829 published a pamphlet, *Walker's Appeal*, which aroused a storm of protest among slaveholders because it incited their bondsmen to revolt.

Walker's white counterpart was William Lloyd Garrison, whose newspaper, the *Liberator*, was read avidly by literate blacks and enlisted many prominent white citizens in the battle to end slavery.

"I will be as harsh as truth, and as uncompromising as justice," Garrison wrote. "On this subject, I do not wish to think, to speak, or write, with moderation. . . . I am in earnest–I will not equivocate–I will not excuse–I will not retreat a single inch–AND I WILL BE HEARD."

Another white editor who was equally determined to be heard paid with his life for his dedication to the abolition of slavery. A native of Maine, Elijah P. Lovejoy was a fiery humanitarian who moved west to St. Louis in the 1830's to become an ordained Presbyterian minister and editor of a religious journal, the *Observer*.

The preacher-writer's early stand on slavery was one that favored gradual abolition of the vicious practice; his position was that the cause was just "but it will take time." Lovejoy's attitude changed dramatically in the spring of 1836, when a free St. Louis black, Francis McIntosh, "was lynched at a slow fire in a revolting and barbaric manner."

Those accused of the horrifying crime were freed by a partisan judge, not on grounds of innocence but because punishment for the murder of a black victim was "beyond human laws." At this, the flames that had destroyed the hapless black ignited in Lovejoy a burning determination to achieve justice for all blacks. The editor soon discovered, however, that his stinging editorials aroused more animosity than sympathy among his fellow townsmen in slaveholding Missouri. They destroyed his printing press and forced him to flee for safety across the Mississippi River to Alton, Illinois.

Although Illinois was a free state, the citizens of Lovejoy's new community had little more sympathy for his antislavery views. When the editor resumed publication of the *Observer*, Alton merchants were warned that they would lose their St. Louis markets if they did not dissuade Lovejoy from attacking slavery from his sanctuary in Illinois. The response of some Alton businessmen was immediate; threatened with economic penalties, they incited a mob to throw Lovejoy's press into the river.

The courageous editor was not so easily dissuaded. He bought another press, and it, too, went into the river. By this time, a man of lesser convictions would have surrendered, but Lovejoy simply ordered new equipment once again, and this time a group of his local friends, admiring his tenacity, determined to help him protect it.

Before the new press was placed in operation, an angry mob of thirty men attacked Lovejoy and his supporters and set fire to the warehouse in which the equipment was stored. In the exchange of gunfire that ensued, the editor's pen was finally stilled. He died with five bullets in his body.

Lovejoy's death aroused national indignation and drew increased white support for the efforts of the black abolitionists who were engaged in the antislavery crusade. Aid in the cause was also mustered by the eloquent appeals of men like Henry Highland Garnet, who was born a Maryland slave but had escaped to become a Presbyterian minister and "the Thomas Paine of the abolitionist movement."

For the most part, the white abolitionists were concerned only with ridding the nation of the institution of slavery, while the black ones were also determined to wipe out the discriminatory practices that were directed toward free blacks. As increasing numbers of them won their freedom, the nation's slaveholders felt growing concern over the influence of free blacks on those who were still in bondage. They sought means of limiting the capacity of the freemen to take advantage of their status in attacks on the institution of slavery.

In order to perpetuate the denigration of black Americans, even after they had achieved freedom, many states began to impose "black codes" that severely restricted the movements of free blacks and even barred them from slaveholding states. These early segregation laws, which set the pattern for those imposed against all blacks after emancipation, established separate schools for freemen and determined where they might sit in places of public accommodation, or on a railroad train. These laws were leveled against their victims not because they were *black*, but because they were *free*. Thus, a black slave who accompanied his master on a railroad train could sit where his master chose to sit; but a free black sat where he was told.

The distinction between the objectives of the white abolitionists and the broader ones of the black men who were fighting for freedom *and* equality was to become significant after the Emancipation Proclamation was signed. With that victory achieved, many of the white abolitionists considered that the battle was over and the cause won. They retired from the field. The black American knew that the struggle had only begun; that the achievement of legal freedom was only the first step in the quest for equality.

So it was that, throughout the Reconstruction period, the black leadership of the nation found itself with little white support in the continuing struggle for freedom. Yet the scores of black leaders who emerged before and after the Civil War fought their lonely battle with great bravery and determination.

Many black Americans, while fighting slavery, fought discrimination as well. William Cooper Nell, in the mid-1850's, led a campaign that ended separate schools for blacks in Massachusetts. Later, in 1861, he attacked discrimination in federal employment and won appointment as a clerk in the Boston post office, thus becoming the first black employed in the federal service. James W. C. Pennington and William Still, in 1867, successfully fought segregation in the streetcars of New York and Philadelphia.

Among all the black leaders of the 19th century, the name of Frederick Douglass stands out as the giant of his race. White historians have largely favored Booker T. Washington in the role of leader of his people because of his emphasis on the need for blacks to *earn* a place in society. Douglass agreed that men must progress through their own efforts, but in addition he expressed what Washington delicately left unsaid: that no man should be required to earn his own birthright. This distinction speaks volumes about the difference in stature that white society has accorded the two men.

Douglass was born in 1817 on a farm near Easton, Maryland. His mother, who named him Frederick Augustus Washington Bailey, was virtually a stranger to him. The child lived with his slave grandparents, and his mother saw him only at night, when she could find the strength to walk to and from her place of employment twelve miles away. Even those visits ended with her death when Frederick was only seven.

A year later, the child was sent to Baltimore as the servant and playmate of the eight-year-old son of Hugh and Sophia Auld. There, over the objections of her husband, Mrs. Auld taught Frederick to read, and he taught himself to write by copying words from drawings in Hugh Auld's shipyard.

Ultimately, Frederick was returned to a Maryland plantation, where he immediately began to resist the oppressive treatment imposed upon him by his master. Turned over to a "slave breaker," he proved that even this could not break his spirit. Finally, after years of brutality, he escaped to New Bedford, Massachusetts. He was just twenty-one years old, and in honor of his new freedom he took a new name. The career of Frederick Douglass had began.

It was William Lloyd Garrison's newspaper, the *Liberator*, that first aroused in Douglass an interest in the abolitionist cause. In August, 1841, he heard Garrison speak at a New Bedford antislavery meeting and became so fired with enthusiasm that he joined Garrison and a group of abolitionists who were traveling the next day to a meeting in Nantucket. Someone called on him for a speech, and his effort was so impressive that the Massachusetts Anti-Slavery Society hired him as a traveling orator at a salary of $450 a year.

In 1845, against the advice of his friends, Douglass published his autobiography. Their fears were well-founded because, although the book was an overnight sensation, it also focused so much attention on the runaway slave that he was forced to flee to England. He was able to return to America only after his freedom had been purchased by a group of his British friends.

As slave property, Douglass' owner had valued him at $710.96. To those who were concerned with ending slavery in America, his worth was beyond price. The vigorous black leader set up a printing plant in Rochester, New York, and in 1847 began publishing a newspaper, the *North Star*, changing the name to *Frederick Douglass' Paper* in 1851. He crusaded against slavery throughout the North, and when the Civil War began he battled to secure for blacks the right to fight. After winning that crusade he helped to recruit volunteers for the black Fifty-fourth and Fifty-fifth Massachusetts Regiments. His sons, Lewis and Charles, were the first volunteers.

When the war ended, Douglass resumed his crusade against efforts to put free blacks—and now all blacks were free—"in their place." When President Rutherford B. Hayes appointed him as United States marshal for the District of Columbia, Douglass used his new post as a platform from which to launch a vigorous attack on Jim Crow conditions in the nation's capital.

Before Douglass' death in 1895, a succession of presidents of both political parties had appointed him to responsible positions in the United States government, including that of minister to Haiti. Although he did not live to see an end to segregation and discrimination in America, his efforts were an effective early force in the battle against injustice.

There were many others to take up where Douglass left off, and many who were inspired by him. Today, under new black leaders who again have the support of many white Americans in the effort, the struggle against poverty and injustice continues. It will end only when the nation can say that it has met the challenge posed by President Franklin Delano Roosevelt in 1938:

"The test of our progress is not whether we add more to the abundance of those who have much; it is whether we do enough for those who have too little."

BIBLIOGRAPHY

Many primary sources—manuscript collections, documents, official records—in the collections of state historical societies, public and private libraries, and state and federal archives, were examined in the preparation of this book. For the most part these sources are not accessible or of interest to the general reader and are not included in this bibliography.

The reader who wishes to delve more deeply into the subject will, however, find the following one-volume works generally available and of interest:

Adams, Ramon F. (ed.). *The Best of the American Cowboy*. Norman, Oklahoma, 1957.

Allen, Richard. *The Life, Experience and Gospel Labors of the Rt. Rev. Richard Allen, Written by Himself*. Philadelphia, 1887.

Allyn, Charles. *The Battle of Groton Heights*. New London, 1882.

Aptheker, Herbert. *American Negro Slave Revolts*. New York, 1943.

———. *The American Revolution*. New York, 1960.

——— (ed.). *A Documentary History of the Negro People in the United States*. 2 vols. New York, 1951.

Bailey, Thomas A. *Diplomatic History of the American People*. New York, 1940.

Bakeless, John. *Lewis and Clark: Partners in Discovery*. New York, 1947.

Bardolph, Richard. *The Negro Vanguard*. New York, 1959.

Barry, Williams. *A History of Framingham, Massachusetts*. Boston, 1847.

Beard, Charles A. and Mary R. *A Basic History of the United States*. New York, 1944.

Beasley, Delilah T. *The Negro Trail Blazers of California*. Los Angeles, 1919.

Beckwourth, James P. *The Life and Adventures of James P. Beckwourth*, ed. Bernard De Voto from T. D. Bonner's 1856 edition. New York, 1951.

Bennett, Lerone, Jr. *Before the Mayflower: A History of the Negro in America 1619-1964*. Chicago, 1962.

Beyer, Walter F., and O. F. Keydel (eds.). *Deeds of Valor*. Detroit, 1903.

Billington, Ray Allen. *The Far Western Frontier: 1830-1860*. New York, 1962.

Brown, William Wells. *The Negro in the American Rebellion*. Boston, 1867.

Carruth, Gordon (ed.). *The Encyclopedia of American Facts and Dates* (4th ed.). New York, 1966.

Cashin, Herschel V., et al. *Under Fire with the Tenth Cavalry*. Chicago, n. d.

Catton, Bruce. *A Stillness at Appomattox*. Garden City, 1954.

———. *This Hallowed Ground: The Story of the Union Side in the Civil War*. Garden City, 1956.

Cobrun, Frank W. *The Battle of April 19, 1775*. Lexington, Mass., 1912.

Conkling, Roscoe P. and Margaret B. *The Butterfield Overland Mail, 1857-1869*. 3 vols. Glendale, Calif., 1947.

Cornish, Dudley T. *The Sable Arm: Negro Troops in the Union Army, 1861-1865*. New York, 1966.

Cutter, Benjamin and William R. *History of the Town of Arlington, Mass.* Boston, 1880.

Dobie, J. Frank. *The Longhorns*. Boston, 1941.

———. *A Vaquero of the Brush Country*. Boston, 1943.

Dobler, Lavinia, and Edgar A. Toppin. *Pioneers and Patriots: The Lives of Six Negroes of the Revolutionary Era*. Garden City, 1965.

Dodd, William E. *The Cotton Kingdom*. New Haven, 1919.

Douglass, Frederick. *Life and Times of Frederick Douglass, intro. by Rayford W. Logan*. New York, 1962.

Durham, Philip, and Everett L. Jones. *The Negro Cowboys*. New York, 1965.

Dyer, Frederick H. *A Compendium of the War of the Rebellion*. Des Moines, 1908.

Emilio, Luis F. *History of the Fifty-Fourth Regiment of Massachusetts Volunteer Infantry, 1863-1865*. Boston, 1891.

Fast, Howard. *April Morning*. New York, 1961.

Fishel, Leslie H., Jr., and Benjamin Quarles. *The Negro American: A Documentary History*. New York, 1967.

Franklin, John Hope. *From Slavery to Freedom: A History of American Negroes* (3rd ed., rev.). New York, 1967.

Fremont, John C. "*A Narrative of the Exploring Expedition to Oregon and North California,*" *The Daring Adventures of Kit Carson and Fremont among Buffaloes, Grizzlies, and Indians*. New York, 1885.

Gipson, Frederick B. *Fabulous Empire: Colonel Zack Miller's Story*. Boston, 1946.

Glass, Edward L. N. *History of the Tenth Cavalry, 1866-1921*. Tucson, 1921.

Greene, Lorenzo J. *The Negro in Colonial New England*. New York, 1942.

Guthrie, James M. *Campfires of the Afro-American*. Philadelphia, 1899.

Hakluyt, Richard. *Hakluyt's Collection of Early Voyages, Travels, and Discoveries of the English Nation*. London, 1810.

Haley, James Evetts. *Charles Goodnight, Cowboy and Plainsman*. Norman, Okla., 1949.

Hansen, Harry (ed.). *California: A Guide to the Golden State*. New York, 1967.

Herr, John K., and Edward S. Wallace. *The Story of the United States Cavalry, 1775-1942*. Boston, 1953.

Heywood, Chester D. *Negro Combat Troops in the World War: The Story of the 371st Infantry*. Worchester, 1928.

Higginson, Thomas Wentworth. *Army Life in a Black Regiment*. East Lansing, Mich., 1960.

Hill, Howard C. *Roosevelt and the Caribbean*. Chicago, 1927.

Hodges, Carl G., and Mrs. Helene H. Levene. *Illinois Negro Historymakers*. Chicago, 1964.

Hunter, John Marvin. *The Trail Drivers of Texas*. Nashville, 1925.

Jackson, Luther P. *Virginia Negro Soldiers and Sailors in the Revolutionary War*. Norfolk, 1944.

Johnson, Edward A. *History of Negro Soldiers in the Spanish American War*. Raleigh, 1899.

Katz, William L. *Eyewitness: The Negro in American History*. New York, 1967.

Kidder, Frederic. *History of the Boston Massacre*. Albany, 1870.

Lang, Lincoln A. *Ranching with Roosevelt*. Philadelphia, 1926.

Lea, Tom. *The Wonderful Country*. Boston, 1952.

Leckie, William H. *The Buffalo Soldiers: A Narrative of the Negro Cavalry in the West*. Norman, Okla., 1967.

Lee, Irvin H. *Negro Medal of Honor Men*. New York, 1967.

Lewis, Meriwether. *History of the Expedition Under the Command of Lewis and Clark*. Philadelphia, 1814.

Little, Arthur W. *From Harlem to the Rhine: The Story of New York's Colored Volunteers*. New York, 1936.

Logan, Rayford W. *The Negro in American Life and Thought: The Nadir, 1877-1901*. New York, 1954.

Lord, Walter. *Day of Infamy*. New York, 1957.

Love, Nat. *The Life and Adventures of Nat Love, Better Known in the Cattle Country as "Deadwood Dick," by Himself*. Los Angeles, 1907.

Lovejoy, Joseph C. and Owen. *Memoir of the Rev. Elijah P. Lovejoy Who was Murdered in Defense of the Liberty of the Press*. New York, 1838.

Lynk, Miles V. *The Black Troopers, or the Daring Heroism of the Negro Soldiers in the Spanish American War*. Jackson, Miss., 1899.

McCarthy, Agnes, and Lawrence Reddick. *Worth Fighting For*. Garden City, 1965.

May, Samuel J. *Some Recollections of our Antislavery Conflict*. Boston, 1869.

Medal of Honor of the Navy 1861-1948. Washington, D. C., Government Printing Office, 1949.

Medal of Honor of the U. S. Army. Washington, D. C., Government Printing Office, 1948.

Meltzer, Milton (ed.). *In Their Own Words: A History of the American Negro*. 3 vols. New York, 1964.

A Memorial to Crispus Attucks, Samual Maverick, James Caldwell, Samuel Gray and Patricia Carr, from the City of Boston. Boston, 1889.

Merriam, John M. *Five Framingham Heroes of the American Revolution*. Framingham, 1925.

Miles, General Nelson A. *Personal Recollections of General Nelson A. Miles*. Chicago, 1896.

Moore, George H. *Historical Notes on the Employment of Negroes in the American Army of the Revolution*. New York, 1962.

Myrdal, Gunnar. *An American Dilemma: The Negro Problem and Modern Democracy*. New York, 1944.

The Negro Handbook. Chicago, 1966.

Nell, William C. *The Colored Patriots of the American Revolution.* Boston, 1855.

———. *Services of Colored Americans in tre Wars of 1776 and 1812*. Boston, 1851.

Ploski, Harry A., and Roscoe C. Brown. *The Negro Almanac*. New York, 1967.

Quarles, Benjamin. *The Negro in the American Revolution*. Chapel Hill, 1961.

———.*The Negro in the Civil War*. Boston, 1953.

———. *The Negro in the Making of America*. New York, 1964.

Roosevelt, Theodore. *The Rough Riders*. New York, 1899.

Russell, John H. *The Free Negro in Virginia, 1619-1865*. Baltimore, 1913.

Santee, Ross. *Cowboy*. New York, 1928.

Schar, John T. *History of Maryland*. Baltimore, 1879.

Schoenfeld, Seymour J. *The Negro in the Armed Forces*. Washington, 1945.

Scott, Emmett J. *Official History of the American Negro in the World War*. Chicago, 1919.

Smith, Samuel Abbot. *West Cambridge on the Nineteenth of April, 1775*. Boston, 1864.

Spangler, Earl. *The Negro in Minnesota*. Minneapolis, 1961.

Stampp, Kenneth M. *The Peculiar Institution: Slavery in the Ante-Bellum South*. New York, 1956.

Steiner, Bernard C. *A History of Slavery in Connecticut*. Baltimore, 1893.

Sterling, Dorothy, and Benjamin Quarles. *Lift Every Voice*. Garden City, 1965.

Sterling, Philip, and Rayford Logan. *Four Took Freedom*. Garden City, 1967.

Steward, Theophilus G. *The Colored Regulars in the United States Army*. Philadelphia, 1904.

Tourtellot, Arthur B. *William Diamond's Drum*. New York, 1959.

Towne, Charles Wayland, and Edward Norris Wentworth. *Cattle and Men*. Norman, Okla., 1955.

Turner, Frederick J. *The Frontier in American History*. New York, 1920.

Villard, Oswald Garrison. *John Brown*. Boston, 1910.

White, Walter. *A Rising Wind*. Garden City, 1945.

Whitman, S. H. *The Troopers.* New York, 1962.

Wilkes, Laura E. *Missing Pages in American History.* Washington, 1919.

Williams, Charles H. *Sidelights on Negro Soldiers.* Boston, 1923.

Williams, George W. *A History of the Negro Troops in the War of the Rebellion, 1861-1865.* New York, 1888.

Wilson, Joseph T. *The Black Phalanx.* Hartford, 1888.

Woodward, C. Vann. *The Strange Career of Jim Crow.* New York, 1955.

INDEX

A

Abolitionism, 34, 74, 87-88, 215-220, 222
Abrams, Creighton W., Jr., 200
Academy of Science (France), 35
Adair, General, 50
Adams, John, 16, 17, 18
Adams, John (soldier), 115
Adams, John Quincy, 213
Adams, Samuel, 17, 25
Agassiz, Louis, 87
"Alabama" (warship), 93
Allen, Ethan, 25-26
"Almeranto Oquenda" (ship), 159
American Expeditionary Forces, 174
American Red Cross, 190-191
"Amistad" (slave ship), 211
Anderson, Osborn Perry, 74
Andrew (slave), 17-19
Andrew, John A., 87, 217
Anthony, Robert, 68
Antietam, Battle of, 80, 81
Antony (slave), 2
Apache Indians, 95, 98, 107-111, 114-117, 151, 153
Arapaho Indians, 98, 102
Argonne Forest, Battle of, 171, 173
Arikara Indians, 56, 57
"Arizona" (battleship), 177, 178
"Ark" (ship), 7
Armes, George, 98
Armistead, William, 32
Ashley, William H., 63
Attucks, Crispus, 16-8, 87
Augustana, A. T., 82
Auld, Hugh, 222
Auld, Sophia, 222
Avocourt, Battle at, 171
Ayers, Charles G., 150
Aztec Indians, 11

B

Bacon, John, 110
Baker, Edward L., Jr., 153-154
Baker, Vernon L., 184-185
Baldwin, T. A., 154
Banderas, Quíntin, 146
Banks, Nathaniel P., 84, 85
Banks's First Engineers, 84-96
Banneker, Benjamin, 34-35
Barrett, James, 22
Barry, James, 32
Batherick, Mother, 24
Bautista de Anza, Juan, 53
Beauman, William, 97
Beauregard, P. G. T., 88
Beckwith, Henry, 121, 130-131, 137
Beckwourth, Jim, 63-64
Belknap, Jason, 23
Belknap, Joe, 23
Bell, B. F., 151
Bell, Dennis, 156
Belleau Wood, Battle of, 171
Bennion, Mervyn, 178
Benton, Thomas Hart, 65, 66
Bigbow, Chief, 103
Big Tree, Chief, 103, 104, 105
Billy the Kid, 95
Black, Primas, 26
Black codes, 220
Black Sam, 123
Black Springs Ranch, 133
Blackman, Epheram, 26
Blackman, Pomp, 22
Blake, James, 42

Blood plasma banks, 190-191
Boardman, Cato, 22
Bodamer, J. A., 102
Boddie, James T., Jr., 203
Bonal, Stephen, 150
Bonga, George, 72
Bonga, Jean, 72
"Booker T. Washington" (liberty ship), 181
Boston Evening Journal, 88
Boston Massacre, 16-18
Boston Tea Party, 18
Boyer, Eli, 108
Bradley, Omar N., 196
Brazeale, Thomas, 103
Brewer, Johnny, 139
Bridger, Jim, 63
Brock, Isaac, 39
Brodas, Edward, 216
Brooks, Robert, 188-189
Brown, Caesar, 27-28
Brown, Heywood, 74
Brown, Jesse L., 198
Brown, John, 73, 74, 75, 76
Brown, John (soldier), 80
Brown, Wesley A., 194
Brown, William Wells, 81
Budge, James, 23
Buell, George, 106, 116
Buffalo Bill, 139
Bulge, Battle of the, 182-183
Bull Run, Battle of, 78, 80
Bunker Hill, Battle of, 26
Burgoyne, John, 26
Burr, Seymour, 28
Bush, George William, 70-71, 72
Bush, William Owen, 71-72
Butler, Benjamin F., 78, 81
Butler, Matthew C., 146
Butler, T. C., 153

C

Caesar (soldier), 28
Caesar (tailor), 32-33
Cailloux, André, 86
Calamity Jane, 123
Caldwell, James, 18
Calvert, Cecilius, 7
Cameahwait, Chief, 59
Cameron, Simon, 77
Campbell, "Aunt Sally," 72
Carmichael, Stokely, 211
Carney, William H., 89
"Carolina" (gunboat), 48
Carpenter, Louis H., 97, 100-101
Carr, Eugene, 116
Carr, Patrick, 18
Carroll, General, 50
Carroll, Henry, 111, 112, 118
Carson, Kit, 63, 65, 77
Cass, Lewis, 72
Castillo, 12
Casualties
  Civil War, 82, 86, 90, 94
  Indian skirmishes (Western frontier), 98, 100, 101, 102, 104-105, 108, 110, 115
  Korean War, 196
  Revolutionary War, 25, 27-28, 30
  Spanish-American War, 149, 152, 160
  War of 1812, 38, 50-51
  World War I, 182, 187
  World War II, 182, 187
Cattle ranches, 121-124
  feudal structure of, 124
  See also names of ranches
Cervera y Topere, Pasqual, 149, 159-160
Champagne, Battle of, 171
Chandler, Winthrop, 157
Charbonneau, 58, 61
Charles V, King, 10
Charleton, Cornelius H., 197-198
Château-Thierry, Battle of, 171
Chauncey, Isaac, 39
Cherlain, Augustus, 81
"Chesapeake" (vessel), 35, 36
Cheyenne Indians, 98, 99-101
Chicago, settlement of, 8
Chicago Daily News, 202
Chipo-ri, Battle at, 197
Chippewa Treaty, 72
Chiricahua Apache Indians, 114-115, 117
Chisholm Trail, 122-123, 127-128
  northern terminus of, 128
"Choctaw" (warship), 86
Choctaw Indians, 48
Christian, Marcus, 48-49
Christy, William, 87, 98
Cinque, Joseph, 211-214
Civil War, 73-94, 107, 121-122, 143, 192, 195, 217, 222
  all-black regiments, 77, 79-80, 82-90
  beginning of, 76
  casualties, 82, 86, 90, 94
  contraband, 78

Medal of Honor, 89, 92
naval warfare, 91-93
Claiborne, William C., 44-45
Clark, Mark W., 182
Clark, William, 55-62, 70
Clay, Henry, 139
Clinton, Sir Henry, 26
Cobb, Irvin, 164-165
Coburn, Titus, 28
Cochise, Chief, 114
Coffee, General, 50
Coffey, Alvin Aaron, 69
Coffey, Raymond R., 202
Coleman, Kenneth W., 185
"Columbia Rediviva" (ship), 9
Columbus, Christopher, 5, 6
Comanche Indians, 95, 98, 99, 102, 105-107, 109-111, 113
Committee Against Jim Crow in Military Service and Training, 193
Committee on Equality of Treatment and Opportunity in the Armed Services, 193-194
Committee on Fair Employment Practices, 190
Concord, Battle of, 21-22, 25, 28, 37
Conquistadores, 10-14
"Constitution" (vessel), 37
Continental Congress, 19, 26
Contraband, 78
Cooper, Grant, 28
Copeland, John A., Jr., 73-75
Cornwallis, Charles, 30, 32
Coronado, Francisco Vásquez de, 11-12, 14, 52, 113
Corps d'Afrique, 84-86
Cortés, Hernando, 10-11
Cotton industry, 3, 4
Couch, William, 118-119
Cowboys, 121-142
loyalty of, 130
number of Negro, 123
organization of, 124
trail cooks, 126-129
trail drive routes, 122-123
See also names of cowboys
Creoles, 48
"Cristobol Colon" (ship), 159
Crosby, Oscar, 67
Crow Indians, 61, 62, 63, 64
Cruzat, 57, 61
Cuban slave revolt of 1868, 145
Cuffe, Paul, 218
Cureton, Jack, 124-125
Cusack, Patrick, 109
Custer, George Armstrong, 72, 101
Cutter, Ammi, 23

D

Dakota territory, 72
Dana, Charles, 87
Daquin, Louis, 46, 48, 50
Davidson, John W., 105, 106
Davis, Benjamin O., Jr., 185-188, 199
promoted to general, 188
Davis, Edmund J., 105
Davis, Franklin, Jr., 200
Davis, John, 38
Davison, Frederic E., 199, 202
Dawes, William, 20
Deadwood Fourth of July celebration (1876), 123
Decatur, Stephen, 32, 37
Declaration of Rights, 19
Delaney, Martin, 82
Delano, Ensign, 178
Deming, Edward, 213
Dennis, Elias S., 87
de Soto, Hernando, 10-11
DeSousa, Mathias, 7
Detroit Military Guard, 77
Dewey, George, 148, 149
Diamond, William, 21
Dick (miner), 68
Dickerson, Caesar, 28
"Discovery" (craft), 1
Dobie, J. Frank, 126
Dodson, Jacob, 65, 77
Dorantes, Andres, 12-13
Douglass, Charles, 87, 223
Douglass, Frederick, 81-82, 87, 221-223
appointed minister to Haiti, 223
Douglass, Lewis, 87, 90, 223
"Dove" (ship), 7
Drew, Charles Richard, 190-191
Drexel Mission, 119
Du Bois, W. E. B., 11, 210
Dudley, N. A. M., 115
Dunmore, Lord, 31
DuPuy, James E., 202
du Sable, Jean Baptiste Pointe, 8
Dutch East India Company, 6

E

Eagle Heart, Chief, 103, 104
Edgel, Simon, 21

Eighth Illinois Infantry Regiment, 147, 159, 173
Eisenhower, Dwight D., 183
El Caney garrison, 152-155
Ellicott, George, 35
Emancipation Proclamation, 3, 81, 131, 217, 221
"Enterprise" (ship), 179
Epps, Richard, 115
Estabrook, Prince, 21, 22
Estevanico, 12-14, 52
Europe, James Reese, 168-169
Eustis, William, 30-31

F

Fabulous Empire, The (Gipson), 138
"Falgout" (destroyer), 199
"Fanny" (brig), 33
Ferdinand, Archduke, 166
Ferdinand V, King, 10
Field, Phillip, 31-32
Fields, Elija, 203
Fields, Mary, 72
Fifteenth New York Infantry, *see* 369th Infantry Regiment
Fifth Massachusetts Regiment, 27
Fifty-fifth Massachusetts Regiment, 223
Fifty-fourth Massachusetts Regiment, 222-223
First Air Cavalry Division, 203
First Kansas Volunteers, 81
First Louisiana Native Guards, 84-86
First North Carolina Regiment, 82
First South Carolina Volunteers, 79, 92
503rd Infantry Regiment, 206
Flake, Green, 67
Flake, James Madison, 67
Flake, Mrs. James Madison, 67-68
Flake, Liz, 67-68
Flora, William, 31
Floyd, J. F., 167
Folk music, 4
Foone, 213
Forrestal, James V., 180-181
Forsyth, George, 100, 101
Fort Apache, 117
Fort Bayard, 114
Fort Benning, 206
Fort Boise, 65
Fort Clark, 108
Fort Clatsop, 60
Fort Concho, 106, 110, 112, 113
Fort Davis, 107-108
Fort Dearborn, 39
Fort Dodge, 99, 102
Fort Duncan, 108, 113
Fort Gibson, 99, 101
Fort Grant, 117
Fort Griffin, 106
Fort Lancaster, 108
Fort Laramie, 70
Fort Larned, 99
Fort McKavett, 110, 111, 112
Fort McKinney, 119
Fort Phantom, 10
Fort Polk, 206
Fort Quitman, 108
Fort Reno, 117, 118
Fort Richardson, 103, 105, 106
Fort Riley, 97-98, 99
Fort Robinson, 119
Fort Sill, 101-102, 103, 106, 112, 117, 206
Fort Snelling, 72
Fort Stockton, 107-108, 109
Fort Sumter, 76
Fort Supply, 101, 117
Fort Thomas, 117
Fort Ticonderoga, 25-26
Fort Vancouver, 65
Fort Verde, 117
Fort Wagner, Battle of, 84, 88-90
Fort Wallace, 99, 100, 101
Fort Zarah, 99
Forten, James, 32, 218
Fortier, Michel, 46, 49
Forty-second Massachusetts Regiment, 86
Foster, John, 207
450th Anti-Aircraft Artillery Battalion, 182
Fourth Massachusetts Regiment, 33
Fowler, Vance, 178
Frederick Douglass' Paper, 222
Fredericksburg, Battle of, 80
Freedmen's Bureau, 108
Freeman, Corporal, 102
Frémont, John C., 65-66, 77
Frémont Peak, 65
French and Indian Wars, 22
Frohock, William, 108
From Harlem to the Rhine (Little), 168
Frontenac, Comte de, 7-8
Frye, Colonel, 28

G

Gage, Thomas, 19, 21
Gandy, Charles F., 184
Gannett, Deborah, 33
Garnet, Henry Highland, 220
Garrison, William Lloyd, 81, 87, 218-219, 222
Geronimo, 95, 114, 117
Ghent, Treaty of, 51
Gibbs, Josiah W., 213
Gillmore, General, 90
Gipson, Fred, 138, 140-142
"Godspeed" (craft), 1
Gone with the Wind (motion picture), 4
Goode, W. T., 147, 159
Goodnight, Charles, 124, 126, 132-137, 138
  death of, 133
Goodnight-Loving Trail, 122-123, 133, 134-136
Gould, Edward, 23
"Gov. Tompkins" (privateer), 38
Goybet, General, 171, 172
Graham, G. W., 99-100
Grant, Ulysses S., 69, 84, 87, 93-94, 96
Gravely, Samuel L., Jr., 199
Gray, Robert, 9
Gray, Samuel, 18
Great Bridge, Battle of, 31
Greaves, Clifton, 115
Green, Christopher, 30
Green Mountain Boys, 25-26
Greens, Shields, 74
Gridley, Richard, 27
Grierson, Benjamin H., 96-99, 101-105, 112-113, 116, 117
  criticism of, 102-103
Guadalcanal, Battle of, 189
"Guerrière (vessel), 37
Gui-tan, 106

H

Haley, J. Evetts, 133, 134
Hall, Governor, 99
Hall, Charles B., 186
Hall, Prince, 28
Hamilton, Alexander, 29
Hamlet, James Frank, 203
Hannibal Guards, 77
Harmon, Leonard Roy, 179
Hastie, William H., 185
Hatch, Edward, 96, 97, 107, 108, 110-115, 118-119
Hayes, Cuff, 28
Hayes, Rutherford B., 223
Haynes, Lemuel, 26
Hayward, William, 167-168, 169-170
Hegel, George Wilhelm, 210
Henry, Major, 119
Henry, Patrick, 19
Henry the Navigator, Prince, 5
Hessian mercenaries, 30
Hickock, Wild Bill, 123
Higginson, Thomas Wentworth, 79-80, 83-84, 92, 217
Hilton, Henry, 129-130
Hitler, Adolf, 187
Hoffman, William, 97
Holliday, Presley, 155
Hopkins, Jim, 139
Horner, Reuben, 185
Hotchkiss, Benjamin, 119
Howe, Sir William, 26, 27
Hudner, Thomas J., Jr., 198
Hudson, C. L., 106
Hudson, Henry, 6
Hudson's Bay Company, 70
Hull, Lieutenant, 23
Hull, William, 38-39
Hunter, David, 78-79, 80, 83, 217
Hunter, John M., 128

I

Ikard, Bose, 121, 132-137
  death of, 133, 136-137
Ikard, M., 133
Imperialism, 161
Impressment, British policy of, 36
Indentured servants, 2
Indian Bureau, 114, 115
Indian Peace Commission, 98
"Indiana" (battleship), 148
Indians
  Medicine Lodge treaties, 98-99
  wagon train raids, 103, 109
  Western frontier and, 95-102
  See also names of Indians, names of Indian tribes
Ingraham, Joseph, 37
Intolerable Acts, 19
"Intrepid" (ship), 179

"Iowa" (battleship), 148, 160
Irving, Washington, 62
Isabella (slave), 2
Isolationism, 166

J

JA Ranch, 138
Jackson, Andrew, 43-51, 52
Jackson, Saunders, 66
Jackson, Waller, 68
Jacoby, Edmond, 177, 178
James Island, Battle of, 88
Jamestown colony, 1-2, 5, 6
Jazz music, 4
Jefferson, Thomas, 4, 34, 35, 37, 53-54, 55, 60
Jeffords, Tom, 114
Jenkins, Ernest, 185
Jim Crow laws, 165
Joel, Lawrence, 204-205
Johnson, C. P., 156
Johnson, Doir, 178
Johnson, Henry, 162-165, 167
Johnson, John, 38
Johnson, Lyndon B., 188, 205, 207, 208
Johnson, Nathan, 108
Johnson, Thomas A., 201
Joliet, Louis, 7-8
Jones, E. T., 108
Jones, John Paul, 32
Juh, Chief, 114

K

Kansas Pacific Railroad, 97
"Kearsarge" (ship), 93
Kendrick, John, 9
Kickapoo Indians, 107, 108, 111-112, 117
  hit-and-run raids (1869), 109
Kickapoo Road, 111
Kidd, Major, 102
King, Martin Luther, 210-211
Kiowa Indians, 95, 98, 99, 102-107, 109, 110
Knox, Frank, 155, 180
Korean War, 194-198
  beginning of, 194
  casualties, 196
  end of, 198
  Medal of Honor, 196-198
Kuni-ri, Battle at, 195

L

LaCoste, Pierre, 46, 47, 50
"Lady Washington" (sloop), 9
Lafayette, James, 32
Lafayette, Marquis de, 32
Laffite, Jean, 48
Lake Erie, Battle of, 39-40, 42
Lamson, David, 23-24, 31
Lane, James H., 81
Lang, Lincoln, 132
Lang Ranch, 132
Lanham, General, 183
La Salle, Robert Cavelier de, 533
"Lawrence" (flagship), 40
Lay, Hark, 67
Leary, Lewis, 74
Lee, Fitzhugh, 146, 156
Lee, James H., 93
Lee, Robert E., 74, 93-94
Lend-Lease Act, 189
L'Enfant, Pierre, 34-35
Leonard, Zenas, 62
"Leopard" (man-of-war), 35
Lew, Barzillai, 27
Lewis, Meriweather, 55-62, 70
Lewis and Clark Expedition, 55-62
Lewis and Clark Pass, 61
Lexington, Battle of, 20-21, 24, 25, 28
Liberator (newspaper), 218-219, 222
Lincoln, Abraham, 3, 75-79, 81
Lipan Apache Indians, 107, 108, 117
"Liscome Bay" (carrier), 179
Little, Arthur W., 164-165, 168, 169
Livingston, Robert R., 54
Locke, Benjamin, 22, 23
Loepus, Markus, 9
London Company, 2
Lone Wolf, Chief, 104, 106
Loud, 119
Louisiana Territory
  Lewis and Clark Exploration of, 55-62
  purchase of, 36, 54
Louisiana Volunteers of African Descent, 86-87
Love, Nat, 123
Lovejoy, Elijah P., 219-220
Loving, Oliver, 133-135
Lowell, James Russell, 90

M

MacArthur, Douglas, 195
McCaleb, J. L., 127-128
"Macedonian" (vessel), 37
Maceo, Antonio, 146
Mackadoo, Richard, 115
Mackenzie, Frederick, 24
Mackenzie, Ranald S., 103
McKinley, William, 146
MacKinney, 62
Madison, James, 36, 41, 44
Madison, Mrs. James, 41
Madison, John, 185
"Maine" (battleship), 146, 148, 154
Malcolm X, 211
Mandan Indians, 56, 57, 61
Mangus, Chief, 117
"Maria Teresa" (ship), 159
Markley, A. C., 158
Marquette, Jacques, 7-8
Marshall, T., 214-215
Martin, Daniel, 36
"Massachusetts" (battleship), 148
Massachusetts Anti-Slavery Society, 222
Massachusetts Committee of Safety, 20, 25
Massachusetts Fifty-fourth Infantry, 87-88
Maverick, Samuel, 18
May, Samuel, 87
Mead, Israel, 23
Medal of Honor
  for cavalry warfare, 111, 112, 115
  Civil War, 89, 92
  Korean War, 196-198
  Spanish-American War, 154, 157, 160
  Vietnam War, 204
Medicine Lodge treaties, 98-99
Mendoza, Antonio de, 13
Menéndez de Avilés, Pedro, 5, 6
Meredith, James, 211
Merimon, Clifton, 172-173
Merrifield, Ed, 174
Merritt, Wesley, 108-109
Mescalero Apache Indians, 107, 111, 114
Michigan Territory, 72
Miles, Nelson A., 158, 160, 172
Miller, Albert P., 213-214
Miller, Dorie, 176-179
Miller, G. W., 137-138
Miller, George, 138
Miller, Joe, 138, 140, 141
Miller, Zack, 138, 141
Miller Brothers rodeo show, 137, 139-141
Milliken's Bend, Battle of, 84, 86-87
Mix, Tom, 139
Monmouth, Battle of, 33
Monroe, George, 69
Monroe, James, 54
Montgomery, Hugh, 18
Montgomery, James, 217
Monthois, Battle at, 171
Montojo, Admiral, 149
Moreau, Vice Admiral, 172
Mormons, 67, 67
Morrison, Alan, 183
Morrow, Albert P., 108, 115
Mulzac, Hugh, 181

N

Napoleon I, 35, 41, 53
Narváez, Pánfilo de, 12
National Editor's Association, 139
National Intelligencer, The, 42
National Militia Act of 1792, 76
Navaho Indians, 114
Naval warfare
  Civil War, 91-93
  Revolutionary War, 32-33
  Spanish-American War, 148, 149, 159-160
  War of 1812, 37-41
Neal, Burr, 151
Negro, Diego el, 5
Negro Masonic Order in America, 28
  first Annapolis graduate, 194
  first born in U.S., 2
  first U.S. general, 188
  slave population (1790-1860), 3-4
Nell, William Cooper, 221
Nelson, W. R., 151
Neve, Felipe de, 53
New Netherland colony, 7
New Orleans, Battle of, 43-51
New York Evening World, 164-165
New York Herald, 73
New York Mail and Express, 154
New York Times, The, 85, 167
New York Times News Service, 201
Newby, Dangerfield, 74
Newport raid (Revolutionary War), 32

Nez Percé Indians, 59-60
Nez Percé National Historical Park, 59
"Niagara" (ship), 40
Nigger Jeff, 123
Niles Register, The, 50
Nimitz, Chester W., 179
92nd Negro Division, 184
93rd Negro Division, 189
99th Pursuit Squadron, 185-187
969th Field Artillery, Battalion, 182
Niño, Pedro Alonso, 5
Ninth Cavalry Regiment, 95-120, 143-144, 147, 148, 150, 151, 153, 155, 158-159, 167
  organized, 96
Ninth United States Infantry Regiment, 194
Nixon, John, 27, 28
Niza, Marcos de, 13-14
Noble, Jordan B., 48
Nolte, Vincent, 50
North Star (newspaper), 222

O

Observer (journal), 219
"Oklahoma" (battleship), 178
Olive, Milton L., III, 205-207
Oliver, Elbert H., 179
One-hundredth New York Regiment, 89
101 Ranch, 137-139, 140, 141
157th French Division, 171
173rd Air Brigade, 204, 206
196th Light Artillery Brigade, 199-200
199th Light Infantry Brigade, 200
Ord, E. O. C., 112-113
"Oregon" (battleship), 148, 159
Oregon Trail, 66, 70
Osage Indians, 128
Ottawa Indians, 56
Oberlin College, 73

P

Pace, Frank, Jr., 197
Pakenham, Sir Edward, 47-48, 50-51
Parker, John, 20-21, 22
Paso, Oro, 139
"Patriot" (schooner), 33
Patton, George S., 182
Payne, David L., 117, 118
"Peacock" (sloop-of-war), 10
Pearl Harbor, bombing of, 176-179
Pease, Joachim, 92-93
Pelton, Captain, 31
Penn, Robert, 160
Pennington, James W. C., 221
Percy, Earl Hugh, 22-23, 24
Peres, Francisco, 7
Perry, Jim, 124
Perry, Oliver H., 39-40, 42
Pershing, John J., 144, 155, 174-175
Pétain, Henri Philippe, 171-172
Petersburg, Battle of, 93
Pharaoh (soldier), 28
Phillips, Wendell, 87
Philosophy of History (Hegel), 210
Pickett, Bill, 121, 137-142
  death of, 141
Pinckney, William, 179
Pine Ridge Agency, 119
Pitcairn, John, 21, 28
Pitcher, Molly, 33
Pitts, Riley Leroy, 205
Pitts, Mrs. Riley LeRoy, 205
Pizarro, Francisco, 10
Plains Indians, 99
"Planter" (gunboat), 91-92
Plauche, Major, 48, 50
Pocahontas, 2
"Pocahontas" (transport ship), 170
Pompey (army private), 21
Pompey (spy), 32
Ponca Indians, 137
Pony Express, 69
Poor, Salem, 28-29, 31
Pope, John, 114, 115, 117
Population
  Afro-Cubans, 146
  free Negro (1860), 4-5
  slave (1790-1860), 3-4
Port Hudson, Battle of, 84-86
Porter, David, 32, 37
Portolá, Caspar de, 52
Potawatomi Indians, 39
Prescott, Richard, 32
Prescott, William, 26-28
Preston, Thomas, 17
Price, John, 7
Progressive Party, 165
Prosser, Gabriel, 44
Putnam, Israel, 27

Q

Quakers, 35
Quarles, Dr. Benjamin, 189

R

Ranching with Roosevelt (Lang), 132
Randolph, A. Philip, 189-190
Randolph, John, 4
Ray, Charles B., 81
Reconstruction period, 123-124, 125, 221
Red Otter, Chief, 106
Reed, Lieutenant Colonel, 82
"Reina Mercedes" (ship), 159
Reservations, Indian, 98, 102, 103, 114-116, 117, 119
Revere, Paul, 20
Revolutionary War, 15-33, 34
  all-black regiments, 30-31
  beginning of, 21
  casualties, 25, 27-28, 30
  female soldiers, 33
  naval warfare, 32-33
  spies, 32
Reynolds, Grant, 193
Reynolds, Kurt, 139
Rhode Island First Regiment, 30-31, 77
Ridgway, Matthew B., 195
Rising Wind, The (White), 186
Rivera y Moncada, Fernando de, 53
Rivers, Sergeant, 80
Roberts, Needham, 162-165
Robideau, 70
Robinson, Bernard W., 180
Robinson, Roscoe, 203
Rocky Mountain Fur Company, 63
Rodgers, Moses, 69
Rogers, Will, 139
Rolfe, John, 2
Rome campaign (World War II), 184
Roosevelt, Franklin D., 187-190, 223
Roosevelt, Theodore, 132, 165
  Spanish-American War, 144, 148, 150-152, 158, 159, 161
Rose, Edward, 63
Ross, Robert, 41
Rough Riders, 144, 148, 150-152, 154, 158
Rowan, Charles H., 68
Russell, Charles M., 125
Russell, Jason, 25
Russian Revolution, 166

S

Sacajawea, 55, 57-61
Sadler, M. W., 152-153
Scamman, James, 28
St. Augustine colony, 5, 6
St. Gaudens, Augustus, 90
St. Ignatius, mission of, 7
St. Mihiel, Battle of, 171, 173
Salem, Peter, 21, 27, 28
Sam (trail cook), 126-127
Sampson, William T., 149, 159
San Carlos Reservation, 114, 115, 116
"San Francisco" (ship), 179
Santa Fe Trail, 66
Santee, Ross, 130
Satank, Chief, 103, 104, 105
Satanta, Chief, 102, 103, 104, 105
Saule, James D., 9-10
Savannah, siege of, 93
Savary, Joseph, 46, 48, 49, 50
Saxton, Rufus, 83
Sayre, Benjamin F., 156
Scribner's Magazine, 158
Sealy, Lon, 139
Second New York Regiment, 31-32
Selective Service Act of 1940, 181
79th Pursuit Group, 185, 186
761st Tank Battalion, 182
Shafter, William R., 113, 149, 160
Shaler, Nathaniel, 38
Sharpe, William, 108
Shaw, Francis, 90
Shaw, Robert Gould, 87-90
Shawnee Trail, 122-123
Sheridan, Philip, 96, 101, 112, 114
Sherman, William T., 96, 99, 103, 104
Shoshone Indians, 58-59
Shurtliff, Robert, *see* Gannett, Deborah
Siegfried Line (World War II), 184-185
Simmons, George, 70, 71, 72
Simmons-Bush party, 70-72
Simons, Wesley J., 183
Sioux Indians, 95, 119-120
Sissle, Noble, 168-169
Sisson, Jack, 32
Sitting Bull, Chief, 119
614th Tank Destroyer Battalion, 184-185

Skinya, Chief, 114
Slavery, 2-4, 121-122, 124
  abolitionist movement and, 215-220, 222
  auctions, 3
  beginning of U.S., 2
  Cuban revolt of 1868, 145
  escapes from, 211-215
  indentured servant, 2, 3
  population (1790-1860), 3-4
  revolts, 6, 44, 73-75, 211-215
Smalls, Robert, 82, 91-92
Smith, Bill, 129-130
Smith, Francis, 20-21, 22, 23
Smith, Joseph, 67
Society of California Pioneers, 69
Sons of the American Revolution, 28
Spanish-American War, 143-161
  beginning of, 146
  casualties, 149, 152, 160
  end of, 160-161
  events leading to, 144-146
  Medal of Honor, 154, 157
  naval warfare, 148, 149, 159-160
  in the Philippines, 148, 149
  significance of, 161
Sparks, Bill, 130, 132
Stance, Emanuel, 111-112
Stanford, Jimmy, 207
Stanton, Edwin M., 83, 84
Stars and Stripes, 183
Stedman, 119
Stedman, Cato, 22
Stevens, Lieutenant, 118
Still, William, 221
Stowe, Harriet Beecher, 81, 218
Strachan, John, 36
Strong, George Crockett, 88
Styron, William, 214
Sullivan, John, 30
"Susan Constant" (craft), 1
Susquehanna Indians, 7

T

Taft, William Howard, 165
Talbot, Sampson, 28
Talleyrand-Périgord, Charles de, 54
Tarrant, Carter, 33
Tatum, Lawrie, 102, 103
Tau-ankia, 106
"Taussig" (destroyer), 199
Taylor, Bill, 135
Taza, Chief, 114
Tecumseh, Chief, 40
"Tennessee" (battleship), 176, 178, 179
Tenth Cavalry Regiment, 95-120, 143-144, 147, 150-151, 153-159, 167
  organized, 96
Tenth Connecticut Regiment, 88
Terrazas, Joaquin, 116
Texas Convention of 1875-76, 124
Texas Rangers, 107, 124-125
Thames, Battle of the, 40
Thatcher, Samuel, 22
Third Louisiana Native Guards, 84-86
Thomas, Charles L., 185
Thompkins, William H., 156-157
Thompson, William, 196
332nd Fighter Group, 187-188
367th Infantry Regiment, 174
369th Infantry Regiment, 167-171, 175
  awarded Croix de Guerre, 170-171
  redesignated, 170
370th Infantry Regiment, 173
371st Infantry Regiment, 171-172
372nd Infantry Regiment, 171, 172
Time (magazine), 203
Tonkawa scouts, 110
Toral, General, 160
Traegerman, Richard, 201-202
Trail cooks, 126-129
Trail Drivers of Texas, The (Hunter), 128
Trimble, Andrew, 108
Trowbridge, John, 79
Truman, Harry S, 192-194
Truth, Sojourner, 215-216
Tubman, Harriet, 215-218
Tubman, John, 217
Tucker, William, 2
Tufts, Cato, 28
Tunnell, Elijah B., 149
Turner, Nat, 214
Turner, Seth, 21
Twenty-fifth Infantry Regiment, 147-153, 167
Twenty-fourth Infantry Regiment, 147-148, 157-158, 189, 194, 195-197
  deactivated, 195

U

Ullman, General, 85
Uncle Tom's Cabin (Stowe), 218
Underground Railroad, 215, 216
  development of, 40-41

"United States" (vessel), 37
United States Army Air Corps, 185
United States Colored Troops, 82
United States First Army, 183
United States Seventh Regiment, 48
United States Supreme Court, 213

V

Vaca, Cabeza de, 12
Van Alen, Clarence R., 172-173
Van Buren, Martin, 213
Vásquez de Ayllón, Lucas, 5-6
Vavasour, Mervin, 9
Verriers, Battle at, 171
Victorio, Chief, 115-116, 117
Victorio War, 115-116, 117
Vidmer, George, 151
Vietnam War, 198-208
  casualties, 203
  Medal of Honor, 204-207
  number of Negroes in, 201, 202-203
  Tet offensive of 1968, 206
"Viscaya" (ship), 159

W

Walker, David, 218
Walker's Appeal, 218
Wall, John, 89
Walley, Augustus, 151
Wanton, George H., 156
War of 1812, 35-51
  beginning of, 36
  casualties, 38, 50-51
  end of, 51
  events leading to, 35-36
  naval warfare, 37-41
  at New Orleans, 43-51, 52
Ward, Artemas, 26-29
Ware, William, 36
Ware, William D., 195-196
Warm Springs Apaches, 114-115
Warre, Henry J., 9
Washington, Booker T., 221
Washington, George, 28, 34, 35
  Delaware River crossing, 31
  elected commander of Continental Army, 26
  at Valley Forge, 31, 32
Washington, Madison, 214
"Washington" (frigate), 212
Washington, D.C.
  architectural design of, 34-35
  British capture of, 41-42
Wayne, Anthony, 32
Webster, Daniel, 16
Weitze, Godfrey, 94
"West Virginia" (battleship), 176, 177-178, 179
Western frontier soldiers, 95-120
  warfare casualties, 90, 100, 101, 102, 104-105, 108, 110, 115
Western Trail, 122-123
Westmoreland, William C., 200
Wheeler, Joseph, 143-144, 146
Whipple, Prince, 31
White, A. C., 151
White, Thomas, 21
White, Walter, 186
White Horse, Chief, 102
Whittmore, Cuff, 22, 27
Wilderness, Battle of the, 93
Wilkes, Charles, 10
Wilkins, Roy, 211
Williams, Bill, 132
Wilson, 135
Wilson, William O., 120
Wilson, Woodrow, 165-166
  executive order on segregation, 166
Winchester, Private, 102
"Winslow" (torpedo boat), 149
Wood, Cato, 22
Wood, Leonard, 144, 148
Wood, O. C., 77
World War I, 162-175
  armistice, 173, 193
  beginning of, 166
  casualties, 170, 171
  last battle of, 173
  number of Negro troops in, 165
World War II, 176-191
  air force pilots, 185
  bombing of Pearl Harbor, 176-179
  casualties, 182, 187
  end of, 192
  first Negro naval commission, 180
  Italian campaign, 184, 185, 187
  Liberty ships, 181
  naval warfare, 179, 189
  number of Negroes in, 180, 182, 189
  Siegfried Line, 184-185
  tank battalions, 182
Wounded Knee, Battle of, 119
Wright, Captain, 119
Wright, Henry H., 114
Writhe, Emanuel, 108

Wynkoop, E. W., 99
Wynn, Ellison C., 195

X

XIT ranch, 124, 138

Y

Yeo, Sir James, 41
York (slave), 55-60
  death of, 62
Yorktown, Battle of, 30, 32
Young, B. M., 150
Young, Brigham, 67
Young, Hiram, 66
Young, John, 126
Young, Whitney M., Jr., 211

Drotning, Phillip T. c.2
Black heroes in our nation's history

DATE DUE			
FEB 14 '72			
12/21/76			
FEB 8 1984			
FEB 22 1984			
SEP 21 1991			
OCT 1 1992			